To



# Guide to East Africa

## Kenya, Tanzania and the Seychelles

by Nina Casimati

Travelaid

HIPPOCRENE BOOKS, INC.

Photo credits: Michael Haag: giraffe and Nairobi; Philipp Kyriakos, Masai woman; Kim Naylor: Masai herdsmen and fishing boats; Andrew Powell: lion and Serengeti; Hilton International: Salt Lick Lodge; Tanzania Information Service: Dar es Salaam, Bagamoyo, Wasukuma women; Seychelles News Bureau: Seychelles sunset.



The author wishes to thank Travintal Limited for having helped supply the information in this guide

Cover illustration by Colin Elgie

Typeset by Witwell Limited, 92 The Albany, Old Hall Street, Liverpool L3 9EJ

Printed in Great Britain by litho at The Pitman Press, Lower Bristol Road, Bath BA2 3BL

Copublished by Travelaid Publishing (Michael Haag Limited), PO Box 369, London NW3 4ER, England and Hippocrene Books Incorporated, 171 Madison Avenue, New York, NY 10016, USA

British ISBN 0 902743 25 2

US ISBN 0 88254 716 X

# CONTENTS



*Practical Information sections follow each chapter, and there is an index at the rear.*

# ABOUT THIS GUIDE

This is the most detailed Guide yet published to these exotic yet increasingly popular countries and islands. Descriptions of cities, game parks and beaches are matched by up-to-date information on accommodation, restaurants, shopping, travel, etc – including useful tips on safaris, scuba diving and game fishing.

The traveller's pattern is often to spend part of his stay in East Africa on safari and then to relax on the beaches of the Indian Ocean coast. This can be done either in Kenya or Tanzania. But many travellers will want to combine their visit to the East African mainland with a stay on the more distant Seychelles islands, enjoying their untouched charm and creole culture. This Guide describes and points the way to all these possibilities.

At the end of each chapter is a *Practical Information* section full of helpful details for that area. These sections make it easy for the traveller to plan his journey, get the most for his means, and enjoy his stay. The information is for all price ranges and degrees of adventurousness.

The *Background* chapters for each country provide the information you need before you go; explain in general terms what you can expect when you arrive; and also serve as reference sections on the spot, with tables of weights and measures, names of local foods and drinks, a Swahili vocabulary, and so on.

This is a complete Guide to Kenya, Tanzania and the Seychelles. But while the *Practical Information* sections and *Background* chapters were up to date when going to press, inflation and changing circumstances have their effect. Also the traveller might like to add his own recommendations of places to visit, things to do, where to stay, for inclusion in the next edition. The reader is asked, therefore, to help with the next edition of this Guide by sending information and comments to the *General Editor, Travelaid Publishing, PO Box 369, London NW3 4ER, England.* Thank you.

# KENYA BACKGROUND

### Basic Facts

Kenya is a republic within the Commonwealth. Its area is 582,646 sq kms, which includes 13,395 sq kms of inland water. Its Indian Ocean coastline stretches for 480 kms.

The population of the country according to the 1979 census is 15.5 million, while its current urban populations are currently estimated as follows: Nairobi (the capital) 950,000, Mombasa (principal seaport) 375,000, Kisumu (principal port on Lake Victoria) 100,000, Nakuru 72,000, Eldoret 38,000, and Malindi 19,000.

The national language is Swahili, but English is the official language. French and German are often spoken in tourist areas.

### Country

Kenya is situated on the east coast of Africa and extends from about 5 degrees north to 5 degrees south of the equator.

**Regions**

There are four main regions in the country: an arid thornbush-covered plain with a small nomadic population in the northeast; a similar but practically uninhabited area in the southeast; low, arid land but including Lake Turkana and mountains in the northwest; and the southwest quarter in which 85 percent of the population and nearly all economic production are concentrated.

**Rift Valley**

The southwest region comprises a plateau rising to mountains 3300 metres high, as well as part of the Great Rift Valley which is often 700 to 1000 metres lower than the surrounding country. This mighty valley is a vast geological fault in the earth's surface running from Lake Baikal in Russia down through Lebanon and the Red Sea to Zimbabwe. It is seen at its most dramatic where it cuts through the highlands of Kenya before descending into the Masai plains.

**Mountains**

The highest mountains in the country are Mount Kenya, 5886 metres; Mount Elgon, 4726 metres, on the border of Kenya and Uganda (the summit is actually in Uganda); and the Aberdare Range, 4368 metres.

**Tana River**

The Tana is Kenya's longest river, draining off the slopes of Mount Kenya and the Aberdare Range and flowing into the Indian Ocean north of Malindi. When it floods, which it does almost annually, the people living along its lower reaches are marooned for several weeks. However, the Tana is navigable only by small craft.

**Lake Turkana**

Lake Turkana, which lies in the Rift Valley and stretches for 288 kms up to the Ethiopian border, is the largest lake wholly within Kenya (6430 sq kms), although Lake Victoria (63,180 sq kms), the largest lake in Africa and the second largest in the world, lies partly within Kenya.

The smaller Kenya lakes include Baringo (130 sq kms), Naivasha (117 sq kms), Bogoria (34 sq kms), Nakuru (31 sq kms) and Elmenteita (11 sq kms). Most of them are fairly shallow and alkaline, supporting large populations of flamingoes and other birds. Lake Magadi, lying in the Rift Valley near the Tanzanian border, is an important source of soda ash and salt. Lake Amboseli, within Amboseli National Park, is no longer a permanent lake, but fills up after heavy rain.

Only Lake Victoria has any commercial craft, although fishing boats ply Lake Turkana, and also Baringo and Naivasha.

## Climate and What to Wear

In general Kenya's climate is cool and invigorating, except at the coast where it is hot and humid, and in the lowlands behind the coastal belt where it is hot and dry. It is altitude which largely governs Kenya's climate, and land above 1600 metres enjoys moderate temperatures and a fairly good rainfall. Nairobi, therefore, at 1800 metres, offers an agreeable climate.

**Dry and rainy seasons**

As the country is located on the equator, there are no marked seasonal changes, and for the most part seasons are differentiated solely by the amount of rain. In eastern Kenya, including Nairobi, there are two rainy seasons: the long rains from the end of March to the end of May, and the short rains through November to mid-December. However, rain seldom falls for more than a few hours each day. The climate in the two dry seasons differs: June to September is cool and cloudy; January to March is sunny and warm. But there are no hard and fast rules – no month in Kenya is invariably wet or dry. As Kenya enjoys a good year-round climate, sport and outdoor recreation are extremely popular.

Summer clothes are worn the year round, but

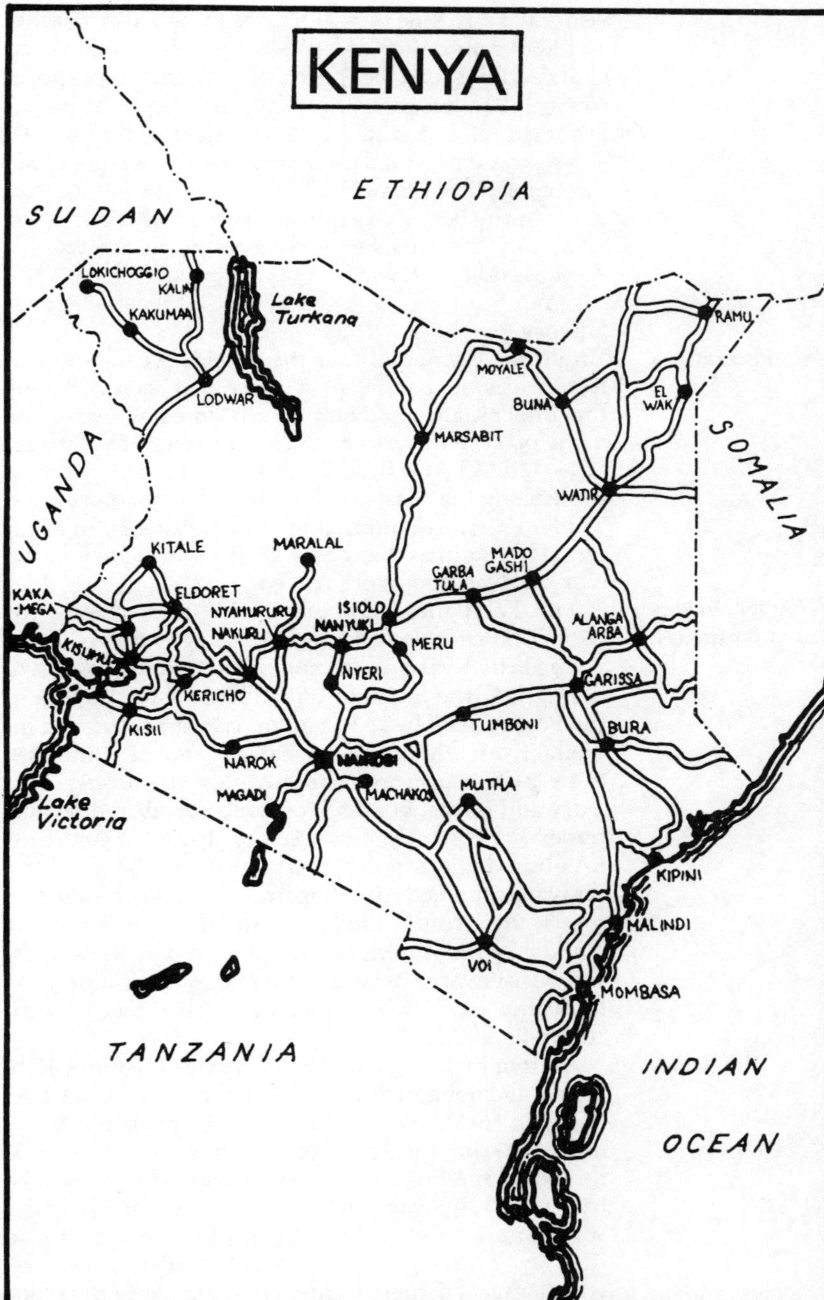
KENYA
ETHIOPIA
SUDAN
LOKICHOGGIO
KALIN
KAKUMAA
Lake Turkana
LODWAR
UGANDA
MOYALE
RAMU
EL WAK
BUNA
MARSABIT
SOMALIA
WATIR
KITALE
MARALAL
MADO GASHI
GARBA TULA
KAKA-MEGA
ELDORET
NYAHURURU
ISIOLO
NANYUKI
NAKURU
MERU
ALANGA ARBA
KISUMU
NYERI
GARISSA
KERICHO
TUMBONI
KISII
BURA
NAROK
MAGADI
MACHAKOS
MUTHA
Lake Victoria
KIPINI
MALINDI
VOI
MOMBASA
TANZANIA
INDIAN
OCEAN

visitors at any time of year should bring a warm jacket and light raincoat or collapsible umbrella. Good cheap khaki clothes can be purchased locally. No special tropical headwear is required, although a broad-brimmed felt hat is advisable for safaris and tours. Always carry dark sunglasses. Informal dress is generally acceptable, though men will require a dark suit for evenings in the better city hotels. Further information on what to wear on safari will be found in the *Safari in Kenya* section, following.

## History

**Phoenicians**

Until the 19th C, all that the outside world knew of Kenya was the coastal strip which had been visited by the Phoenicians *circa* 600 BC. Mombasa, under the name of Tonike, was certainly referred to by Ptolemy in the 2nd C AD. By the 7th C, Arabs had begun to settle along the coast and Hindu traders followed later. Trade flourished and sailing vessels came from as far off as China to exchange goods for Africa's spices and ivory. Slaves, too, were traded.

**Arabs, Indians and Portuguese**

The Portuguese dominated the coast during the 16th C, but after long and bitter struggles the Arabs reclaimed the forts and trading posts, and by the end of the 17th C the Imam of Oman had ousted the last of the Portuguese. In 1837 Sultan Sayyid Said moved his capital from Oman to Zanzibar and at once stimulated trade in the principal commodities of East Africa – ivory and slaves, in search of which, Arab and Swahili traders, frequently financed by Indian merchants, penetrated the interior of the country. Most of the caravans marched from Bagamoyo to Ujiji, the alternative route from Mombasa into the interior being blocked by the waterless Taru plain and by the aggressive Masai warriors who were raiding the country extensively, and who decimated the Bantu agriculturalists.

**The British**

Although the German missionaries Johannes Rebmann and Johann Ludwig Krapf had explored East Africa in the 1850s as far as Mount Kenya, it was not until 1883 that the direct route through Masailand was forged by the English explorer Joseph Thomson, who thus paved the way for trading caravans and later the surveyors who staked out the route for the Ugandan Railway. Masai power was weakened by rinderpest which ravaged their herds, an epidemic of smallpox and internal feuding. In 1888 the British East Africa Navigation Company was entrusted with the development of Kenya, but its charter was surrendered to the British government in 1895 and the Protectorate of British East Africa was proclaimed. The completion of the railway from Mombasa to the shores of Lake Victoria in 1903 opened up a new era in the country's history, and within a few years white settlement began, strongly encouraged by Lord Delamere. In 1920 the East Africa Protectorate became the Kenya Colony and Protectorate, named after lofty Mount Kenya.

**Mau Mau**

Resentment against European domination and the iniquitous distribution of arable land led to the eruption of the Mau Mau (a secret Kikuyu society) rebellion in 1952, lasting four years. Franchise was granted to the Africans and in 1963 the Kenya African National Union (KANU) won a majority of seats in the House of Representatives, its leader Mzee Jomo Kenyatta becoming Prime Minister.

**Independence**

Kenya gained full independence on 12 December 1963 and was admitted to the United Nations four days later. On 12 December 1964 the constitution was revised in an attempt to centralise the state and combat tribalism. At the same time, Kenya became a republic within the Commonwealth, with Mzee Kenyatta as its first President. He remained in office until his death in August 1978, after which the former Vice-President Daniel arap Moi assumed the presidency.

## Government

Kenya is a parliamentary republic with a single political party, KANU (Kenya African National Union). The country is headed by the President and a cabinet of ministers. Ministers are answerable to the National Assembly, by which all government expenditure must be approved. The country is divided into constituencies, each electing one member of parliament.

## Religion

**Islam**

There is freedom of worship in Kenya and most religious groups are represented. Islam influenced coastal communities many centuries ago and to some extent has spread into the interior. Today it is fairly well established among the Hamitic tribes of the Northern Frontier, especially the Somalis.

**Christianity**

Christian missionaries began their work in Kenya in 1844, first at the coast and then inland through Kamba and Kikuyu country to the African peoples in Nyanza Province. Today there are numerous Protestant denominations at work throughout Kenya and several Roman Catholic orders.

Also represented are Hindus, Sikhs and some Zorastrians. Most religions enjoy their own radio programmes, and major Christian and Moslem celebrations are observed as public holidays throughout the country.

## People

**Asians, Europeans and Arabs**

Kenya's population is 98 percent African, with the remaining two percent Arab, Asian and European. The Asians comprise a variety of linguistic and religious groups who came originally from India and Pakistan, and who are mainly involved in commerce. Their numbers have been gradually decreasing since independence. European settlers, once widely spread on the highlands around Nakuru, in the Laikipia district northwest of Mount Kenya, and around Kitale and Eldoret, have had their land bought out for African settlement and a great number have left the country. Of those remaining, many have become citizens of the new nation, as have the Asians. Of the non-Africans, only the Arabs, who are especially in evidence along the coast, have been assimilated into African society, inter-marrying to create the Swahili-Arab-Bantu mixture, as well as the Swahili language, which is now the national tongue.

**African groupings:**

The Africans, who comprise over 30 different ethnic groups divided roughly into four main language families (Bantu, Nilotic, Hamitic and Nilo-Hamitic), are of several different stocks, most arriving in the country from the north or northeast between the 14th and 19th C. Only the Dorobo remain as remnants of Kenya's first historically recorded population.

**a) Bantu**

The Bantu, related to the extensive group spread over southern Africa, comprise some of the largest tribes in Kenya. Traditionally agriculturalists, they cultivate the slopes of the country's numerous mountains – The Embu, Meru and Kikuyu around the base of Mount Kenya, the Baluhya around Mount Elgon, the Taita on the mountainous range north of Tanzania's Kilimanjaro and the Kisii in western Kenya. The

Kamba, Gusii, Luhya and Nyika are also Bantu.

**b) Nilotic** The Nilotic group is represented in Kenya by the Luo, who live on the shores of Lake Victoria and predominate in the west of Kenya. Their origin can be traced by language and culture to the Sudan, their migration route the Nile valley. The Luo are the main rivals of the dominant Kikuyu for political power.

**c) Hamitic** The Hamitic peoples, of which the largest group in Kenya is the Somali, roam over the vast northern half of the country. Nomads all, they count their wealth in camels, sheep and goats.

**d) Nilo-Hamitic** The tribes holding the greatest attraction for visitors are undoubtedly those belonging to the Nilo-Hamitic peoples, rich in ceremonials and spectacular in dress. Nilo-Hamitic is a misnomer, as it implies a mixture of the Nilotic and Hamitic, but there is no evidence to support this, nor has the language any similarity to that of the Nilotes. It is among the Nilo-Hamitics that we find the famous Masai, who still occupy a great area of Kenya and extend south into Tanzania. Even more picturesque are the nomadic Samburu, who roam about in the tumbling, volcanic country between Lake Turkana and northwest Mount Kenya. Appropriately, Samburu means butterfly. West from Samburu country lies the land of the colourful Suk (Pokot) and beyond that is Turkana country.

Two tribes which do not fit into these main classifications are the Dorobo, in the Mau forest beyond Nakuru, and the tiny community of the El Molo on the barren shores of Lake Turkana.

## Visitors Information

**Sights** The main tourist attractions are photographic and specialist safaris (see the *Safari in Kenya* section, following); a visit to snow-capped Mount Kenya on the equator; bird watching and fishing at the Rift Valley lakes; swimming, surfing and big game fishing at the coral resorts along the Indian Ocean; and all varieties of sport and recreation, including private flying. There is a rich diversity of tribal life, with its customs, costumes and ceremonials.

The best season for visiting Kenya is from November through March, though along the coast September and October are the best months. All months, however, have their attractions.

Kenya Tourist Offices in London, New York, Los Angeles, Frankfurt, Paris, Stockholm and Zurich, as well as the Ministry of Tourism, Kencom House, PO Box 30027, Nairobi, Kenya (Tel: 331030), provide a wide range of tourist pamphlets in English, German, French and Japanese.

## Entry and Exit Formalities

**Visas** Visas are required for all visitors except British citizens and nationals of the Bahamas, Bangla Desh, Barbardos, Botswana, Canada, Cyprus, Denmark, the Dominican Republic, Ethiopia, Fiji, Gambia, the German Federal Republic, Ghana, Grenada, Guyana, India, the Irish Republic, Italy, Jamaica, Kiribati, Lesotho, Malawi, Malaysia, Malta, Mauritius, Nauru, the Netherlands, New Zealand, Norway, Papua New Guinea, Samoa (Western), San Marino, the Seychelles, Sierra Leone, Singapore, Solomon Islands, Spain, Sri Lanka, Santa Lucia, Swaziland, Sweden, Tanzania, Tonga, Trinidad and Tobago, Turkey, Tuvalu, Uganda, Uruguay, Zambia and Zimbabwe (all normally for a stay of up to three months). Nor is a visa required for transit passengers holding confirmed onward or return tickets and reservations and valid entry documents for the country of destination. All other visitors must obtain a visa prior to embarkation for Kenya. In special cases visas may sometimes by obtained on arrival in Kenya, but considerable delay is involved. All British passport holders of Asian origin require visas for entry into Kenya and must hold the equivalent in convertible currency of Kshs 4000/-.

Kenya refuses admission to holders of South African passports, although they are allowed to transit Kenya provided they do not leave the airport.

Kenya issues visas through its consular offices abroad. In countries where Kenya has no diplomatic representation, visas for Kenya will be issued by British consulates.

A visitor's pass is required by all visitors and is obtainable free of charge upon arrival. A visitor who has no onward or return ticket may be required to make a refundable deposit of up to Kshs 5000/-. Visitors to Kenya wishing to visit Tanzania, Uganda, the Seychelles or Mauritius and then return to Kenya should request visitor's passes for a sufficient time to cover the whole period of their sojourn in East Africa.

Note that the border between Kenya and Tanzania is closed and there is no through surface transportation without specific government clearance. (See the section *Travel to and within Kenya*, following.)

Normally there are no vaccination requirements, but see the *Health* section, following.

**Customs regulations**

Customs regulations permit the free import by travellers 16 years of age or older of 200 cigarettes or 50 cigars of 250 grams of tobacco, one bottle of alcoholic beverage and half a litre of perfume. The import of fruit, plants, seeds, imitation firearms, children's toy pistols, etc., is prohibited. Firearms and ammunition require a police permit. Export of gold and diamonds is prohibited, as is the export of skin articles or game trophies unless obtained from authorised government personnel. Persons wearing any ivory articles should be able to prove by licence or receipt in which country the ivory was purchased.

## Travel to and within Kenya

**The Kenya-Tanzania border**

*Note: At the time of writing there are no passenger communications between Kenya and Tanzania by air, sea, rail or road. This may change. But meanwhile it is possible to fly from Nairobi to Dar es Salaam or Kilimanjaro via Addis Ababa on Ethiopian Airlines (around Kshs 5500), or via Entebbe on Uganda airlines (around Kshs 2750), or via Kigali in Rwanda on Sabena (around Kshs 4400).*

*It is also possible to travel overland from Nairobi to Arusha through the border crossing at Namanga, but permits must be obtained in advance, first from the Inspector General of Police in Dar es Salaam and then from the police in Nairobi. Your embassy in Nairobi might assist you with these formalities, which take about three weeks. You must state in advance the date on which you intend to cross into Tanzania and your length of stay there.*

*You can get a shuttle car* (matatu) *from Nairobi to Namanga for around Kshs 90, from where you must cross the border on foot, though you will be subject to interminable police and customs scrutiny (allow at least two hours). Once across, you can usually pick up a Tanzanian matatu to Arusha for about Tshs 220 per seat. Your welcome on the Tanzanian side will be warmer if you carry gifts of toilet soap, toothpaste or chocolate, which are either impossible to obtain or exhorbitant in price.*

**International flights**

**Air.** Kenya is served internationally by over 20 air carriers including Aeroflot, Air Burundi, Air France, Air India, Air Madagascar, Air Malawi, Air Mauritius, Air

Zaire, Alitalia, British Airways, Cameroon Airlines, Egyptair, El Al, Ethiopian Airlines, Iberian Airlines, Kenya Airways, Olympic, PIA, Pan Am, Royal Swazi Airways, Sabena, SAS, Somali Airlines, Sudan Airways, Swissair, Uganda Airlines, Yemen Airways and Zambia Airways. Several other airlines maintain liaison offices in Nairobi. There are regular daily services to Europe and frequent scheduled services to Asia, the Middle East, the United States and to other parts of Africa.

Kenya Airways' international network includes Accra, Addis Ababa, Athens, Bahrain, Bombay, Cairo, Copenhagen, Djibouti, Dubai, Entebbe, Frankfurt, Harare (formerly Salisbury), Jeddah, Karachi, Lagos, London, Lusaka, Mauritius, Mogadishu, Paris, Rome, the Seychelles, Vienna and Zurich. Inaugurated in 1977, the national airline has captured over 85 percent of the market once enjoyed by East African Airways.

**Domestic flights**

Kenya Airways operates domestic flights several times daily to Malindi and Mombasa, and twice weekly to Kisumu.

Nairobi's Jomo Kenyatta International Airport, long the aviation gateway to East Africa, has been completely renovated and is destined to become a major aircraft maintenance centre offering a wide range of technical services. The Moi Mombasa International Airport, Kenya's second airport, can now accommodate heavy international traffic enabling wide-bodied aircraft to land or be diverted from Nairobi.

**Sea.** Once-popular sea services to Kenya are on the decline and no scheduled passenger ships operate at the time of writing, except for a passenger service linking Mombasa with India via the Seychelles. Regular cargo ships operate to all parts of the world, but very few carry passengers. The port of Mombasa, linked by rail and road with Nairobi, serves as gateway to international markets not only for Kenya but also for neighbouring African countries.

**Lake Victoria.** Kenya's Lake Victoria services are hardly worth travelling on these days; you cannot sail to Tanzanian or Ugandan ports, but are restricted to the Kenyan wedge of lakeshore. The ferries operate two to six times per week (depending on destination) between Kisumu, Kendu Bay, Homa Bay and

Karungu. Enquiries should be made through Kenya Railways.

**Land transport.** The greater part of Kenya's domestic supplies as well as those for export are carried by surface transport, Kenya's system being one of the most advanced in Africa. Rail and road networks reach all parts of the country, in addition to maintaining valuable links with neighbouring states. Kenya handles an enormous volume of traffic passing to and from Uganda, Rwanda, Burundi and Zaire to the Sudan, Ethiopia and Somalia.

**Rail** Kenya's rail system includes over 1000 kms of main line between Mombasa and the Uganda border, and a further 1000 kms of branch lines serving such vital points as Magadi, Taveta, Nanyuki, Butere and Kericho. The principal passenger train services operated daily by Kenya Railways are between Nairobi and Mombasa, Nairobi and Kisumu, and Nairobi and Nanyuki via Thika and Nyeri. The Nairobi-Mombasa line runs through Tsavo National Park (28 Indian labourers were eaten by lions during its construction) – if you get up early you have a good chance of seeing game from the safety of your compartment. For information, phone Nairobi 21211, or Mombasa 312221.

**Roads** Kenya boasts some 50,000 kms of classified (major and minor) roads, as well as a further 100,000 kms of unclassified roads and tracks. Some 5000 kms of roads are bitumenised. Main routes connect Kenya with its immediate neighbours and further to central and southern Africa, Zaire, the Sudan, Ethiopia and Somalia. There is a highway between Nairobi and Addis Ababa and an agreement has been signed for the construction of a road to link Lodwar in Kenya with Juba in southern Sudan. In general road links with Ethiopia, Uganda and Tanzania are good, but those with Somalia and the Sudan are poor.

**Bus** Regular bus services connect Nairobi with the main towns, but the buses tend to be crowded. Scheduled coach services on which seats may be reserved are operated by several companies in Nairobi and Mombasa.

**Taxis** Visitors are strongly advised to consult their hotel managers regarding specific taxi fares and to agree on the price with the driver before commencing the journey. Shuttle or share taxis (*matatus*) operate between major towns providing more rapid travel than coaches at little extra cost – except on the nerves: they are sometimes driven by maniacs and can be dangerous (matatu, roughly translated, means 'always room for three more'!).

### Driving in Kenya

Driving in Kenya is on the left, petrol stations are fairly frequent along main highways, and police highway cars, dark with blue and white roofs, patrol these routes. Also the Automobile Association's patrol cars cover the major trunk roads. Their service is for members only, but visitors may obtain on-the-spot membership.

On minor roads drivers should be prepared for unexpected hazards, such as cattle, game and pedestrians, unsignposted drifts through which streams flow in the rainy season, and sudden changes in road surface and camber. They should also beware at night the single approaching headlamp behind which lurks almost invariably not a motorcycle but a large truck or bus. Main roads, however, are relatively free of traffic and generally well maintained, permitting high average speeds. The speed limit is 100 kms per hour unless otherwise stated by signs in built-up areas.

**Off the beaten track**

Basic precautions are necessary for travel into Kenya's more outlying districts. Even when dry, some earth and sand surfaces can be treacherous, especially when the driver swerves or stops suddenly. Special care should be taken until experience is gained. In the event of breakdown or accident, it may be several hours or even days before any other traffic or help arrives. The motorist should therefore always carry some food and drink, a first-aid outfit, a basic kit of tools and spare parts, and he should be able to mend a puncture. Temporary membership of the Flying Doctors Society of Africa, PO Box 30125, Nairobi (Tel: 501301), costs very little and provides insurance against air ambulance fees should an accident occur.

**Maps**

Excellent maps of Kenya's national parks are published by Survey of Kenya, PO Box 30046, Nairobi. Each sheet has illustrations of the animals commonly found in the park and a list of birds. The following are available: Nairobi, Maru, Tsavo, Amboseli, Marsabit, Samburu and Masai Mara. There is also a beautiful topographical map of Mount Kenya. The Shell company has produced an excellent road map. Further details about general driving conditions in Kenya may be obtained from the Automobile Association of East Africa, AA Headquarters, Westlands, PO Box 40087, Nairobi (Tel: 742926).

**Driving documents**

Visiting motorists entering Kenya must be in possession of the following documents: vehicle registration book, certificate of insurance valid for Kenya, driving licence, international plate showing country of vehicle registration, valid passport or other proof of identity, health certificates, visa if required, and visitor's pass obtainable at the frontier post. Foreign vehicles must within seven days of arrival acquire an International Circulation Permit from the Licencing Officer, Nairobi. Valid international driving licences are recognised in Kenya. Visitors over 18 years of age may use their own driving licence for up to 90 days provided it is endorsed at the Road Transport Office in Nairobi. A Kenya driving licence can be obtained on any valid Commonwealth driving licence or on a valid international driving licence. Further information may be obtained from the Registrar of Motor Vehicles, Gill House, Government Road, PO Box 30440, Nairobi (Tel: 26624), or from any District Commissioner's Office in Kenya.

**Car hire.** The following rates are indicative only and subject to increase.

*Selfdrive:* VW Beetle 105/- per day, 625/- per week, plus 1/6 per km; VW Golf 140/- per day, 825/- per week, plus 2/10 per km; Audi 100 or Safari Minibus 275/- per day, 1650/- per week, plus 3/90 per km; Range Rover 330/- per day, 2000/- per week, plus 5/50 per km. VW Polos, Audi 80s and Mercedes 200s are also commonly available. Rates are exclusive of petrol and oil. The driver must be over 23 and have had a valid licence for at least 24 months.

*Chauffeur-driven:* Rates are about 65 percent higher (eg Range Rover 550/- per day, 3300/- per week, plus 6/60 per km), but include petrol and oil, and the chauffeur's service from 8am to noon and 2pm to 5pm. Chauffeur's overtime is charged at 11/- per hour, and he gets an out-of-town safari allowance of 100/- per day.

## Accommodation

**Nairobi** Kenya boasts a wide range of accommodation, both in style and price. In Nairobi the centrally located Hilton, Inter-Continental, Six-Eighty and New Stanley offer all modern conveniences at international standard. There are delightful country club-style hostelries in the suburbs, notably the historic Norfolk, Nairobi's oldest hotel, the Nairobi Serena and the Jacaranda. These are excellent for family holidays. For the budget-minded traveller there are very cheap lodgings near Nairobi's Central Market and along River and Digo Road – and throughout the country. Sometimes you will have to rough it, but not always: there are some inexpensive yet pleasant hotels and guest houses, as well as youth hostels, YMCAs and YWCAs, and camping.

**At the game parks** Game parks offer an abundance of imaginatively designed luxury lodges, and attractive African-style bandas or thatched huts with surprisingly sophisticated comforts within. Salt licks are strategically placed to attract animals for easy viewing; you sip your sundowner on the terrace while the wildlife parades before you. Kenya's most famous game-viewing lodge is Treetops, built in the trees of Aberdare National Park. In the same park is The Ark, shaped like Noah's, though in this case man is inside, the animals all outside. Apart from lodges, there are numerous permanently tented camps with facilities from the luxurious to the basic throughout Kenya. Most parks have organised camping sites within or just outside the park perimeter. Some sport a complete range of services, eg hot and cold running water, electricity, petrol pump, service station, and a store usually well stocked with provisions. In others you need to be completely self-sufficient. You must never camp outside the specified camping sites, at least not without a professional escort.

**Along the coast** At the coast you will find a bewildering variety of beach hotels vying with one another in luxury and the unusual. Amongst the best south of Mombasa are Two Fishes Hotel and Robinson Baobab, at Diani. To the north, Bamburi Beach, Serena Beach, Mnarani Club and Seafarers are a few of the many top class establishments. Hotels at Malindi are mostly in the traditional style, and on the island of Lamu there is Swahili Petley's Inn dating back to the early 1800s.

Along the entire length of the coast there are also medium- to low-priced hotels, self-service bandas, rondavels and camping sites. There are some extremely cheap hotels in both Mombasa and Malindi. Most beach hotels provide evening entertainment: barbeques, traditional dancing, film shows and discos.

Note that both along the coast and in the game parks greatly reduced accommodation rates are available in the low season from mid-April to mid-July. This is the rainy season and roads in some of the game parks often become impassable.

**Self-service accommodation.** The Forest Department operates 21 rest houses in various parts of the country; these are available for public use when not required by forestry officers on duty. Details may be obtained from the Automobile Association's handbook, or from the Public Relations Officer, Forestry Department, PO Box 30513, Nairobi; Tel: 22141. Bookings must be made in advance. Two other government rest houses are available at Tot, 120 kms northeast of Eldoret (bookings through the District Commissioner, Tambach, via Eldoret) and at Kabichbich, north of Kitale (bookings through the District Commissioner, West Pokot, PO Kapenguria via Kitale).

Four fishing camps (three in central Kenya, one near Kericho) are operated by the Fisheries Department, PO Box 40241, Nairobi; Tel: 24865 and 23592. Others near Kitale are run by the Kapalet Fishing Association, PO Box 332, Kitale, and by Suam and Kaptagat Angling Club, PO Box 168, Kitale. Bookings for the Kiandorongo Fishing Camp in Aberdare National Park can be made through PO Box 24, Meiga.

In the national parks there are self-service camps at Kitani and Ngulia Safari Camp (Tsavo West), Aruba (Tsavo East) and Leopard Rock (Meru). Bookings should be made through the Automobile Association/Bunson Travel Service, PO Box 45456, Nairobi; Tel: 742926 – they also handle the Lake Baringo self-service camp and the bandas at Buffalo Springs (Samburu). The Travel Bureau, PO Box 43230, Nairobi (Tel: 21716), accepts bookings for Ol Tukai bandas (Amboseli). Naro Moru River Lodge, PO Box 18, Naro Moru (Tel: 23), handles bookings for the Mount Kenya self-service lodge.

Self-service accommodation is also available at the following places: Ologesaile, bookings through PO Box 30239, Nairobi (Tel: 22684); Bushwhackers Safari Camp, about 30 kms off the Nairobi-Mombasa road, PO Kibwezi; Narok Club, meals available, bookings through the District Commissioner, Narok; Naro Moru River Lodge, Nguruman Park, bookings through PO Box 15028, Nairobi.

**Camping**. As mentioned above, camping in Kenya can vary from the basic to the deluxe. The better sites provide running water, toilet facilities and a shop. But many others, especially in game areas, provide little except atmosphere, so campers should travel self-contained, with adequate water and food supplies. For those who would like some of the freedom of camping without its possible discomforts, the growing number of do-it-yourself banda camps may provide the answer. These are huts built in various styles, often rondavels with thatched roofs, with beds, kitchen, toilet and shower or bath facilities. It is necessary only to take food and sometimes bedding; hire costs are low. This type of accommodation must usually be booked in advance through agents in Nairobi, and demand is often high at weekends and on public holidays. Apart from camps within and near game parks, there are forestry and fishing camps; these can only be booked through local officials. Campers should see *Camping in Kenya* by J D Arkle.

Note that camping can be widely defined, so that as well as referring to the information below, you should read the section above on self-service accommodation.

All national parks have specified camping sites. Also there are organised camping sites with varying facilities and charges at: Carnelly's Camp, Marina Club and Safariland Club (Lake Naivasha); Lanet Camp and ASK Showground (Nakuru); Namanga River Hotel, Naro Moru Lodge and New Wagon Wheels Hotel (Eldoret); Bushwhackers Safari Camp (Kibwezi); Machula River Farm (Kitale); Eliye Springs (Lake Turkana); and at Youth Hostels.

In addition, camping is permitted in most forest areas (inform the local ranger), and on private land (with the landowner's permission). In practice, anyone camping discreetly in a sparsely populated area other than a game park is unlikely to cause offence. However, intending campers should take precautions against theft, which is increasingly becoming a problem even in apparently uninhabited areas.

**Youth centres**. The Kenya Youth Hostels Association, PO Box 48661, Nairobi (Tel: 26045); the YMCA, PO Box 30330, Nairobi (Tel: 337468); and the YWCA, PO Box 40710, Nairobi (Tel: 338689) – all offer accommodation both in Nairobi and round Kenya. There are Youth Hostels at Kanamai on the north coast, Kitale, Malindi, Mount Elgon, Mount Kenya, Nairobi, Naivasha, Nanyuki and Nyeri. Camping is also possible at these.

**Special note**. Accommodation rates throughout this Kenya section are exclusive of tax and service charges. There is a 15 percent government tax on the accommodation element of hotel bills, plus a two percent training tax on the entire bill. Also, some hotels may impose a five to ten percent service charge on the entire bill. As a rule of thumb, therefore, you should probably add 25 percent to the rates shown in the listings.

Many hotels offer special rates for children. The rate for single occupancy of a double room is higher than the normal single rate. Some hotels offer reduced rates to Kenyan citizens.

## Food and Drink

**Cuisine**

Most hotels and game lodges serve European food, with occasional African or Indian dishes on the menu. Outside the hotels, however, eating places in the larger towns offer a more adventurous range of cuisines, including Continental, Oriental and Creole. The visitor can find good Chinese, Korean and Japanese places, French and Italian cafes, Kenyan roast meat stalls, burger joints, marvellous seafood restaurants, and endless variations on the vegetarian theme. Meat, despite its excellent quality, is largely absent from local diets.

Some typically African dishes:

*Githeri*: beans and maize
*Irio*: peas, vegetables and maize
*Matoke*: steamed bananas
*Matumbo*: cooked intestines
*Mkate mayai*: flour and eggs

*Mrere*: green vegetables cooked with magadi soda
*Muhogo ya kuchoma*: roasted cassava with chillies and lemon
*Nyama ya kuchoma*: roasted meat
*Sukuma wiki*: boiled spinach
*Ugali*: maize meal, often covered with a vegetable and meat sauce, and served in a clay pot

Mention should be made of the *samosa*, the Kenyan version of the Greek pita, the Cornish pasty or the Chinese spring roll. It consists of a thin, crisp and light pastry neatly folded round a filling of firmly packed mince cooked with spices and chopped onions. A samosa may be an instant snack, served as a quick lunch, or as an accompaniment to drinks.

Beef, pork, butter, cheese, vegetables and fruits (mangoes, oranges, pineapples, paw paws, avocados, grapefruits, bananas) are outstanding. Trout, tilapia (a local white fish) and Nile perch are easily obtained, and seafood delicacies include lobster, shrimps, prawns and Mombasa oysters.

Strongly spiced food, especially curry, has become popular, not only among Europeans and Asians, but also among Africans.

**Spirits and wine**

While dining in Kenya can be anything from expensive to cheap, drinking wine and spirits is usually on the expensive side. Both Tanzania and Ethiopia have vineyards, but Kenya has none and so all wine from the grape must be imported. (Kenya is studying the feasibility of developing its own vineyards, and is fermenting its tropical fruits, especially paw paw juice, to produce its own wines, vermouths and sherries.) Shortages of foreign exchange can make foreign wines and spirits scarce and expensive, though Kenya makes Smirnoff vodka and Gilbey's gin under licence, while many other brands are locally blended or bottled. Kenya's own spirits include Kenya Cane, from sugar cane, and an international prize winning coffee liqueur called Kenya Gold which rates well against Kahlua and Tia Maria.

**Beer**

Beer is the national drink, and it is preferred warm – if you cannot make that cultural shift, be sure to order your beer 'baridi'. The standard is high, and Kenya Breweries Limited produces Tusker Lager, White Cap, Tusker Premium, Tusker Export, Guinness Stout and Pilsner. The most popular is White Cap, which comes in a large bottle sufficient for two glasses. Export and Premium come in smaller bottles, the latter the most expensive Kenyan beer.

**Water** Tap water is safe to drink in large towns and along the coast, unless otherwise stated.

Approximate hours for meals are: breakfast 7.30am-9.30am, lunch 12.30pm-2.30pm, and dinner 7pm-9pm, although hours may be extended in larger cities. Bars are open from 11am to 2pm and from 5pm to 11pm.

### Health

Care should be taken when swimming in lakes and rivers as some are infected with bilharzia. Precautions should be taken against sunburn.

Vaccination against cholera and yellow fever is strongly recommended at all times and mandatory for those arriving from or via an infected area. Kenya itself is included in the cholera infected zone. Yellow fever vaccination is recommended for those intending to travel outside the main cities and may be compulsory for departure from Kenya and entry into the next country. Typhoid and paratyphoid vaccinations are also strongly advised. Malaria risk exists in the whole country including the urban areas, except for Nairobi and the highlands of the Central Rift Valley. Therefore a malaria prophylactic should be taken two weeks before arrival and two weeks after departure.

### Entertainment and Sport

There are nightclubs, modern cinemas and drive-ins in both Nairobi and Mombasa, and the capital supports an active film society. There are two live theatres in Nairobi and one in Mombasa. Occasional concerts are given by the Nairobi Orchestra.

Sport and outdoor recreation are very popular in Kenya. At the coast there are ample opportunities and facilities for swimming in the sea or in fresh water pools, big game fishing, deep sea diving under the supervision of qualified instructors, goggling, water skiing, para-sailing, surfing, wind surfing, sailing and yachting. There are also several yacht clubs up-country. Numerous rivers provide good sport for anglers, especially on the slopes of Mount Kenya and the Aberdares. Horse racing, motor rallies and racing are popular. There are many opportunities for mountaineering, while organised sport includes golf, athletics, polo, football, hockey, rugby, cricket, tennis, judo, squash and netball. Most of Kenya's numerous sport clubs welcome temporary members.

### Publications and Broadcasting

Kenya's press is possibly the most professional in black Africa. There are two national daily newspapers in English, the *Daily Nation* and *The Standard*; weekly publications are the *Nairobi Times*, the *Sunday Standard*, the *Sunday Nation* and the *Weekly Review*. Useful fortnightly or monthly publications are *What's On* (a guide to current events), the *Nairobi Handbook*, *Safari* (the East Africa tourist magazine) and *Swara*, published by the East African Wildlife Society.

Newspapers and magazines from most parts of the world are available in Nairobi and Mombasa shortly after publication.

The Voice of Kenya radio and television services provide news in English, Swahili and tribal languages. The BBC World Service and other overseas radio services broadcast regularly to East Africa.

### Money Matters

**Currency** The unit of currency is the Kenya shilling (Kshs), divided into 100 cents. Kshs 20 (or 20/-) equals K£1 (though currency denominations are always in shillings, not pounds). The following denominations are in circulation:

*Coins*: 5, 10 and 50 cents, and Kshs 1.

*Notes*: Kshs 5, 10, 20 and 100.

**Rates** The approximate rate of exchange is UK£1 equals Kshs 19, and US$1 equals Kshs 13. But rates are subject to fluctuation and should be checked.

Residents of Kenya, Tanzania and Uganda must offer all foreign currency notes for sale to an authorised dealer. Import of foreign currency by other visitors is without restriction, but must be declared on arrival or you will not be able to take it out of the country again. Travellers may carry Kenyan, Tanzanian and Ugandan currency up to the equivalent of Kshs 100. Foreign currency should be exchanged only at an authorised dealer, ie banks as well as leading hotels and travel agents, but not shops. It is important that you obtain and keep exchange receipts until your departure, especially if you want to reconvert any unused Kenyan currency. There are banks at both

Nairobi and Mombasa airports.

There is little black market demand for hard currency and dealing on the street is risky.

**Credit cards** American Express, Diners Club and Visa cards are accepted by many hotels and shops.

Tipping is customary at about ten percent of the bill for most services, though waiters may be tipped less if service is included in the bill. Hotel porters are tipped 2/- to 3/- per article. For other hotel staff, little and often is a good rule. Safari drivers and guides should get 10/- to 100/- depending on the length of the trip. Tipping airport porters is not required.

Banking hours are from 8.30 am to 2 pm Monday to Friday, though banks are also open on the first and last Saturdays of each month. Some exchange bureaux have longer hours.

## What to Buy in Kenya

*Note: The sale of game skins and game trophies, including ivory articles, is strictly prohibited.*

Cow horn bracelets are now substituting for the traditional ones of elephant hair entwined with gold, worn as a protection against evil spirits. The likeliest skin for sale will be sheepskin, in the form of rugs, slippers and coats. The skin needs to be properly cured, so you should buy only from a reputable dealer. Traditional items include ceremonial drums; hunting spears; string and wood instruments (geniune ones are available but hard to find; examine the museum collection first); *kitenge, kanga* or *kikoi* (colourful wrap-around lengths of material worn locally); brass, copper and silverware in the form of lanterns; incense burners (*chetezo*); rose water sprinklers (*mrashi*); and shell necklaces.

Wood carvings skilfully executed by Africans can be purchased at very good prices. They include three-legged folding stools carved from a single piece of wood, and hand-carved chess sets, book ends, salad bowls, table lamps and buttons. Brass-studded wooden chests are made in Zanzibar (Tanzania). Genuine old tribal carvings are hard to find, but you can buy the weired and striking Makonde sculpture from Tanzania and similar Akambe carvings from Kenya.

Stoneware carvings by the Kisii in western Kenya – animals, fruit bowls, ashtrays and so on – are made from light-coloured soapstone, sometimes darkened. Verdite carvings, though not produced in Kenya, can be bought here. Verdite, a stone found only in Africa, is mottled green and looks rather like malachite. Items are hand-carved and polished.

Pleochrosmatic tansanite (blue zoisite) is a characteristic stone of East Africa, faceted into a dazzling aurora of reflected colours. Most zoisites are cut so that the blue facet is face on, hence the name. Agate, amethyst, topaz, beryl and tiger's eye are other precious and semi-precious stones. Tribal bracelets, beadwork armbands, headbands and belts may also be worn as jewellery.

Heartbeat of Africa recordings reproduce authentic East African sounds (animals' voices, bird songs, drums, folk music and traditional instruments) with descriptive notes in four languages.

**Hours of Business**

Government and business hours are from 8.30am to 12.30pm and from 2pm to 4pm Monday through Friday, and 8.30am to noon Saturday.

Banks are open from 8.30am to 2pm Monday through Friday, and on the first and last Saturdays of each month. Bureaux de change sometimes have longer hours.

Main post offices are open from 8am to 6pm, others from 8am to noon and from 2pm to 4pm.

Shops open from 8.30am to 1pm and from 2pm to 5pm, though some will remain open during lunch, or until 7pm or even on Sunday. Normally shops are closed on Sunday and on Saturday afternoons.

Bars are open from 11am to 2pm and from 5pm to 11pm.

**Time and Public Holidays**

Kenya is three hours ahead of Greenwich Mean Time. Noon GMT is 3pm in Kenya. When quoted a departure time for transport, check that it is not Swahili time, which begins at 6am, the hour of sunrise. (See *Swahili Vocabulary*, following, for an explanation of Swahili time.)

Official public holidays are 1 January, New Year's Day; Good Friday; Easter Monday; 1 May, Labour Day; 1 June, Madaraka Day, ie the anniversary of self-government; 20 October, Kenyatta Day; 12 Decem-

*Masai woman and child near the Kenya-Tanzania border. Turkana decorations (see cover) are similar.*

ber, Independence Day; 25 December, Christmas Day; and 26 December, Boxing Day. In addition, Id-ul-Fitr, marking the end of Ramadan, and Id-ul-Azhar, the start of the pilgrimage to Mecca 70 days after the end of Ramadan, are Islamic holidays of variable date – the first is celebrated as a public holiday, the second among Moslems only. (See the *Practical Information* section under *Lamu* for an explanation of the Moslem calendar.)

**Weights, Measures and Electricity**

Electrical voltage is 240AC, 50 cycles. Lamp sockets are the bayonet type and domestic and power plugs are the two-pin round and three-pin square types. It is useful to carry adaptors to meet these variations.

Kenya formerly used the British system of weights and measures, but has now entirely changed over to the metric system.

**Temperature**

| Fahrenheit | = | Centigrade/Celsius |
|---|---|---|
| 122 | | 50 |
| 113 | | 45 |
| 110 | | 43.3 |
| 107.6 | | 42 |
| 104 | | 40 |
| 102.2 | | 39 |
| 100 | | 37.8 |
| 98.6 | | 37 |
| 96.8 | | 36 |
| 95 | | 35 |
| 93.2 | | 34 |
| 91.4 | | 33 |
| 90 | | 32 |
| 87.8 | | 31 |
| 86 | | 30 |
| 84.2 | | 29 |
| 80 | | 26.7 |
| 75 | | 23.9 |
| 70 | | 21 |
| 65 | | 18.3 |
| 60 | | 15.6 |
| 55 | | 12.8 |
| 50 | | 10 |
| 45 | | 7.2 |
| 40 | | 4 |
| 32 | | 0 |
| 23 | | -5 |
| 14 | | -10 |
| 0 | | -17.8 |

*Fahrenheit into Centigrade/Celsius:* subtract 32 from Fahrenheit temperature, then multiply by 5, then divide by 9. *Centigrade/Celsius into Fahrenheit:* multiply Centigrade/Celsius by 9, then divide by 5, then add 32.

**Linear Measure**

| | |
|---|---|
| 0.39 inches | 1 centimetre |
| 1inch | 2.54 centimetres |
| 1 foot (12 in.) | 0.30 metres |
| 1 yard (3 ft.) | 0.91 metres |
| 39.37 inches | 1 metre |
| 0.62 miles | 1 kilometre |
| 1 mile (5280 ft.) | 1.61 kilometres |
| 3 miles | 4.8 kilometres |
| 10 miles | 16 kilometres |
| 60 miles | 98.6 kilometres |
| 100 miles | 160.9 kilometres |

| | |
|---|---|
| 1 sq. foot | **Square Measure** |
| 1 sq. yard | 0.09 sq. metres |
| 0.84 sq. metres | |
| 1.20 sq. yards | 1 sq. metre |

**Weight**

| | |
|---|---|
| 0.04 ounces | 1 gram |
| 1 ounce | 28.35 grams |
| 1 pound | 453.59 grams |
| 2.20 pounds | 1 kilogram |
| 1 ton (2000 lbs.) | 907.18 kilograms |

**Liquid Measure**

| | |
|---|---|
| 0.22 imperial gallons | 1 litre |
| 0.26 US gallons | 1 litre |
| 1 US gallon | 3.79 litres |
| 1 imperial gallon | 4.55 litres |

## Swahili Vocabulary

The Swahili language evolved along the East African coast from the intermixing of African Bantu with Arabic and Persian. The word Swahili itself derives from the Arabic *sahil,* meaning coast, and today it is a lingua franca throughout Tanzania and to a lesser extent in Kenya, Uganda, Burundi, Malawi, Zambia, Somalia, Sudan and even Oman on the Persian Gulf.

Swahili uses our alphabet and is entirely phonetic. Pronunciation of the vowels is approximately as follows: A as in *father,* E as in the *a* in *say,* I as the *e* in *be,* O as in *hoe,* and U as the *oo* in *too.*

The consonants are generally pronounced as in English, but note the following: F as in *fat*, never as in *of*; G as in *got*, never as in *ginger*; S as in *sin*, never as in *is*.

Syllables always end with a vowel. Therefore *jambo* (hello) is composed of the two syllables *ja + mbo*. *Asante* (thank you) is *a + sa + nte*. The stress is always on the penultimate syllable.

Swahili is spoken by about one-seventh of the world's population, and is one of the easiest languages to learn. The well-known *Teach Yourself* series has a book on Swahili, and phrase books are for sale in East Africa. Some words and phrases are listed below to get you started.

**General**

| | |
|---|---|
| Hello | *jambo* |
| Please | *tafadhali* |
| Thank you (very much) | *asante (sana)* |
| I am sorry | *pole* |
| Goodbye | *kwaheri* |
| Yes | *naam* |
| No | *la* |
| Good | *mwema* |
| Bad | *mbaya* |
| I want | *nataka* |
| Do you have? | *una?* |
| How much? | *Pesa ngapi?* |
| This | *huyu* |
| That | *yule* |
| Big | *kubwa* |
| Small | *kidogo* |
| Quickly | *upesi* |
| Slowly | *polepole* |
| Another/more | *ingine* |
| Much/many | *mwingi* |
| And | *na* |
| Or | *au* |
| Not/is not | *si* |

**People**

| | |
|---|---|
| I/me | *mimi* |
| You (sing.) | *wewe* |
| He/she | *yeye* |
| We | *sisi* |
| You (pl.) | *ninyi* |
| They | *wao* |
| Man | *mwamamume* |
| Woman | *mwanamke* |
| Child | *mtoto* |
| Father | *baba* |
| Mother | *mama* |
| Son | *mwana* |

| | | |
|---|---|---|
| | Daughter | *binti* |
| | Husband | *mume* |
| | Wife | *mke* |
| | Friend | *rafiki* |
| | Name | *jina* |
| | Sir/mister | *bwana* |

| | | |
|---|---|---|
| **Medical** | Doctor | *dokitari* |
| | Hospital | *hospitali* |
| | Medicine | *dawa* |
| | Where is the nearest doctor? | *Wapi dokitari karibu?* |
| | Where is the nearest hospital? | *Wapi hospitali karibu?* |

| | | |
|---|---|---|
| **Hotel** | Where is a hotel? | *Wapi hoteli?* |
| | I want a room (with bath) | *Nataka nyumba (na bafu)* |
| | How much? | *Pesa ngapi?* |
| | Cheap | *rahisi* |
| | Expensive | *ghali* |

| | | |
|---|---|---|
| **Food and Drink** | Food/meal | *chakula* |
| | Beer | *pombe* |
| | Coffee | *kahawa* |
| | Tea | *chai* |
| | Hot | *moto* |
| | Cold | *baridi* |
| | Ice | *barafu* |
| | Sweet | *tamu* |
| | Sugar | *sukari* |
| | Milk | *maziwa* |
| | Water | *maji* |
| | Meat | *nyama* |
| | Chicken | *kuku* |
| | Fish | *samaki* |
| | Vegetables | *mboga* |
| | Rice | *wali* |
| | Fruit | *tunda* |
| | Dessert | *tamu tamu* |
| | Bread | *mkate* |
| | Butter | *siagi* |
| | Salt | *chumvi* |
| | Pepper | *pilipili* |
| | Enough | *basi* |
| | Another/more | *ingine* |
| | Big | *kubwa* |
| | Small | *kidogo* |
| | A lot/plenty | *mingi* |
| | How much? | *Pesa ngapi?* |

## Shopping

| | |
|---|---|
| Shop | *duka* |
| Market | *soko* |
| I want | *nataka* |
| Do you have? | *una?* |
| How much? | *Pesa ngapi?* |
| Cigarettes | *sigareti* |
| Newspaper | *gazeti* |
| Clothes/dress | *nguo* |
| Shoes | *viatu* |
| Money | *fedha* |
| Expensive (very) | *ghali (sana)* |
| Cheap | *rahisi* |
| Please give me a discount | *Tafadhali nipunguzie* |

## Numbers

| | |
|---|---|
| Half | *nusu* |
| One | *moja* |
| Two | *mbili* |
| Three | *tatu* |
| Four | *nne* |
| Five | *tano* |
| Six | *sita* |
| Seven | *saba* |
| Eight | *nane* |
| Nine | *tisa* |
| Ten | *kumi* |
| Eleven | *kumi na moja* |
| Twelve | *kumi na mbili* |
| Twenty | *ishirini* |
| Twenty-one | *ishirini na moja* |
| Thirty | *thelathini* |
| Thirty-five | *thelathini na tano* |
| Forty | *arobaini* |
| Forty-seven | *arobaini na saba* |
| Fifty | *hamsini* |
| Sixty | *sitini* |
| Seventy | *sabini* |
| Eighty | *themanini* |
| Ninety | *tisini* |
| Ninety-nine | *tisini na tisa* |
| One hundred | *mia* |
| One hundred and one | *mia na moja* |
| One hundred and ten | *mia na kumi* |
| Two hundred | *mia mbili* |
| Two hundred and fifty | *mia mbili na hamsini* |
| Nine hundred and ninety-nine | *mia tisa tisini na tisa* |
| One thousand | *elfu* |

## Time and the calendar

| | |
|---|---|
| What time is it? | *Saa ngapi?* |

The answer to this depends upon whether the African or the European system of reckoning hours is used. There are 24 hours in the African day, but the counting begins with sunrise and with sunset. What would therefore be 7am by European reckoning is one o'clock (*saa moja*) by the African system – there is always a six hour difference. 8am is *saa mbili*, 9am *saa tatu*; 7pm is also *saa moja*, 8pm *saa mbili*, midnight *saa sita*.

| | |
|---|---|
| Today | *leo* |
| Tomorrow | *kesho* |
| Yesterday | *jana* |
| Nighttime | *usiku* |
| Daytime | *mchana* |
| Morning | *asubuhi* |
| Afternoon | *alasiri* |
| Evening | *jioni* |
| Day | *siku* |
| Week | *wiki* |
| Month | *mwezi* (pl. *miezi*) |
| Year | *mwaka* (pl. *miaka*) |
| Sunday | *Jumapili* |
| Monday | *Jamatatu* |
| Tuesday | *Jumanne* |
| Wednesday | *Jumatano* |
| Thursday | *Alhamisi* |
| Friday | *Ijumaa* |
| Saturday | *Jumamosi* |
| January | *Januari* |
| February | *Februari* |
| March | *Machi* |
| April | *Aprili* |
| May | *Mei* |
| June | *Juni* |
| July | *Julai* |
| August | *Agosti* |
| September | *Septemba* |
| October | *Oktoba* |
| November | *Novemba* |
| December | *Desemba* |

## Animals

| | |
|---|---|
| Lion | *simba* |
| Leopard | *chui* |
| Cheetah | *duma* |
| Giraffe | *twiga* |
| Buffalo | *nyati* |

| | |
|---|---|
| Rhinoceros | *kifaru* |
| Hippopotamus | *kiboko* |
| Elephant | *tembo* |
| Hyena | *fisi* |
| Baboon/Monkey | *nyani* |
| Chimpanzee/ape | *sokwe* |
| Zebra | *punda milia* |
| Impala | *swala* |
| Warthog | *ngiri* |
| Boar | *nguruwe mwitu* |

**Demise of the East African Community**

**The Economy.** The former East African Community had united Kenya, Tanzania and Uganda together in a customs union with shared taxation, currency, airways, railways, posts and telecommunications. The Community suffered a blow from the events in Uganda, and collapsed completely in February 1977 with the abrupt closure of the border between Kenya and Tanzania. Since November 1977 no scheduled flights have been permitted between Nairobi and Dar es Salaam, and mail and telephone links have been curtailed. This has cut Kenya off not only from most of its trade with Tanzania, but also from the greater part of its flourishing export trade with Zambia and Malawi, which used to pass through Tanzania. Nonetheless, Kenya handles a large volume of traffic passing to and from other countries, from Uganda, Rwanda, Burundi and Zaire to the Sudan, Ethiopia and Somalia.

**Trade**

Uganda remains Kenya's most important market in Africa, but a determined effort is being made to develop export trade with other African countries and with the Seychelles for the supply of its thriving tourist industry. Zimbabwe holds great potential, as goods can be shipped from Mombasa to Beira without being affected by the Tanzanian border closure. Moreover, Kenya will more easily be able to supply its important market of Zambia through Beira and Zimbabwe. The traditionally important trade with the Sudan is expected to increase still further with the construction of the road link between Lodwar in Kenya and Juba, in southern Sudan. Further afield, Kenya is endeavouring to profit from the lucrative markets in the Middle East and the Gulf area, to which it is comparatively close.

**Agriculture**

Coffee, tea and tourism are Kenya's most important foreign exchange earners and the high prices of the two first, coupled with record crop yields, contributed significantly to the country's economic recovery after the recession of 1976. Since 1978, however, prices have been levelling off due to world market fluctuations, the weather and the fact that the country's capacity for production is nearing saturation. Kenya's traditional livelihood comes from agriculture, which also provides the basis for much of the country's industry, from grain milling to sugar production, and from a flourishing dairy industry which figures prominently in the country's exports, to specialised food products such as breakfast foods, cereal, pasta, sweets and confectionery. After coffee and tea, the most significant exports are pyrethum and soda ash, but there are also considerable quantities of livestock, dairy products, wheat, maize and cotton, even if much maize and livestock is consumed locally.

**Industry**

Industry in general has been expanding fast since 1976 with important increases in the output of food products, chemicals, leather, rubber, plastic and metal products, as well as a sizeable rise in such fields as beverages, tobacco, textiles, paper, cement and pharmaceuticals. Vehicle assembly plants have been set up in Thika, Nairobi and Mombasa which moreover provide an unprecedented market for Kenya-made components ranging from tyres and radiators to seats and batteries. The sugar industry has been expanded to virtual self-sufficiency, and the rise in the standard of living ensures continued prosperity for the brewing industry. Large new plants are producing footwear, biscuits, confectionery, flour and paper products, and an ever-increasing range of small and medium-size industries produce everything from bicycles to plastic goods. Major mills at Thika, Kisumu, Eldoret, Nanyuki and Mombasa reflect the size of investment in the textile industry, which is hampered, however, by Kenya's limited production of cotton, previously imported from Tanzania.

**Natural resources**

Kenya's natural resources include agricultural and ranching land, forests, fisheries and minerals, as well as wildlife and varied scenery. The first two, land and forest, have been under development for many years; particular emphasis is now placed on the raising of yields, the prevention of erosion and the provision of water supplies. The country's fisheries have been largely neglected, but a programme has been initiated to exploit the potential of the fresh-water lakes, including Lake Turkana, and coastal fisheries as a source of food. Wildlife, whose existence in Kenya has often been taken for granted, is likely to be affected outside the game parks by land development schemes. Hence, a research programme has been begun to investigate the possible ways of obtaining better returns from wildlife through game cropping schemes, as well as viewing.

Minerals have, to date, been of marginal importance in the economy and there are no major mines of the more valuable commodities. Twenty-five years of oil exploration have yielded scanty results. But Kenya does have many minor minerals and traces have been found ranging from gold and copper to anglesite and villiqumite (sodium flouride). Trona, or soda ash, mined at Lake Magadi, is one of the most valuable minerals, and the raw materials for cement, coral rock, limestone, volcanic ash and weathered sand, are freely available. The cement plant at Athi River supplies the local market and that at Bamburi the export. Deposits of lead, silver ore, fluorspar and kyanite are being mined, and gemstones are being produced both for the local and export markets. Kenya has the largest ruby mine in the world, and there are deposits of silver, diatomite, beryl, tanzanite, tasavoite, garnet and zirconium.

## Tourism

**Ban on hunting**

The traditional pattern of Kenya's tourism, the country's third most important foreign exchange earner, has been affected by three major factors: the ban on hunting, the closure of the Tanzanian border, and the collapse of East African Airways.

The ban on hunting was imposed in May 1977 in an attempt to preserve the country's spectacular game heritage. Over the years a number of animals, including lion, leopard, rhino, zebra, elephant and black colobus monkey have been decimated, and there was growing fear that they would be extinct within a few years. The ban which cost Kenya an estimated four million US dollars in trophy and licence fees, has been hailed by conservationists throughout the world. Further effort toward conservation was made when the government ordered the closure of all curio shops and took over the business. New style tourists with cameras are now being attracted, and photographic safaris being substituted for big game hunting.

To replace the tourist circuits in Tanzania, Kenya has been opening up new areas in the western and northern parts of the country, as well as expanding the already popular coastal zone. Communications links with Europe are being provided by the national airline, Kenya Airways, and development of tourism is materially assisted by the country's political and economic stability. The most significant development in the sphere of tourism has been the division early in 1980 of the Ministry of Tourism and Wildlife into a separate Ministry of Tourism, with responsibility for wildlife now falling under the newly created Ministry of Environment and Natural Resources.

**National Parks and Reserves**

Kenya's national parks and reserves, where all fauna and flora are protected, are a major tourist attraction and are normally open from sunrise to sunset. They are usually feeding grounds for the herbivorous animals, who, in turn, attract the great predators. For obvious safety reasons, visitors may only circulate in these areas by vehicle, with a maximum speed of 30 kms per hour, and may only leave their cars at clearly indicated points. Park wardens control the parks, with the assistance of a staff of rangers who may be recognised by their khaki uniform, kepi-like headgear and official badge. These rangers have an intimate knowledge of animal habits and will advise the visitor as to the most likely places where the different species of fauna may be found. Accommodation and camping facilities are provided within or close to the parks or reserves, all of which have roads; most also have airstrips. Game reserves are also being developed on private land.

**Safari in Kenya**

Deriving from the Arabic *safariyah* meaning trip or journey and the old Swahili verb to travel, the safari originated in East Africa. Others adopted the word and applied it to real life adventures everywhere. But a true safari can still only take place in the area where it

*The world's tallest animal*

was born and where it is now being perfected. Today in Kenya, the safari has become a collective noun that means excitement and variety in travel of every kind. For reasons of conservation, the Kenyan government imposed a ban on hunting in May 1977, a move which was hailed by conservationists throughout the world as helping to preserve one of the last great reservoirs of wildlife on earth. The hunting safari has been replaced by equally exciting photographic or game-viewing safaris which are available in all shapes and sizes, as well as specialists' safaris, and spectacular deep sea fishing safaris for the giants of the Indian Ocean.

**Overland safaris**

Traditional safaris make use of four-wheel drive vehicles for travelling over difficult terrain. There are, however, many reasonable roads and it is possible to see large areas of Kenya from a more comfortable vehicle. Nearly all safari companies use micro-buses that seat five or seven people and have large sliding roof panels. The most popular routes run from Nairobi: via Lakes Naivasha and Nakuru to the Aberdares; to one of the lodges on Mount Kenya or the Aberdares up to Meru and Samburu National Parks; past Lake Naivasha to Masai Mara; and to the Amboseli and Tsavo National Parks. Tours can be arranged for any length of time, one day upwards.

It is also possible to hire a vehicle and arrange your own itinerary, though you might have difficulty getting reservations at the lodges. If you stay at second class hotels or camp out, you can explore territory that tourists seldom, if ever, see. In Kenya the whole northern frontier desert waits to be explored. There are pockets of development at Samburu, Marsabit and on the shores of Lake Turkana, but an area the size of France is still in the hands of nomadic pastoral people whose way of life remains unaltered since prehistory. On exploratory excursions of this kind you will need a guide or at least a working knowledge of Swahili. Local firms will provide camping equipment, and the services of a driver/guide and cook/camp attendant for all-inclusive charges. It should be noted that special permits are required to visit certain areas.

**Air safaris by plane or balloon**

Because of the long distances involved, many places in East Africa are best visited by air. Air charter services operate from every main centre, and there are numerous airfields close to the game lodges, hotels and town centres; there are also scheduled safari tours. It is, of course, possible to charter your own plane and go wherever you like, because there are usable bush strips in almost every part of Kenya. Flying is often less expensive than going by car, and is safer, faster and more comfortable. A novel variation is the balloon safari where vast balloons, which are subject to normal civil aviation regulations float free on the wind, offering passengers alternate bird's eye and close-up views of the game below. The flights usually cover several kilometres and last an hour or so, followed by a champagne breakfast.

**Water safaris**

An unusual way to explore Kenya is by water. Kenya Railways operates a ship on Lake Victoria which calls at Kisumu, Kenda Bay, Homa Bay and Karungu, and there are fascinating canoe safaris along the Tana River.

**Railway safaris**

Kenya Railways offers an old-fashioned train journey in carriages which recall the heyday of the British Empire, complete with wooden shutters and a xylophone summoning travellers to dinner. This is the overnight journey between Nairobi and Mombasa. In the small but charming restaurant car a five-course meal is served by waiters who sometimes outnumber the diners. As the sun rises over Tsavo, lions might be spotted in the dry bush country, descendants of the man-eaters of Tsavo, which three-quarters of a century ago held up construction of the railroad for many months.

**Horseback safaris**

Horse-riding safaris are operated over the Ngong Hills near Nairobi and on to Lake Naivasha. A few small firms offer pony trekking in wild areas, some with a caravan of camels and zebroids carrying camping equipment into thornbush country north of Mount Kenya. Camel safaris are sometimes conducted from Marsabit to Lake Turkana.

**Safari on foot**

But perhaps the best way of all to travel on safari is on foot. Foot safaris are organised, amongst other places, to the Mathews Range through the magic landscape of the Great Rift Valley into the Namanguseri and Lebetero Hills north of Lake Magadi. Groups are accompanied by a number of porters and an experienced guide. Safari members carry packs with their own personal effects and the porters follow on behind with tents, cooking equipment, latrines, bedding and food. Each party also has its own floodlight for game-viewing around the waterholes, where camp is pitched at night.

**Photographic safaris**

Photography offers the perfect substitute for the old-style hunting safari without endangering the species. This often requires considerable patience and skill, but you have the advantage of being able to do it from your safari car, which was not permitted for hunting. In the national parks and reserves, where the protected animals fear men and vehicles less than in the past, you can approach much closer to the game than any hunter ever did. As with the old hunting safaris, you have the advantage of a professional escort and it is still possible, for a price, to have the comfort of an equipped safari camp complete with drivers, cooks, waiters, hot baths and iced drinks. Vehicles carry immense loads including double sleeping tents with attached bathrooms and ground sheets, spring beds with foam rubber mattresses, insect-proof dining tents, toilet tents, shower tents, cooking tents, refrigerators, lamps, silverware and champagne buckets.

**Types of cameras and lenses**

To take advantage of Kenya's exciting photographic opportunities, the ideal camera is a 35mm single lens reflex that has a behind-the-lens exposure meter. This makes it possible to see exactly what you are taking and to set the controls quickly without taking your eye from the viewfinder. Double lens reflex cameras are inadvisable as they are impossible to use through a car window. It is also vital that the still camera should be capable of taking interchangeable lenses and that you bring several with you. The standard lens will be useful for general pictures, but you will also need a wide-angle lens to capture the incredible vistas and a telephoto for animal pictures. A zoom lens moving between 135 and 250 mm is ideal for mammals and a 300 or 350 mm for birds. All these long lenses can be hand-held with the aid of a pistol grip or chest tripod, but for very sharp focus you will find it useful to rest the lens on a sand bag draped over the window or open roof. To save weight, bring your own small bag with you and fill it with sand on safari.

The best all-purpose cine camera is a super 8 or 16mm with a zoom lens and an automatic diaphragm. Both still and cine cameras should be permanently fitted with a lens hood and an ultra-violet filter. Animals have a way of getting between you and the sun and can only be captured with a hood that shields the lens from direct sunlight. The UV filter not only cuts out glare, but also protects the lens from dust and damage. When not in use, all cameras should be further protected from dust in a case or plastic bag with a small bag of moisture-absorbing silica gel inside. This will prevent humidity from eroding the apparatus and spoiling the film.

**Photographic tips**

Keen photographers will find that they use about 2000 metres of cine film or about 1500 still exposures in a month on safari. Most of this will be colour and all can be bought in Kenya. Agfa, Fuji and Kodak (not Kodachrome) films can be processed locally. If a large part of you itinerary involves work in the high humidity of coastal areas, it is advisable to have film in short length so that it can be exposed quickly and replaced in an airtight container again with moisture-absorbing silica gel. All film everywhere should be kept as cool as possible and no camera should be exposed to direct sunlight for longer than is necessary to get your picture.

Other useful tips to remember are to watch out for the high reflection from white volcanic ash and bare ground; never to risk flare by resting a camera on the white painted roof of your safari vehicle; to pan slowly with a cine camera to allow the automatic diaphragm time to adapt when moving from light to shade and to remember to have the engine turned off when using a cine or long lens from inside a vehicle. A very useful extra piece of equipment is a changing bag which provides complete darkness for camera repairs. It is a rare cameraman who will not jam his equipment at least once in the excitement of photographing big game in action on safari.

One word of warning: some tribes are still afraid of the camera, whilst others demand large 'posing fees'. It is best to seek advice from your guide or driver before you do something which might offend local prejudice or superstition.

It is possible to engage a professional photographer who will join you on safari and take all the pictures, leaving you free to enjoy the trip without distraction.

**Bird and butterfly watching**

More and more visitors to Kenya are coming, not to take photographs, but just to look. There is much to see. Perhaps too much to take in all at once, so some safaris are to concentrate on single aspects of the varied scene. One of the most popular attractions is the wealth of bird life. Visitors from Europe and America enjoy seeing spectacular species completely unknown in northern climes – groups such as bulbuls, pittas, trogons, hornbills, coucals, turacos and barbets. It is by no means uncommon to have a big day or century run on which you see a hundred different species of birds. With careful planning, it is even possible to find as many as 250 in a single day – more species than most active bird watchers in Britain or America see in a whole year. It is, however, vital to have an expert guide to help you find and put names to things. A local ornithologist might take you to famous sites such as Lake Nakuru, where millions of flamingoes create what is probably the greatest bird spectacle in the world. Or he might take you way off the beaten track to the Mathews Range in the desert north, where there is said to be a long-tailed bird that is completely unknown to science. Many areas like this that have never been explored zoologically await the visitor who would like to do something really different.

A rival attraction to the birds are the butterflies. There are about 3000 species in Africa and many of them can be seen in Kenya. Butterflies are most common in moist, forested areas and so the best places to see them are on the coast. Diani is a collector's paradise, as is Kakamega Forest in western Kenya. The best time is in June or late October.

**Flowers and plants**

The climate of East Africa is so varied that it supports a complete cross section of the world's plant life. It is said that from whatever part of the world you come from, you will find some part of Kenya that reminds you of home. It is possible to devote a whole safari to an examination of the flowering plants alone. You should see high altitude heaths in the Aberdares, the montane forest on Mount Kenya, the dry bush country in Tsavo and the dunes along the coast. The best time for flowers in all these areas is right after the long rains in June and early July. November is also good in higher areas. The National Museum in Nairobi will put visiting botanists in touch with local experts.

**Prehistoric man**

East Africa was the cradle of mankind. A month-long safari could easily be filled with visits to some of the more dramatic sites in man's prehistory. It would be best to begin, as man himself perhaps did, at Olduvai Gorge in Tanzania and go on up the Rift Valley to Olorgesailie with its 200,000-year old living site. Further north are the Stone Age 'museums on the spot' at Kariandusi, Gamble's Cave, Hyrax Hill, and Richard Leakey's discoveries near Lake Turkana. Late Stone Age and early Iron Age sites abound in western Kenya and around Lake Victoria, and evidence of fishermen and potters lies everywhere around Lakes Naivasha and Nakuru.

**Contemporary African life**

Others prefer to study the traditions of contemporary Africans and a novel idea has been introduced in the form of 'meet the people' tours, with itineraries complementing the usual game park trips and designed to familiarise visitors with the local way of life. These tours include visits to African farms, markets, schools and places of interest, as well as the opportunity for tourists to sample local foods in houses, farms or simply in the bush al fresco style.

**Mountaineering**

One of the most startling features of Kenya is that there is snow on the equator. This means high mountains and the opportunity for some interesting climbs. The highest in the country is Mount Kenya (5686 metres), described in the section 'Longer Excursions in Kenya', as are Mount Elgon and the Aberdare Range.

**Fishing**

Kenya provides some fascinating fishing especially at the coast where big-game deep sea fishing is at its peak from November to March with marlin, sailfish and barracuda running. Record catches compare with any in the Atlantic and no licence is required. There is also excellent spear fishing inside the coral reefs all along the coast, except in the marine national parks and reserves where only goggling is permitted. There is inland big-game fishing which is best in Lake Turkana where Nile perch abound. Trout fishing is best in January and February in the highlands of the country, where rivers have been stocked with brown and rainbow trout. Licences are required, but there is no closed season.

**Golf**

The last, but by no means the least popular specialist safari is that offered to golfers. There are first class courses at Mombasa, Nairobi, Eldoret and Limuru, the premier one probably that at Karen Country Club near Nairobi which has an SSS rating of 72. All these courses are built through very attractive country and some have the most unusual hazards in the golfing world. There are special rules to deal with puff adders wrapped around balls, and balls that come to rest in a hippo's footprint.

**What to wear on safari**

Most of the safari areas lie inland between 700 and 1700 metres above sea level, where the days are warm, the evenings cool and the early mornings often quite cold. Your outfit should be adaptable to these conditions. It must include a warm pullover and a wind and waterproof jacket. For both men and women, slacks are advisable; skirts and shorts are not recommended. Shirts should have long sleeves that can be rolled down the protect you against the sun and occasional insects. The high altitude in some areas makes the air deceptively cool and disguises the fact that you are on the equator and may get sunburned very easily. A hat, preferably with a broad brim, is essential.

On a hunting safari, ankle boots of the veld-skoen type are ideal, but much of the time you will be more comfortable in rubber-soled gym shoes or substantial sandals. Three sets of cotton shirts and slacks (or bush suits) will be ample, as laundry is done in camp and in the lodges every day. Non-iron clothes are unnecessary and usually too warm for comfort. It is traditional to wear neutral colours – jungle green or khaki – on safari, but the value of this is doubtful, as few game animals see colour and on most trips you will spend a great deal of time in your vehicle. Bush jackets and matching trousers can be made to measure in Nairobi within 24 hours. Locally made boots and shoes are also good and inexpensive. The main game viewing areas are, on the whole, very healthy. It is advisable, however, to take a recognised malaria prophylactic before, during, and after your safari.

Insects are not nearly as troublesome as you might expect, but there are a few occasions when a repellent cream will be useful. Suntan oil is also recommended. All toilet articles should be brought with you as there is a heavy duty on these in Kenya. Two further essential items of equipment are sunglasses (which should ideally be ones with unbreakable polarised lenses) and a pair of binoculars. The best sizes for general use are 7 × 35 or 8 × 30, both of which can be purchased quite cheaply in local camera shops.

# NAIROBI

**Metropolis of East Africa**

Its name in Masai meaning 'the place of cold water', Nairobi is the largest city between Cairo and Johannesburg. Although only 160 kms south of the equator, it is situated at a bracing altitude of 1800 metres above sea level and thus temperatures are never very high despite the abundance of sunshine. Its marvellous climate is one of the city's chief attractions. Half a century ago Nairobi was a town of mud streets and tin houses. Today it is a strikingly modern city with skyscrapers, dual carriage-ways, nightclubs, theatres, cinemas, drive-ins, art galleries and a university. Its main avenues blaze with colour from the tropical bushes and trees which line them.

Born in the spirit of adventure, Nairobi originated as a collection of tents and shacks marking the 500-km peg on the historic Mombasa to Uganda railway. It was located in open, game-teeming country on the border between Masailand and Kikuyu country. In 1900 township regulations were issued, and five years later Nairobi succeeded Mombasa as capital of British East Africa. During the First World War it played an important role as a base in the campaign against the Germans in Tanganyika, although severely restricted in its commerce and productive capacity. In 1919 Nairobi became a municipal council with corporate rights, during the Second World War it once more assumed significance as a military base, and in 1950 became a city by Royal Charter. Nairobi's importance today as a commercial, industrial and political centre is matched by its popularity as a tourist city and its advantageous position on African and intercontinental air routes.

**Points of Interest in Nairobi**

Founded in 1910 as the Coryndon Memorial, the **National Museum** is on Museum Hill, 2 kms from the city centre. It is well worth a visit for its habitat groups depicting wildlife in natural settings and its fine collections of African fauna and flora, tribal crafts and costumes (ceremonial masks, headdresses, weapons, witch doctors' paraphernalia, etc.), finds from prehistoric sites (Olorgesailie, Fort Ternan, Lake Turkana), home-made weapons of 1950s freedom fighters and tribal portraits from the Joy Adamson Painting Fund exhibited in the Ethnographic Reference Section. Multi-lingual guided tours are available. The museum is open daily from 9.30am to 6pm including holidays. Phone 20141, extension 17, for information.

Adjacent to the National Museum is the **Snake Park**, which contains over 50 species of snakes, as well as crocodiles and other reptiles. On certain days visitors may see the poisonous snakes being milked of their venom (which is used for anti-snake-bite serum). Opening hours are as for the museum. The **Aviary** next to the Snake Park contains innumerable colourful birds.

**City Park** in the northern suburbs, 4 kms along Limuru Road, was originally an excision from an indigenous forest. It contains the Boscowen collection of rare plants, the city nurseries, gardens, lawns and an amusing labyrinth of high hedges. Women should preferably visit with a male escort. The park is open daily from dawn to dusk; to visit the Boscowen collection phone 45371 for an appointment.

The **Arboretum**, 2.5 kms along State House Road, has an extensive collection of exotic indigenous trees. It is open daily from dawn to dusk.

The **Parliament Buildings**, at the intersection of Parliament Road, Harambee Avenue and Uhuru Highway, were built in 1955 and form an impressive architectural complex dominated by a 12-storey high clock tower which visitors may ascend. Mosaics, friezes and African carvings decorate the interior of the buildings, 12 giant African-style sculptures adorn the public entrance and a fine bronze statue of Kenyatta stands outside. Visitors may obtain a permit for a seat in the Public Gallery to follow debates of the National Assembly. Tours of the buildings can be arranged when Parliament is not in session: phone 21291 extension 256.

The **University** is at University Way and Moi Avenue. The main campus houses the faculties of arts, sciences, architecture, commerce and education. The faculties of medicine, agriculture and veterinary science, and African studies are located at various points away from the main campus. In all the University has a teaching staff of over 700, and more than 5000 students. Theatres, concerts and exhibitions held at the University's Taifa Hall are sometimes open to the public.

*Nairobi: skyscrapers on the plain*

The **Railway Museum**, at the corner of Uhuru Highway and Haile Selassie Avenue, contains a variety of historical exhibits on the construction, development and daily running of the railways in East Africa. Outside the museum hall, steam locomotives, coaches and other rolling stock are on display. Open weekdays from 8.30am to 4pm, Saturdays from 8.30am to 1pm.

Displays of over 50 species of salt water fish and invertebrates found off the Kenya coast are in the **Marine Aquarium** on Mama Ngina Street near the Hilton. Closed on Sundays, the aquarium is otherwise open daily from 9.30am to 5.30pm.

The beautiful **Jamia Sunni Mosque** in Banda Street, whose white dome and minarets are one of Nairobi's landmarks, and the **Ismailia Mosque** (for the adherents of the Ismaili Moslem sect whose head is the Agha Khan) in Moi Avenue, are illuminated on special occasions. Visitors must remove their footwear before entering.

The **Municipal Market** on Muindi Mbingu Street is a spacious indoor market for local and imported fruits, vegetables and flowers. Adjacent stalls sell African carvings and curios.

The nation's cultural centre is **Bomas of Kenya**, one kilometre up the Langata Road from Nairobi National Park. Here, in the main auditorium, displays of traditional dancing are given daily by the Harambee Dancers, the country's only professional troupe. Also on display are cultural villages representative of Kenya's 16 main ethnic groups, and visitors can take a guided tour of the tribal villages located in the forest.

**Ngong Racecourse**, 8 kms from the city centre, is the attractive setting for horse races held every Sunday afternoon. There is a smaller course at Limuru, where meetings are held two or three times a year.

**Nairobi National Park** is the capital's greatest attraction, and with good reason, for where else would you find lions prowling in complete freedom only a ten-minute drive from an ultra-modern city centre? A mere 115 sq kms in area, the park teems with an astonishing variety of wildlife which can be viewed and photographed within the space of a couple of hours. The park lies on the outskirts of Nairobi, close to the airport, a slender fence the only partition between the animals' playground and the city. The southern side is unfenced to allow the animals free access to and from the Athi plains.

Nairobi Park comprises a hilly, forested area where giraffe, rhino and buffalo can be seen, and a shallow escarpment descending to wide-spreading grass plains where zebra, wildebeest, kongoni, Thomson's gazelle, Grant's gazelle and impala abound. Of the 'big five', only the elephant is missing. At a certain spot along the Athi river you can leave your car to view hippos and crocodiles, but beware of monkeys, who are not above filching objects from open vehicles. The park's main fascination, however, is its lions. It is not uncommon to find a pride on the kill or relaxing in deceptive amiability after a hearty meal. The best time to visit the park is at sunrise or sunset.

## A Walk Around Nairobi

A walk around central Nairobi will take about an hour, ignoring detours, shopping and other diversions. Start next to the Hilton and walk up Kimathi Street toward the New Stanley. Turn left here into Kenyatta Avenue. The right hand side of this broad boulevard is the more interesting for shopping. The central islands contain several statues and memorials, which are often overlooked. About 150 metres along you will see on your right, at the end of Wabera Street, the McMillan Library, and beyond it the Jamia Sunni Mosque. (A 30-minute detour in this direction will allow you to see the Bazaar area.)

Returning to Kenyatta Avenue, continue along it, passing the Post Office, to the roundabout at the junction with Uhuru Highway. In front of you on the right is Central Park, on the left Uhuru Park with its ceremonial dais and boating pool. Both parks are filled with colourful crowds at weekends. Turn left and walk through Uhuru Park or along the Highway to the junction with Harambee Avenue. On this corner are the Parliament Buildings, easily identified by their clock tower, statue of Kenyatta and sculptures.

Harambee Avenue itself is lined with government offices and you will probably find it more interesting to turn left again into Parliament Road. Near the Inter-Continental Hotel is the Jomo Kenyatta Mausoleum with its eternal flames and dress-uniformed military honour guard. If you turn right into City Hall Way you will pass the Catholic Cathedral and City Hall on your left and return to your starting point.

# PRACTICAL INFORMATION

## ACCOMMODATION

See the *Kenya Background* chapter for general information on Kenyan hotels and other accommodation.

Hotel rates shown below are exclusive of tax and service charges. Throughout Kenya there is a 15 percent government tax on the accommodation element of hotel bills, plus a two percent training tax on the entire bill. Also, some hotels may impose a five to ten percent service charge on the entire bill. As a rule of thumb, therefore, you should probably add 25 percent to the rates shown below.

Many hotels offer special rates for children. The rate for single occupancy of a double room is higher than the normal single rate. Some hotels offer reduced rates to Kenyan citizens.

The rates shown below are indicative only and subject to increase at any time.

Accommodation, particularly in the more expensive hotels, can sometimes be difficult to obtain and you should therefore make reservations well in advance of your arrival.

**Warning:** Gangs of panga-wielding thieves make Nairobi a dangerous place after dark. This is particularly true around the River Road area, where many of the cheaper hotels are found. As one traveller has said: 'Personally I feel far safer walking through a forest of gorillas, elephants and buffaloes than through Nairobi centre at night.' So after dark, don't walk – take a taxi.

*Deluxe*:

**Nairobi Serena Hotel**, Central Park, PO Box 46302. Tel: 720760. Telex: 22613. Considered Nairobi's finest hotel, the

Serena is designed in African themes and is set amidst beautifully landscaped gardens and ponds with views across Central Park and towards the downtown skyline half a kilometre away. The rooms are spacious, with panoramic windows, and are equipped with bath, shower, radio, phone and air conditioning. There is a restaurant, grill room, coffee shop, barbecue terrace and cocktail lounge, plus boutiques, heated pool (with pleasant dining alongside) and, nearby, golf, tennis and squash. 670/- single, 850/- double, 1155/- triple, suites from 1575/- to 3150/-.

**New Stanley Hotel**, Kimathi Street and Kenyatta Avenue, PO Box 30680. Tel: 333233. Telex: 22223. More historic and atmospheric than luxurious, the New Stanley, rebuilt and renovated several times since its establishment in 1907, has long been a favourite with world travellers. It is located near both train and airline terminals. Its attractive rooms are equiped with bath, radio and phone, and some with air conditioning and private balcony. Its facilities include a restaurant, bar, shops and the popular Thorn Tree sidewalk cafe. 525/- to 610/- single, 730/- double, suites from 1050/- to 1730/-.

**Inter-Continental Nairobi**, City Hall Way, PO Box 30353. Tel: 335550. Telex: 22631. Located at the city centre. All rooms have air conditioning, phone, radio and private balcony. TV with in-house films is available on request. There is a rooftop supper club and cocktail lounge with dancing, plus a coffee shop, safari bar and tavern, and a terrace restaurant overlooking the pool. Shops, hairdressers and a bank complete the facilities. 630/- single, 770/- double, suites from 1450/- to 2200/-.

*First class:*

**Hilton International Nairobi**, Mama Ngina Street and Moi Avenue, PO Box 30624. Tel: 334000. Telex: 22252. This is a 20-storey circular tower rising in the shopping and business district near the railway station and airline terminal. All rooms are air conditioned, with bath, phone, radio and colour TV. There is a restaurant, grill room, trattoria, 24-hour coffee shop, cocktail bar and lounge, and supper club with dancing. Also a rooftop pool with sundeck, health club and shops. 430/- to 545/- single, 545/- to 640/- double, 1360/- to 2460/- for suites.

**Norfolk Hotel**, Harry Thuku Road, PO Box 40064. Tel: 335422. Telex: 22559. Built in 1904 in colonial style, this is the oldest hotel in Nairobi, located opposite the National Theatre and under a kilometre from the city centre. Guests have included Ernest Hemingway and Robert Ruark, and the traditional safari atmosphere and high standard of personal service remain. Accommodation is in hotel rooms or private cottages, all with bath and phone. There is a dining room and bar, grill room, cocktail lounge and ballroom, plus the famous outdoor cafe and aviary terraces. Pool, hairdresser, golf and horse racing are also on tap. From 480/-to 710/- single, 670/- to 755/- double, studio suites 945/-, cottages from 1200/-to 1950/-.

**Six Eighty Hotel**, Kenyatta Avenue, PO Box 43436. Tel: 332680. Telex: 22513. Centrally located, business and convention oriented hotel. Well appointed rooms, all with bath or shower, radio and phone. An entire floor of this high-rise is devoted to a variety of restaurants, indoor and out, including a Japanese restaurant, a cocktail bar and pub. There is also a shopping arcade and beauty parlour. 405/- single, 600/- double, suites 1050/-.

**Excelsior Hotel**, Kenyatta Avenue, PO Box 20015. Tel: 23953. Telex: 23147. A small, old (1928) hotel at the centre of town. All rooms with bath, radio and phone, plus a fine restaurant, resident band and beauty parlour. 355/- single, 510/- double, suites from 670/- to 850/-.

**Ambassadeur Hotel**, Moi Avenue, PO Box 30399. Tel: 336803. Telex: 22223. In the city centre, all rooms with bath, radio and phone. Indian restaurant, grill room, cocktail bar and snack bar. Rates include breakfast. 345/- single, 480/- double, 675/- triple.

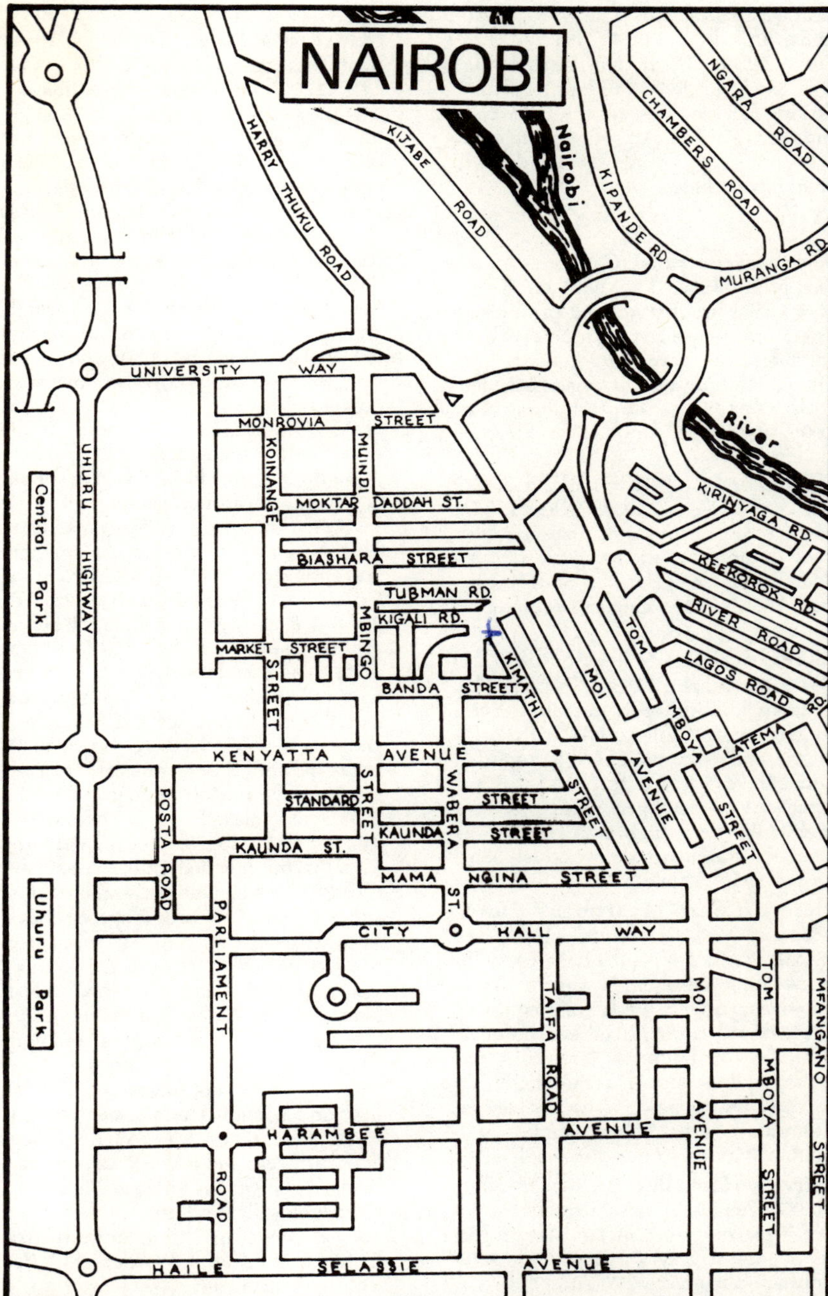
NAIROBI
HARRY THUKU ROAD
KIJABE ROAD
Nairobi River
KIPANDE RD.
CHAMBERS ROAD
NGARA ROAD
MURANGA RD.
UNIVERSITY WAY
MONROVIA STREET
KOINANGE STREET
MUINDI MBINGO
MOKTAR DADDAH ST.
BIASHARA STREET
TUBMAN RD.
KIGALI RD.
MARKET STREET
BANDA STREET
KIMATHI STREET
MOI AVENUE
TOM MBOYA STREET
KIRINYAGA RD.
KEEKOROK RD.
RIVER ROAD
LAGOS ROAD
LATEMA RD.
UHURU HIGHWAY
Central Park
KENYATTA AVENUE
POSTA ROAD
STANDARD STREET
KAUNDA ST.
KAUNDA STREET
WABERA ST.
MAMA NGINA STREET
CITY HALL WAY
PARLIAMENT ROAD
TAIFA ROAD
MOI AVENUE
TOM MBOYA STREET
MFANGANO STREET
Uhuru Park
HARAMBEE AVENUE
HAILE SELASSIE AVENUE

**Jacaranda Hotel**, Chiromo Road, Westlands, PO Box 14287. Tel: 742272. Telex: 22591. Located in a residential area, with gardens, outdoor pool and parking facilities. Restaurant, three bars and pizza garden. All rooms with bath and phone. 290/- single, 440/- double, breakfast included.

*Tourist class:*

**New Mayfair Hotel**, Parklands Road, PO Box 43817. Tel: 742731. Telex: 22954. Set amidst wooded grounds, 4 kms from city centre. All rooms with air conditioning, bath or shower, and phone. Restaurant, bar, snack bar, plus freshwater pool, sauna and parking. 260/- single, 395/- double, breakfast included.

**Grosvenor Hotel**, Girouard Road, PO Box 30471. Tel: 722081. Telex: 22033. Most rooms with bath. Gardens with pool, outdoor bar and barbecue, plus indoor restaurant. Rates include breakfast. 250/- to 285/- single, 335/- to 365/- double.

**Milimani Hotel**, Milimani Road, PO Box 30715. Tel: 720760. Telex: 22613. In-town location with minibus service to city centre. All rooms with bath, phone and balcony. There is a garden and outdoor heated pool, a restaurant (excellent curries), grill and bar, plus a nightclub. Very high standard for its category. Rates include breakfast. 335/- single, 555/- double.

**Heron Court Apartment Hotel**, Milimani Road, PO Box 41848. Tel: 29201. Located in residential area, within walking distance of centre. Two-room apartments with fully equipped kitchen and phone, maid service available. Two restaurants, three bars (one in a London double decker bus), TV lounge, beauty salon, laundry service, pool and sauna. 215/- single, 295/- double. Monthly rates also available.

**Fairview Hotel**, Bishops Road, PO Box 40842. Tel: 331277. An attractive, colonial-style hotel set in landscaped gardens. 140/- to 220/- single, 270/- to 300/- double, suites from 370/- to 750/-.

*Inexpensive:*

**New Kenya Lodge**, corner of River Road and Latema Road, PO Box 43444. Tel: 22202. 58/- single, 70/- double, or 29/- per bed in triple room.

**Iqbal Hotel**, Tom Mboya Street, PO Box 11256. Tel: 20914. Once very popular, the Iqbal has recently become rather seedy, and Mrs Roche's Guest House has replaced it in traveller's affections. Communal shower and toilet. 50/- double, or 20/- for dorm bed.

**Mrs Roche's Guest House**, 3 Parklands Avenue, opposite the Aga Khan hospital in Westlands. Take bus 11 or 12. In a setting of trees and flowers, this very popular place may not have a bed free, in which case you'll have to sleep on the floor the first night. 25/- to 30/- per bed, 40/- for bed and breakfast. For under 20/- you can camp in the garden.

**YMCA**: There are three YMCAs in Nairobi, and for information on them you should contact the YMCA National Council, PO Box 30330, Nairobi; Tel: 337468. Rates, which include full board, are 100/- single with shower, 125/- single with shower and toilet, or 100/- per bed in a four-bedded room. Non-residents can also eat here (excellent value), and there is a pool. Security, however, is poor, and your fellow travellers are likely to steal anything left unguarded.

**YWCA**, Mamlaka Road, PO Box 40710; Tel: 338689. More expensive than the YMCAs, but married couples may share rooms. Rates include bed and breakfast and are geared towards longterm stays.

**Youth Hostel**: For information, contact the Kenya Youth Hostels Association, Ralph Bunch Road, PO Box 48661, Nairobi; Tel: 21789. Rates are under 20/- per day. Security is good and your things can be stored in safety.

Other shoestring accommodation can be found along Biashara Street (near the Central Market), Moi Avenue, Tom Mboya Street and River Road – all particularly dangerous areas at night.

**Camping** is pleasant and cheap (around 10/-) at Rowallan Camp, Jamhuri Park. Contact the Camp Warden, PO Box 41422, Nairobi. Tel: 66911.

## FOOD AND ENTERTAINMENT

*African:*

**African Heritage**, Banda Street; Tel: 28045. Lunchtime is devoted to pan-African cuisine, meals and snacks, indoors or on the open air terrace. In the evening it is Ethiopian. Moderate prices.

**Kariokor Market**, Racecourse Road. The market has a section of stalls where you can get a truly Kenyan meal. Ask for a bit of everything. Cheap.

**Malindi Dishes**, Gabarone Road, off Lithuli Avenue behind the Ambassadeur Hotel; Tel: 333191. Coastal cooking, a blend of African and Indian. Cheap to moderate.

**New Continental Hotel**, Rhapta Road; Tel: 60321. Barbecued meat, including goat and beef, and chicken. Moderate prices.

*Eastern:*

**Mandarin Restaurant**, Tom Mboya Street; Tel: 20600. One of the most popular Chinese restaurants in Kenya. Moderate prices.

**Curry Pot**, Moi Avenue; Tel: 331666. Specialising of course in curries; very popular. Cheap to moderate prices.

**Hashmi Kapuri Pan Shop**, Jainsala Road, close to Tom Mboya Road, behind the Supreme Restaurant. A small place stuck in a parking lot, but jammed with the faithful who come for the succulent chicken tikka, kebabs, or faluda, an Indian milkshake. Dessert is usually pan, a mixture of seeds, betel nut juice, tobacco and God knows what else, folded into a betel nut leaf. Cheap.

**Kwality Hotel**, Argwings-Kodhek Road; Tel: 721285. Despite the silly spelling, the restaurant here is a charming place to enjoy refined Parsee cuisine. Moderate prices.

**Nargis Kapuri Pan Shop**, River Road; Tel: 28654. Similar to the Hashmi, but classier decor and the option of dial-a-take-away food. Cheap.

**Safeer**, Hotel Ambassadeur, Tom Mboya Street; Tel: 336803. Elegant Indian Restaurant with Moghul cuisine, often with Afghan influences. Moderate to expensive.

**Stavrose**, Banda Street; Tel: 24973. A popular restaurant with extensive menu spanning Indian and French cuisines. Many people never win the fight to get inside and eat in their cars instead, or phone up and take it away. Moderately priced.

**Supreme Hotel**, Kilome/Keekorok Road, off Tom Mboya Street; Tel: 25241. Indian vegetarian in stark surroundings. You get a tray which is periodically refilled by roaming waiters. Moderately priced.

**Korean Restaurant**, Safari Park Hotel, Thika Road; Tel: Ruaraka 2311. Simple surroundings but complex and indefinable textures and flavours. Ask for help with the menu. Moderate to expensive.

*Western:*

**The Carnivore**, Langata Road; Tel: 501775. A Brazilian-style open air restaurant arranged round a massive charcoal pit capable of cooking hundreds of kilos of meat at a time. A good bar; memorable meals – and even a vegetarian menu. Also a playground for kids, where they are fed too. Expensive.

**Le Jardin de Paris**, French Cultural Centre, Loita/Monrovia Street; Tel: 336435. Soft music, bistro atmosphere, exquisite food. Moderate to expensive.

**The Tate Room**, New Stanley Hotel, Kimathi Street; Tel: 333233. The menu tends to be French, though on Fridays there is a lavish lunchtime smorgasbord. Expensive.

**Pizzeria**, Hilton Hotel, Mama Ngina Street; Tel: 334000. Not only pizza: quite a range of Italian dishes well prepared. The Pizzeria serves equally well as a place to go for a quick, simple meal (particularly convenient if you have children in tow), or for a late candlelit dinner for two. Moderately priced.

**Stavrose**, already mentioned under Eastern-style restaurants, it offers French as well as Indian cuisine.

*Seafood:*

**Alan Bobbe's Bistro**, Caltex House, Koinanage Street; Tel: 21152. One of the finest restaurants in Nairobi, overseen with the greatest attention to detail, standards and atmosphere by the whimsical eponymous Bobbe himself. Tiny, packed, essential to book. Expensive dinners, but at lunchtime prices are moderate while quality remains high.

**Tamarind Restaurant**, National Bank House, Harambee Avenue; Tel: 338959. As good as Alan Bobbe's Bistro is, the Tamarind is better. Expensive.

*Coffee houses and snack bars:*

**Aatikah**, University Way; Tel: 27242. Strictly take-away: excellent samosas, meat cutlets and other tidbits. Cheap.

**Delamere Coffee Shop**, Norfolk Hotel; Tel: 335422. The verandah of Nairobi's oldest hotel is sodden with atmosphere, glorified by hunters of yesteryear, made famous through Robert Ruark's novels, and a good place to watch the world go by. Strawberry tarts, chocolate eclairs, Norfolk hamburgers and apple pie is the fare. Moderately priced.

**Dil Bahar Hotel**, Ngara Road; Tel: 23066. Samosas and a mind-boggling selection of 300 sweets at this marvellous Indian confectioners, but take-away only. Cheap.

**Ismailia Hotel**, River Road; Tel: 28618. Self-service, with good vegetable and meat samosas, meat cutlets and pastries. Cheap.

**Pool Terrace**, Inter-Continental Hotel; Tel: 335550. For the price of a snack or the daily special, you get to goggle the bikini-clad airline stewardesses sunning themselves by the pool; and for the price of the lavish Sunday buffet, you get to jump in, too. Moderately priced.

**Sunflower and Lamu Coffee Shop**, Kaunda Street at Standard Street; Tel: 335097. Scandinavian-style, with health food menu. Cheap to moderate.

**The Thorn Tree**, New Stanley Hotel, Kimathi Street; Tel: 333233. Famous pavement cafe where you come to watch the passing bustle, though the eats are less than memorable. Moderately priced.

*Entertainment:*

**Bacchus Club**, Wabera Street; Tel: 333233, extension 2855. A classy members-only club (though daily membership is available to overseas visitors), with stylish food, an extensive wine list, and cabaret, often featuring an international entertainer. Jacket and tie in the evening. Expensive.

**Pasha Club**, Kimathi Street; Tel: 331626. Daily membership available at this 'twenties-ambience club. Food and disco, young crowd. Moderately priced.

**The Starlight Club**, top of Kenyatta Avenue; Tel: 26751. Live bands, lots of action, and some of the most beautiful women in town. Not strictly a restaurant, but you can make a meal of the snacks right up to 6am. Moderately priced.

**Bomas of Kenya**, off Langata Road; Tel: 891801. Within this magnificent cultural centre, a resident dance company performs traditional Kenyan dances twice daily, at 2.30pm and 8.30pm (weekends at 3.30pm and 8.30pm). While enjoying the show, you can pick up a snack or simple grill in the small dining area overlooking the large arena. Cheap to moderately priced.

## SHOPPING

Though Nairobi lacks true department stores, a wide range of goods is available at the many western-style, Asian and African shops and markets throughout the city. Prices tend to fall off sharply as you go away from the central area. In all but the most westernised shops discounts are available on cash purchases; often, *if you ask*, the price will be reduced by 10 to 25 percent without further ado.

**Western-style shops** are mostly in the city centre, roughly the area between the New Stanley, Hilton, Inter-Continental and Excelsior hotels.

The **Bazaar**, an area of mainly Asian-owned shops (*dukas* selling fabrics, clothes, made-up goods and numerous other things such as souvenirs, food and hardware), is on the other (northern) side of Kenyatta Avenue. **Biashara Street** is usually full of life, as is the nearby **Municipal Market**.

To the east of the central area, beyond Moi Avenue and Tom Mboya Street, which both contain a wide variety of shops, are **African shops**. Here are small restaurants, general stores selling everything from milk to mattresses, and streetside sellers offering roasted maize. Walk around the circuit of Tom Mboya Street, Luthuli Avenue, River Road and Latema Road for a general impression, but beware of pickpockets. **Kariorkor Market**, next to the main bus station and not far from the railway station, provides a contrast to the more orderly Municipal Market near the centre. Nearby you can watch craftsmen make wooden carvings and hand-printed fabrics.

Apart from the many shops found in the major hotels, and the wide variety of shops you will find by just wandering around Nairobi, here is a shopper's selection:

**Cottage Crafts**, Standard Street, opposite Brunner's Hotel. Jewellery, basketwork, exotic dresses, African-motif toys, handbags, etc; traditional and modern designs; reasonably priced.

**Kenya Canvas**, Muindi Mbingu Street; Tel: 26843. Camping equipment.

**African Drapering**, Nation House, Tom Mboya Street; Tel: 26895. Kitenge, batiks and tie-and-dye.

**Maendeleo Ya Wanawake** (Progress for Women), Muindi Mbingu Street; Tel: 22095. This is the showroom of a nationwide organisation of village women, formed to encourage traditional crafts. Genuine tribal articles, basketware and so on are for sale.

**Maridadi Fabrics**, Tom Mboya Street, opposite Gill House. Visitors are also welcome at the local factory in Digo Road, Pumwani, to see hand silkscreen printing employing colourful African designs. Fabrics, dresses, shirts, etc., are for sale.

**Municipal Market**, at the corner of Market and Muindi Mbingu Streets. A large indoor market with fruit and flower stalls, African curios upstairs, and street stalls where you might find the odd collector's item.

**Sapra Studios**, Vedic House, Kuanda Street; Tel: 34626. Heartbeat of Africa records and East African music, sounds, etc.

**Tourist Haven**, Kimathi Street; Tel: 37074. Safari clothes, shoes, films, souvenirs.

**Treasures and Crafts**, Esso House, Kaunda Street; Tel: 28356. Superior quality Tanzanites, handbags, jewellery, curios; worldwide parcel service.

**Woolworths**, corner of Kenyatta Avenue and Kimathi Street; Tel: 335011. Well-stocked, including a good selection of newspapers and magazines.

**Select Bookshop**, Mutual Building, Kimathi Street; Tel: 21546. Nairobi's largest bookshop, with a wide selection of Africana, guides and maps, plus English, German and French paperbacks.

## INFORMATION

The **Tourist Information Bureau**, Mama Ngina Street (Tel: 23285), near the Hilton, is very helpful, and along with most hotels can provide you with a free copy of *What's On* or *Tourist's Kenya*, both full of useful information. For a detailed map of the city, however, you will probably have to buy one from a bookshop.

Your own **hotel desk** or those of major hotels, as well as such **travel agents** as American Express, and your own **embassy** can all be valuable sources of varied information.

The **Thorn Tree cafe** at the New Stanley Hotel is the traditional place for leaving a message. The bulletin board is the place to find people to form a group for visiting game parks, etc., or to leave notes for friends who will turn up any month now.

## TRAVEL

Nairobi's **Jomo Kenyatta Airport** is entirely modern and with a full range of facilities. These include a restaurant and snack bar, a drinks bar, medical services (first aid and vaccinations), showers, baggage storage, post and telegraph, newsstand, bookshop, souvenir shop and a duty-free shop for both incoming and outgoing passengers (the latter only if the passenger is not scheduled to another destination within East Africa). There is also a bank (open daily from 7am to midnight), a 24-hour information counter, a hotel reservations service, car hire and long term parking.

An **airport tax** of 80/- is levied on all outgoing international passengers.

The airport is linked to central Nairobi, 13.5 kms distant, by a limited access dual carriageway. The airlines provide **transport between the airport and Nairobi** at a cost of about 150/-, and taxis are available at about 150/- to 200/-. There is also a bus for about 20/-.

Some **airline offices** in Nairobi:

**Air Mauritius**, Kencom House, Moi Avenue; Tel: 29166.

**British Airways**, Silopark House, Mama Ngina Street; Tel: 334362. Also Prudential Building, Wabera Street; Tel: 334440.

**Egyptair**, Shankardass House, Moi Avenue; Tel: 26821. Also at the Hilton; Tel: 27683.

**Kenya Airways**, Airways Terminal, Koinange Street; Tel: 29291. Also at Jomo Kenyatta Airport; Tel: 822171; and at the Hilton; Tel: 29291.

**KLM**, Union Towers, Moi Avenue; Tel: 332673.

**Lufthansa**, IPS Building, Kimathi Street; Tel: 335819.

**Pan Am**, Hilton Hotel; Tel: 23581.

**SAS**, Grindlays Building, Kimathi Street; Tel: 338347.

**Sudan Airways**, York House, Moi Avenue; Tel: 21326. Also UTC Building, General Kago Street; Tel: 25129.

**Swissair**, Salama House, Mama Ngina Street; Tel: 331012.

**Uganda Airlines**, corner of Kenyatta Avenue and Muindi Mbingu Streets; Tel: 21354.

**Zambia Airways**, Hilton Hotel; Tel: 24722 or 29908.

**Within Nairobi** the cheapest way of getting around is by **bus**, if you know the system. Fares are about 2/- to 3/-. More convenient are **taxis**, with official ranks at the railway station, the museum and major hotels. But taxis are not permitted to cruise and so can rarely be hailed in the street. Nor are drivers of yellow-band taxis in the habit of putting their meters on; it is advisable therefore to agree on the fare in advance. Taxis can also be hired from **Archers Taxis and Car Hire**, New Stanley Hotel (Tel: 20289 or 21935).

Though Hertz and Avis both have offices (or agents) in Nairobi, the best **car hire** company is again **Archers Taxis and Car Hire** (see above), which offers very reasonable rates, or **Habib's Cars Limited**, Agip House, Haile Selassie Avenue (Tel: 20463 or 23816), one of the longest established car hire firms in Kenya, with a range of campers, caravans and station wagons as well. **Hertz** is represented by the United Touring Company (UTC), Travel House, Muindi Mbingu Street (Tel: 331960); while **Avis** is handled by Kenya Rent A Car, Kenyatta Avenue (Tel: 336703), with branches at the airport and the Hilton.

Drivers may obtain useful information from the **Automobile Association of East Africa** in Westlands; Tel: 742926. In emergencies, Tel: 745084. The AA of East Africa has reciprocal facilities with the AA and RAC in Britain and with other automobile associations elsewhere.

**Intercity travel** is by taxi, bus, train or plane.

There are three types of **taxi**: **a) Matatus**, that is shared vans or trucks, whose principal function is to act as feeders to bus routes and so tend to go only short distances, eg Nairobi to Thika. They cost about half the price of buses, and you can find them everywhere. The drivers are maniacs. **b) Speed taxis**, which are non-stop shared taxis between cities and are quite expensive. **c) Peugeot taxis**, though travel is rarely by Peugeot now, instead by small (25-seat) buses. They run on fixed routes, usually require booking in advance, and are in effect a superior form of bus transport. They cost nearly double the ordinary bus fare. One such company is **Mombasa Peugeot Service** (in Nairobi telephone 557218 or 559565) with departures near River Road for Mombasa, Eldoret, Kericho, Kisumu, Nakuru, etc.

**Buses** are operated by Kenya Bus Services and other companies, with ordinary and express-luxury services covering most parts of the country. Numerous buses travel daily between Nairobi and Mombasa, taking anything from eight to eleven hours and costing about 100/-.

**Trains** take even longer than buses, and departure and arrival times can be erratic, but they are comfortable, especially for overnight travelling. The Nairobi-Mombasa run (through Tsavo National Park) takes about 14 hours, costs about 260/- first class, 110/- second class and 55/- third class. Dinner will cost about 55/-, breakfast 30/-, bedding 17/- and a mattress 10/-. The Nairobi railway station is off Haile Selassie Avenue; information can be obtained from the Chief Traffic Manager, PO Box 30121; Tel: 21211. Outside office hours, Tel: 21212.

**Kenya Airways** flies between Nairobi, Kisumu, Mombasa and Malindi, using Boeings, DC9s and Fokker Friendships. Approximate fares are 670/- from Nairobi to Mombasa or Malindi, except for excursion flights which usually leave early in the morning and cost 440/-, and 450/- from Nairobi to Kisumu. From Nairobi, flight times are about one hour to Kisumu or Mombasa, about an hour and a half to Malindi (via Mombasa). In Nairobi, contact Kenya Airways, Koinange Street; Tel: 29291. There is also an office at the Hilton; Tel: 29291.

In addition, there are a number of air charter companies; among them:

**Air Kenya**, Wilson Airport, PO Box 30357, Nairobi; Tel: 501210.

**Pioneer Airlines Ltd**, PO Box 43356, Nairobi; Tel: 501509.

**Hitchhiking** is easy on main roads, though African drivers may expect you to pay. If hitching to Mombasa take bus 13 to the airport turnoff and start from there. If heading for Uganda take bus 23 from the Hilton to the end of its route and hitch from there. If you are going to Naro Moru, Nyeri, Nanyuki, Embu or Mt Meru take bus 5 from the Central Bus Station up Thika Road to Kenyatta College and start there.

Brochures in hotels, the Tourist Information Bureau and travel agencies will announce the hundreds of **safaris** available from Nairobi. Here are a few contacts to get you started:

**Afrikan Cultural Safaris Limited**, Hilton Hotel Arcade, PO Box 42458; Tel: 335581, or after 6pm 722749. As well as the usual game park safaris, this outfit offers contact with the people of Kenya, in their villages, sometimes in their homes. Specialises in individuals and small groups in private cars.

**Air Kenya**, Wilson Airport, PO Box 30357; Tel: 501210. One-, two- and three-day air safaris.

**Balloon Safaris**, PO Box 43747; Tel: 27217. Balloon safaris in Masai Mara National Reserve.

**Furaha Travels**, Mamujee Building, Tom Mboya Street, PO Box 41641; Tel: 333696 or 26593. Mr Kassam will give his personal attention to devising your individual itinerary and offer many useful tips. Inexpensive.

**Kimbla Kenya Limited**, Banda Street, opposite African Heritage, PO Box 40089; Tel: 337892 or 891288. Camping safari specialists, from the most economical to the most deluxe, as well as camel, canoe and foot safaris for the more adventurous.

**Nilestar Tours**, Norfolk Hotel, Cottage 10, PO Box 42291; Tel: 337392. Inexpensive, organised and scheduled tours and safaris.

**Safari-Camp Services Limited**, Bruce Travel, Koinange Street, opposite the market, PO Box 44801; Tel: 891348. Week-long truck expeditions to Lake Turkana; also wildlife expeditions. Inexpensive.

**United Touring Company**, Travel House, Muindi Mbingu Street, PO Box 42196; Tel: 331960. A leading operator, on the expensive side, offering a wide variety of all-inclusive safaris.

## OTHER THINGS

The **General Post Office**, Kenyatta Street near its junction with Uhuru Highway, is open 24 hours. In addition to post and telegraph facilities (available at any post office), it offers the one public **telex** service in Nairobi. Guests at the New Stanley and Hilton hotels may use the telexes there; the British High Commission (and perhaps other embassies) permits use of its telex facilities to contact Britain if essential. There is a **parcel post office** (also accepting general business) on Haile Selassie Avenue. **Stamps** are also available at hotels and some shops, eg Woolworths, and red post boxes are in abundance throughout the city.

Overseas and inland **telegrams** may be sent from all post offices or telephone from any call box or hotel or private phone: dial 990.

**Telephone** calls may easily be made throughout Kenya, East Africa, to Britain, and to most other parts of the world. Direct dialling is possible to principal towns and cities throughout Kenya, Uganda and Tanzania. For Kenya, dial 900 for the operator, 991 for directory enquiries, 992 for general enquiries, and 999 for emergencies. For most international calls, dial 0196 (0195 for most countries in Asia and Africa).

Barclays Bank operates a **Bureau de Change** at Jomo Kenyatta Airport, open 24 hours. **Barclays'** Kenyatta Avenue branch (Tel: 20523) is open Monday through Saturday, 9am to 4.30pm. Other banks include:

**Citibank**, Wabera Street; Tel: 333524.

**National Bank of Kenya**, head office and main branch, Harambee Avenue; Tel: 26471.

**Standard Bank**, head office, Moi Avenue; Tel: 331210.

For **hospital** treatment:
**Aga Khan Hospital**, Parklands Avenue near City Park; Tel: 45301 (24-hour emergency service).
**Nairobi Hospital**, Argwings-Kodhek Road; Tel: 21401 (24-hour emergency service).

There is no 24-hour **pharmacy** service. Rotas for late openings and restricted weekend service are posted on shop doors, eg **Robsons** in Wabera Street. In dire emergency, try one of the two hospitals above.

For **inoculations**:
**Nairobi City Council Medical Department**, City Hall; Tel: 24281.
**Jomo Kenyatta Airport Medical Officer**; Tel: 822111.

In **Emergencies**:
Dial 999 from any phone (no coins needed from a public phone) for **general emergencies**.
**Central Police Station**; Tel: 22222.
**Fire Department**; Tel: 22481.
**Ambulance**; Tel: 22396.
**Flying Doctor**; Tel: 501301.

Your **embassy** can assist you in a number of ways, possibly by acting as a mail drop, certainly by advising on emergency financial and medical problems, effecting emergency communications home, etc. It should be noted, however, that embassies cannot lend money to stranded travellers, though they can find ways of helping you. A full list of embassies can be found in the free handout *Tourist's Kenya*; a few are listed below:
**Australia**: Development House, Moi Avenue, PO Box 30360; Tel: 334666.
**Egypt**: Chai House, Koinange Street, PO Box 30285; Tel: 25991.
**Sudan**: Shankardass House, Moi Avenue, PO Box 48784; Tel: 20770.
**United Kingdom**: Bruce House, Standard Street, PO Box 30465; Tel: 335944.
**USA**: Embassy Building, corner of Haile Selassie and Moi Avenues, PO Box 30137; Tel: 334141.

Other addresses:
**Immigration Department**, Bima House, Harambee Avenue, PO Box 30191; Tel: 332110 or 337274. To extend your visa.
**Seychelles Tourist Information Office**, 3rd floor, Esso House, Mama Ngina Street.
**American Express**, c/o Express Kenya Limited, Consolidated House, Standard Street, PO Box 40433; Tel: 3347277.

# DAY EXCURSIONS FROM NAIROBI

### To the Southwest

**View of the Rift Valley**

The **Ngong Hills**, 25 kms southwest of Nairobi and rising to a height of over 2700 metres, are the sacred mountains of the Masai, also mentioned by Kipling in his *Just So* stories. A motor road leads to the Ngongs, where a short walk to the summit is rewarded by a splendid view of the Rift Valley and, on a clear day, Mounts Kenya and Kilimanjaro. There are 500 resident buffalo on the hills, as well as some bushbuck, and the rare Chandler's reedbuck, waterbuck, eland and other animals found in this type of wooded, lush countryside. Horse safaris are conducted, ranging from three-hour rides over the hills to five-day excursions continuing through the Rift Valley and on to Lake Naivasha.

In dry weather a pleasant afternoon can be spent on the circular motor route round the hills. From Nairobi take the Langata Road. Shortly after the main gate of the national park, turn left onto the Magadi Road and continue past the Masai Lodge turning and the Kiserian Mission to the southern shoulder of the hills, from where there is a magnificent view over the Rift Valley. Giraffe, zebra and gazelle can usually be seen here. The road climbs up the side of the hill and returns to the village of Ngong. The circuit can be completed from here back to the Magadi Road, but most people will prefer either to take the road leading to the summit or to return directly to Nairobi on the tarmac road through **Karen**. This suburb at the foot of the Ngong

**Isak Dinesen**

Hills was named after Baroness Karen Blixen (Isak Dinesen), the Danish author of *Out of Africa*, whose farmhouse is open to the public (but please phone first: Karen 2366).

To get to the **Olorgesailie prehistoric site**, take the Langata Road out of Nairobi and continue as for the Ngong Hills circular route until Olepole. Here, instead of turning right, continue down a series of steep hills on the road to Magadi. The drive (80 kms) takes about one and a half hours; there are no petrol stations or repair facilities along the way.

The site of Acheulian Stone Age Man consists of a

*Masai herdsmen*

series of levels; the date of the earliest level, discovered in 1942 by the renowned anthropologist Dr Louis Leakey, is estimated to be about 200,000 BC, and the latest 125,000 BC. No human fossil remains have been found, but that this was once a living site is confirmed by the giant animal fossils as well as the hundreds of hand-axes and other stone tools found here. There is a field museum and a rest camp with four bandas to which visitors must bring their own food, bedding and utensils. Enquiries and bookings should be made to the Curator of the National Museum, PO Box 40658, Nairobi.

**Dr Leakey**

Continuing along this same road you reach **Lake Magadi** (110 kms), an almost solid-surfaced soda lake 630 metres above sea level, its temperature often over 32°C. Its soda ash and salt are valuable Kenyan exports. You can drive over the lake on a causeway.

## To the Northwest

**Through the Rift Valley**

An 80-km drive northwest from Nairobi on a tarmac road (built by Italian prisoners during the Second World War) takes you through the rich farming and ranching country of the spectacular **Great Rift Valley** where it narrows to 65 kms. On the way you can enjoy a magnificent view from the top of **Limuru Escarpment**; there is a picnic site nearby. The Limuru branch of the Kenya Red Cross has built **Kimathi Model Village** consisting of eight round clay and thatched houses where poor and illiterate mothers are accommodated with their children for a free two-week practical course in basic nutrition, hygiene and family planning.

Near Kijabe the more energetic may wish to branch left along the Narok Road to visit the 24 **Caves of Mount Suswa**, volcanic in origin, which house hundreds of bats. A guide is necessary as the tracks to the mountain from the Narok Road are unsignposted and indistinct.

Back on the main road, 16 kms before Lake Naivasha, **Mount Langonot** (3040 metres) is a perfect example of an extinct volcano. It is an easy climb to the crater rim where steam jets out and game can be spotted. It is also popular with thieves: do not leave valuables in your car.

The enchanting papyrus-fringed fresh water **Lake Naivasha**, surrounded by volcanic mountains, is one of the loveliest in the Rift Valley. More than 300 varieties of birds have been seen on the lake islands, including spoonbills, herons, egrets, crested grebes, cormorants and fish eagles. Fishing is excellent, particularly for tilapia and black bass. There is an active sailing club which accepts temporary members and yachting races are held most Sundays. Excursions can be made to **Crescent Island**, a game and bird sanctuary. The lake area was the setting for Rider Haggard's *She*. In these tamer days there is a variety of accommodation and excellent facilities for fishing and birdwatching.

Five kms beyond the Lake Naivasha Hotel is a narrow track leading to **Hell's Gate Gorge** with its hot springs, the prehistoric outlet for the lakes which once filled the Rift Valley. The peculiar upright cliff in the centre is locally known as the Statue of the Devil. North of Lake Naivasha, on the road toward Gilgil and Nakuru, is the **Stone Age site of Kariandusi**, which has a small museum of finds from the region.

Still in the Rift Valley, at an altitude of 2035 metres, **Nakuru**, (155 kms from Nairobi) is the unofficial capital of the Kenya Highlands. With a population of 72,000, it is Kenya's main agricultural town (an important agricultural show is held here in June) and is also undergoing considerable industrial expansion. A wide range of reasonably priced sheepskin goods can be bought at the town centre, and excellent local cheeses about 2 kms along the road to Eldoret.

Above the town rises the extinct volcanic **Menengai Crater**, whose inside depth is 483 metres; there are breathtaking views from its rim. The highest point reaches 2490 metres and overlooks one of the world's finest bird sanctuaries, the soda **Lake Nakuru**, home of two million flamingoes and favourite haunt of the colour photographer. The Greater Flamingo, a whitish bird with salmon pink wings standing about one and a half metres tall, can also be found in other parts of the world, but the Lesser Flamingo exists only in the Rift Valley and is the most prolific of the flamingo species. The lake has numerous other bird species, and an ornithological research centre has been developed by the Baharini Wildlife Sanctuary, PO Box 33, Nakuru; Tel: 2563. A lodge and an educational centre are planned.

**Two million flamingoes**

In the surrounding country impala, waterbuck and the colobus monkey can be seen. A visit to **Hyrax Hill**, a prehistoric site on the outskirts of the town, is worthwhile. Application for visiting **Gamble's Cave**, occupied by Stone Age man from around 30,000 BC, must be made in advance to the Centre of Prehistory, PO Box 30239, Nairobi; Tel: 22648.

From Nakuru it is a 70-km excursion to the spectacular **Thomson's Falls**, named after the English explorer Joseph Thomson who in 1883 was the first European to walk from Mombasa to Lake Victoria. There is a lodge at Thomson's Falls (which has been renamed Nyahururu), 196 kms from Nairobi.

### To the North

Nyeri, celebrated by novelists, is 160 kms from Nairobi on a tarmac road. Near **Thika** (48 kms), setting for Elspeth Huxley's *The Flame Trees of Thika*, are the **Chania Falls** and the 2344-metre **Ol Donyo Sabuk** (Hill of the Sleeping Buffalo), haunt of many birds including the African carrier hawk. At a church in **Muranga**, murals by Chagga artist Elimo Njau depict the life of an

African Christ in local surroundings. The main road goes through interesting villages with traditional round thatched huts – this is the fertile **Kikuyu reserve** on the slopes of Mount Kenya.

**Kikuyu country**

The Kikuyu, Kenya's largest tribe, together with their tribal cousins the Embu and the Meru, originally came with the Bantu immigrants up the Tana River, settling in the Fort Hall district. They are rich in tribal legend, which includes the belief that they originated on Mount Kenya (Kirinyaga), dwelling-place of the god Ngai. Jomo Kenyatta, who led the nation to independence, was a Kikuyu.

**Nyeri**, at an altititude of 1913 metres, has many excellent trout streams (including the well stocked Chania River), a nine-hole golf course, and fine hotels which serve as staging points for visits to Aberdare National Park. In the grounds of one of the hotels lies the grave of Lord Baden-Powell, founder of the Boy Scout movement.

**Baden-Powell**

The outstandingly beautiful **Aberdare National Park**, about 360 kms round trip from Nairobi, is unlike most others in that it lies at a high altitude. Covering 788 sq kms of the dense forest and moorlands of the Aberdare Range, it has impressive waterfalls and trout streams, and interesting vegetation of the sub-alpine series not normally found in the tropics. Wildlife is mainly forest animals, naturally shy and mostly nocturnal in habit. However, they often make daytime appearances and are becoming accustomed to cars so that game viewing in the area is improving. The park is frequently closed during and after heavy rain to preserve the main track.

Given a hard day's driving, you could travel through the park from Nairobi via Nyeri and Naivasha, but it would be preferable to break the journey overnight. If you are adventurous, you might decide to camp in the park and savour the crisp, clear morning, but take precautions against the cold because you would be at an altitude of 3300 metres. Hotel accommodation in the park is at a lower altitude, away from the main track. As famous as the park itself is Treetops Hotel, a luxury game lodge perched in the trees overlooking a water hole and salt likc which is regularly visited by a variety of big game. The Ark, a modern architectural achievement, also overlooks a natural water hole and salt lick.

### To the Southeast

Reached from Nairobi via the Mombasa Road, **Machakos** (70 kms) is the chief town of the Wakamba, who are famed for their woodcarving. It is also the centre of an attractive hilly area which the visitor with a good map can explore at will. Particularly worth a visit is **Nzaui**, a dramatic forested peak with excellent views and a nearby rest house. In the rainy season travel in the area is difficult unless you have four-wheel drive, but the road as far as Machakos is all tarmac. Enroute about 10 kms from the Athi River, and set apparently in the middle of nowhere, is a country club offering banda accommodation.

# PRACTICAL INFORMATION

The listings for this chapter are arranged alphabetically. For details on **travel**, sources of **information**, etc, see the *Nairobi* listings. For additional information on **accommodation** throughout Kenya, see the *Background* chapter. Many hotels in this section offer reduced rates during the low season, approximately 15 April to 31 July.

**ABERDARE NATIONAL PARK**

**Accommodation**

**Treetops Hotel**, PO Box 24, Nyeri. Tel: Nyeri 2424. Reservations should be made through Block Hotels, PO Box 47557, Nairobi. Tel: Nairobi 22860. Telex: 22146 Nairobi. This world famous game lodge was built in 1932 on stilts among a cluster of Cape chestnut trees, overlooking a water hole and salt lick which attracts wild animals. The rooms are comfortable but simple, without private bath. There is a bar and dining room. Children under 10 are not accepted. Access is from the Outspan Hotel in Nyeri, 16 kms distant. 620/- per person full board, 820/- per person full board in a suite.

**NAIVASHA**

**Accommodation**

**Lake Naivasha Hotel**, South Lake Road, PO Box 15, Naivasha. Tel: Naivasha 13. Telex: 22146 Nairobi. 3 kms off the main Nairobi-Nakuru road at the edge of the lake, on the floor of the Rift Valley. Hotel, and bungalows under acacia trees, all rooms with bath and verandah. Dining room, bar, lounges, pool, extensive grounds; particularly attractive for fishermen, birdwatchers and photographers. Fishing gear and boats available. A relaxed and cheerful old-style place. 570/- single, 780/- double, with full board.

**Safariland Club**, PO Box 72, Naivasha. Tel: Naivasha 29. Rooms with bath in cottages, also bandas and tents. Pool, tennis, stables and boats available. 330/- single, 440/- double, full board.

**Food**

Apart from meals at the above hotels, on the expensive side, try the following.

**Crescent Island Camp**, access via Marina Club in South Lake Road, 4 kms from main Naivasha-Nairobi turn-off. Moderate to cheap meals, excellent cuisine, on this beautiful island abounding with birds, waterbuck, reedbuck and jumping hares.

**Kenchic Inn**, in Naivasha town centre. Open 24 hours a day. The most popular stop-off spot in Naivasha, with good hot meat pies. Avoid the bar and restaurant indoors, both gloomy; instead eat on the verandah. Moderate to cheap.

## NAKURU

### Accommodation

**Lake Nakuru Lodge**, in Nakuru National Park; PO Box 73667, Nairobi. Tel: Nairobi 20225. Tennis and swimming. 410/- single, 635/- double.
**Lion Hill Camp**, in Nakuru National Park; PO Box 48658, Ken-Com House, Nairobi. Tel: Radio Call 2129 at the park. Highly organised and comfortable tented accommodation. 510/- single, 640/- double.

### Food

Both the above offer meals to visitors.
**Tipsy Restaurant**, Gusii Road. A simple but cheerful place, moderate to cheap, specialising in curries and other Indian dishes. Also try the sister shop, the **Nakuru Sweet Mart**, next door.
**Nakuru Railway Restaurant**. The decor and service hark back to the golden days of the East African railways, and even the moderate prices are old fashioned for what you get. For entertainment, watch the trains go by.

## NYERI

### Accommodation

**The Ark Forest Lodge**, PO Box 449, Nyeri. Tel: Mweiga 17. Located north of Nyeri in the Aberdare Forest. Many rooms small and simple. Game viewing verandahs, permitting sight of the rare bongo antelope. Dining room, bar, exotic aviary. Full board; apply for rates to Across Africa Safaris Ltd, Bruce House, PO Box 49240, Nairobi. Tel: 332744 Nairobi. Telex: 22501 Nairobi.
**Outspan Hotel**, Baden Powell Road, PO Box 23, Nyeri. Tel: Nyeri 2424. Telex: 22146 Nairobi. 2 kms from Nyeri, this old colonial-style mountain resort is situated between the foothills of Mount Kenya and the Aberdare Mountains in its own extensive semi-tropical gardens. All rooms with bath, most with fireplace. Dining room, grill room, terrace, plus pool, tennis, squash, horse riding, golf, playground, and big game and fishing parties. 570/- single, 775/- double, full board.
**White Rhino Hotel**, PO Box 30, Nyeri. Tel: Nyeri 2189 or 2013. A small, friendly place, English-style, some rooms with bath. Golf, climbing and fishing are available. Apply for rates, which are moderate.

### Food

There is decent, standardised fare at the **Outspan Hotel**. Prices are moderate. The restaurant is open to all-comers, and the great bonus is the view of Mount Kenya.

## THIKA

### Accommodation and Food

**New Blue Posts Hotel**, on the Nairobi-Thika road, PO Box 42, Thika. Tel: Thika 22241. A small, welcoming place, recently redecorated, some rooms with bath. Pool and tennis available. The restaurant is open to all-comers, is moderate to cheap, and is a good place to stop for a snack or decent curry after viewing the falls. The hotel is moderately priced; apply for rates.

## THOMSON'S FALLS (NYAHURURU)

### Accommodation

**Thomson's Falls Lodge**, PO Box 38, Thomson's Falls. Tel: 6. Facing the falls; some rooms with baths; fishing, birdwatching and golf the activities. Moderate rates; apply to PO Box 10530, Nairobi. Tel: 24339 Nairobi.

# LONGER EXCURSIONS IN KENYA

*Many of the following trips can be done as standard tours offered by tour operators. Some, however, necessitate the hire of a car, possibly with chauffeur, in which case the* Background *chapter notes on* Motoring in Kenya, *especially in remote areas, should be read carefully. Nearly all the destinations mentioned can also be reached by light plane. If several people share the cost of the charter, this need be little more expensive than travel by road; it will certainly be faster and more comfortable.*

**Tsavo National Park**

Half-way between Nairobi and the coast, on either side of the recently renovated Mombasa highway, lies East Africa's greatest game sanctuary (administratively divided into the Tsavo East and Tsavo West National Parks), famous for its amazing variety of game and scenery. Here roam herds of magnificent elephant, truculent rhinoceros, buffalo and plains game, as well as an abundance of monkeys, warthogs and birds.

**Man-eating lions**

Here, too, is the home of the notorious man-eating lions, whose predilection for railway workers temporarily stopped all work on the Mombasa-Uganda railway line at the turn of the century. The wilderness of the country and the hard battle for survival may be partially responsible for the traditional fierceness of these lions.

A well-known feature of Tsavo West is **Mzima Springs**, where large elephant herds come to bathe and drink. Hippo, crocodile and fish can be watched in complete safety from a specially constructed glass-walled observation tank in the main palm-shaded pool. The wild, rugged scenery retains a savage splendour. Vast tracts of arid bush country, dried to a silver grey in the hot season, burst into delicate flower after the first shower of rain.

Both parks, Tsavo East and West, are well served with game lodges inside, and hotels outside the park boundaries. There are, in addition, a number of self-help bandas and camp sites in both parks, and several tented camps in the vicinity.

Travellers coming from Nairobi on the Nairobi-Mombasa highway may wish to stop off at Hunter's

Lodge (160 kms), where they can fish for their tilapia lunch in a well-stocked dam. It is also possible to enter the park from Nairobi via the beautiful **Chyulu Hills**, source of the Mzima Springs' water, but a good road map or a guide is needed. The road branches off the Nairobi-Mombasa highway at Sultan Hamud (signpost to Amboseli) and follows the water pipeline to Makutano (one shop), before veering back towards the hills. It winds up to the crest (2000 metres), where panoramic views may be enjoyed to the right and left, and continues along it for some 30 kms before descending to the Chyulu gate of the park near the relatively recent lava flows from **Shaitani Volcano**.

## Amboseli National Park and Masai Mara National Reserve

**The Masai**

Masailand extends south of Nairobi and into Tanzania. The once dominant position of this Nilo-Hamitic group over most of the other East African tribes was due to their effective military organisation and their standing army of young warriors, *moran*, not unlike the Zulu *impis*. Today Masai moran still blood their spears on lions which attack their cattle. Proud, extremely good-looking, classically athletic, they dye their tall bodies with ochre clay and fat and wear only a red cloak tied to one shoulder. Earrings have special significance for the Masai, who even have a specific way of cutting out the ear lobe to distinguish persons who have killed a lion in single combat. The hair of the Masai is ochred and braided, except for married women, whose heads are shaved and polished with red clay.

Although a national park, **Amboseli** still accommodates some Masai herdsmen and their cattle, which graze together with the wild game. This is one of the finest areas in Africa for big game photography. The great variety of game, the open nature of the country, and the immense grandeur of the snow-wreathed mass of Mount Kilimanjaro as an impressive backdrop, contribute to its reputation. Much of the fascination lies in the visitor's uncertainty as to just what kind of wild animal he may see round the next fringe of grass. This area, particularly around Lake Amboseli, is an ornithologist's paradise; it is also famous for its rhinoceros. Some of these dangerous, unpredictable animals allow cars to approach quite close, but visitors should be wary. Other well-known animals are the gerenuk

*Salt Lick Lodge, Taita Hills*

and the bushbuck, which are more frequently seen here than in other parks and reserves.

Amboseli is actually the name of a dry lake bed which contains surface water only in seasons of extremely heavy rain. In dry weather, it is smooth enough for cars to drive across, and the extraordinary feature of such a journey is the remarkable mirage formed by the heat haze. At times it is almost impossible to distinguish between mirage and actual surface water.

There are three routes to Amboseli from Nairobi: via Athi River and Namanga (216 kms); via the Mombasa Road to Sultan Hamud, turning off down the pipeline road (216 kms); and the long route via Kilaguni Lodge (385 kms). Accommodation is available in and near the park in lodges, self-help bandas and camp sites.

**Masai Mara National Reserve** in the southwest corner of Masailand has an amazing concentration of wildlife and outstanding scenery. The country ranges from forests and rivers, hills and escarpments, to plains, bush and scrub. Traversed by the Mara river, it is noted for its lion, leopard, rhino and elephant; but above all the Mara is famous for the migrations of thousands of wildebeest and other plains animals which pass through here on their way to and from the Serengeti plains in Tanzania from July to December.

Visits to this area, which many believe now gives the finest game viewing in Kenya, are becoming increasingly popular. All-inclusive tours are organised to suit every pocket and taste, from overnight fly-in safaris using luxury tented camps to budget camping trips lasting a week or more. There are nine accommodation facilities in or near the reserve; two of these are luxury game lodges, the remainder tented camps with varying facilities and special attractions.

Plans are in the pipeline for extending and improving the network of game viewing tracks and for developing other tourist attractions - in two areas of the reserve it is already possible to enjoy the unique experience of viewing game from a hot air balloon floating serenely above the plains. And in the zones adjoining the reserve proper you may go on a walking safari accompanied by an experienced guide, whether for an hour's stroll or for a several-day excursion, living in the style of old time hunting safaris and tented 'fly camps' supplied from your base. Horseback safaris can be arranged at certain times of the year.

Enroute to the reserve, the Masai, whose homeland this is, are very much in evidence, either herding their precious cattle or striding purposefully across the windswept plains.

### Mount Kenya National Park

**Climbing the mountain**

**Mount Kenya**, the country's highest mountain, a snow-capped, long-extinct volcano on the equator, is draped with glaciers and carved into a complex of interesting ridges and faces. It boasts no less than 12 glaciers and the snowline is perennial above about 5000 metres. The highest peaks, **Batian** (5686 metres) and **Nelion** (5674 metres), can be climbed only by experienced alpinists, but **Point Lenana** (5452 metres) and many smaller peaks are accessible also to the amateur. Professional guides are available. There are two climbing seasons: mid-December to mid-March and mid-June to mid-October. On certain routes it is possible to drive up part way, and safaris to the lower slopes can be arranged. The slopes, apart from a break of about 10 kms on th north side, are clothed from an altitude of 1800 metres to 4000 metres in magnificent forests of pencil cedar, African camphor and podocarpus trees. Mount Kenya's many rivers offer excellent trout fishing throughout the year. A self-service lodge has been built at 3300 metres on the Naro Moru (river of black shiny stones) track up the mountain, where there is good trout fishing.

**Nanyuki**, at 3100 metres, provides a good base for mountain excursions. The town takes great pride in its luxurious Mount Kenya Safari Club, an opulent and dull residential club contrived by a group of Americans, including the late William Holden.

Visits may be made to the neighbouring **Solio Game Reserve**, where numerous species of game to be seen include lion, leopard, cheetah, rhino, buffalo, oryx, eland, zebra and hartebeeste. From Nanyuki you can also visit **Secret Valley**, where there is a lodge and where observation structures built into trees offer excellent views of black rhino and buffalo with an occasional elephant. Forest birds are abundant here.

### Tana River Game Reserve

**Rare antelope and monkeys**

The lower part of the Tana, Kenya's longest river, and its basin constitute a genuine remnant of old Africa with a superb heritage of wildlife, local traditions and history. Considered one of the best wild life areas in the country, it offers not only a profusion of wild animals, but also the opportunity to see several unique fauna attractions, such as the rare Hunter's antelope (a hartebeeste with lyre-shaped horns) and varieties of the red colobus and crested mangabey monkeys.

The two last are found predominantly in western Africa, and their occurrence in the gallery forest of the lower Tana, more specifically in a 60-km strip between Wenje and Garsen, indicates the existence in earlier times of forest belts across East Africa. The Garsen-Malindi road passes the Tana River Primate Reserve, established to protect the Mangabey and red colobus monkeys whose future was being severely threatened by the destruction of the forest from Pokomo agriculture. The Hunter's antelope is easily seen around Ijara in the Arawale National Reserve which is passed on the road from Lamu.

Visitors interested in local customs and traditions will be fascinated by the Pokomo, the Orma (a section of the Galla peoples) and the Somalis who inhabit the area. The appeal of Tana River is greatly enhanced by its proximity to Malindi, only two and a half hours away by car when the road is passable.

The Tana River Reserve lies between Garsen and Garissa at a distance of 160 kms from Malindi. Garissa is linked to Nairobi by a fairly fast all-weather road, via Thika, through the famous Nyika thorn country, dropping down to the semi-desert of the Tana basin; the journey takes five to six hours. Garissa may also be reached by the adventurous in rugged vehicles from the northeastern corner of the Meru park, on a track which joins the main road at Garba Tulla. From Garissa, travel south on the B8 route to the reserve.

Although **Garissa** offers no tourist class accommodation, camping is possible and local hostels offer cheap lodging. Special visits may be arranged to Garissa Boys Town, where orphans have succeeded in developing a lush green farm (their melons are particularly famous) in the middle of the semi-desert.

From Garissa two roads lead south: one direct to Lamu via Bura; the other, more heavily travelled, via Garsen to Malindi. Both are dry-weather roads only. The road from Malindi can be covered by ordinary saloon car in about two and a half hours, once the roads have been graded after the long rains, which is usually in August; it should be borne in mind, however, that from around mid-April to mid-July the roads are often impassable. It is also, of course, possible to fly to the Tana River Reserve where an airstrip has been constructed for light craft a few kilometres from the lodge on the reserve boundary.

**A Pokomo village**

If you travel by car over the more popular route from Malindi you can turn off just before Garissa to **Idsowe**, a typical village of the lower Pokomo, known as Malachini. A Bantu people whose folk song is the basis for the country's national anthem, the Pokomo originally came from the Kenya-Somalia border. They are a poor people who have to contend with seasonal flooding of the river and who until recently were not averse to crocodile and hippo poaching as a source of food. Land is sacred to them and they trade their produce for the milk products of the neighbouring Galla. The village of Idsowe, whose Pokomo inhabitants are all converts to Christianity, is remarkable for a heron breeding ground on a nearby lake, and if the river floods in May the whole delta supports innumerable water birds.

Near **Garsen** the flood plain opens into a wide grassy delta which is the main dry season grazing land of the Galla, the people who drove most of the Bantu tribes south and west when they invaded from Somalia about six centuries ago. The Galla are today split into several groups spread between the Ethiopian border and the Kenya coast, the most southerly called the Orma. Like other Hamites they are cattle herders, keeping some sheep and goats. But the Orma differ from most of Kenya's cattle herding tribes in that they have permanent villages. A tall, fine-featured people, they wear bright clothes and their women adorn themselves with numerous arm and leg bracelets.

**The Galla**

Picturesque Garsen, located approximately half way along the road from the Tana to Lamu, is an important local trading centre where the Somalis, Orma and Pokomo congregate daily to exchange their produce. The main Lamu-Garsen road is part of the much used direct route to the north.

The reserve's Baomo Lodge is splendidly sited on the river bank with a magnificent section of the Tana valley lying behind it. Guests may set off for an early morning game run in a Land Rover to see giraffe, zebra, oryx, lesser kudu, waterbuck, impala, gerenuk, Peters gazelle, warthog, dikdik and possibly buffalo. Cheetah are fairly common, as are the lion and the elephant, although the latter, mostly confined to the forest, are more easily seen on a foot safari. In addition to the red colobus and crested mangabey already mentioned, other species of monkeys abound, and baboons perform antics in the trees and on the river banks. After breakfast excursions are organised along the river in fibre-glass motor boats for viewing crocodiles and schools of hippos. There are visits ashore for walks in the untamed forests or for wandering through Pokomo villages located on the river banks. Or you can drop a line for catfish and barbel in the parts where the river runs less swiftly.

### Meru National Park

Established by the Meru County Council, this park is 160 kms northeast of Mount Kenya and borders on the Northern Frontier. It may be reached by car from Nairobi via Meru or Embu or from Isiolo. Most of the country is hot and low, but well watered with nine permanent rivers suitable for fishing, and several springs and swamps. Considerable changes in altitude mean that the local flora varies from tropical riverine to rain forest, with a similar variety of fauna: most species of Kenya's wildlife are found within Meru. This is the only park in Kenya where white rhinos may be seen; it was also the home of the famous lioness Elsa. Lodge and self-catering banda accommodation is available in the park and there are several camping sites.

**The Meru and Embu tribes**

The Mbere section of the Meru tribe is famous for its drummers, who perform on special occasions in Nairobi. They have been enthusiastically received in London on several occasions. Also on the eastern side of Mount Kenya is the district of the Embu, noted for their dancing teams. The pith-hat dance is performed by older men and can be seen only on rare occasions. More frequent is the stilt dance, for which the dancers wear sinister black coats and masks of white animal skins and perform on tall stilts.

## Samburu National Reserve

Samburu and Marsabit National Reserves, wild and remote areas, lie in the fascinating, semi-desert Northern Frontier of Kenya. Within their boundaries are mountain ranges, volcanoes, forests, palm-fringed rivers and rare species of animals not found in the more civilised areas. Samburu extends north of Isiolo along the wide, muddy, but never completely dry Ewaso Nyiro River, where crocodiles and hippos are commonly seen. The riverine country also attracts a wealth of birds; more than 350 species (including migrants) having been recorded. Indeed, practically all indigenous African birds and animals can be found here, even the reticulated giraffe and the beautiful, fuzzy-eared Grevy zebra.

The climate at Samburu is hot, but nearly always dry. The best months for visiting are June to August, but with the low humidity of the desert air even the hot months are not unpleasant and nights are always comparatively cool.

**The Samburu tribe**

A drive through **Buffalo Spring Reserve** to Archer's Post on the boundary of the reserve, may reward you with a glimpse of a traditional settlement (*manyatta*) of the Samburu. These tribesmen, handsome, noble characters with red-ochred pigtails and bodies, are nomadic cattle people of the Nilo-Hamitic group. Their toughness is legendary and it is nothing for a young warrior (*moran*) to walk 100 kms without food or water, or to track a lion with only his spear. Traditional ceremonies, beginning with the initiation at an early age and continuing to mark various stages of development through life, are extremely colourful. The Samburu women are finely adorned with coils of heavy beadery.

Opposite Samburu and Buffalo Springs on the east side of the main Isiolo-Marsabit road is **Shaba,** the newest reserve in the area. The scenery, habitat and wildlife are similar to those in the neighbouring reserves, but there is the added attraction of hot springs and small volcanic cones. A small tented camp is located near the Archer's Post entrance.

The drive from Nairobi to Samburu, via Nanyuki, the Timau Escarpment and Isiolo is nearly all tarmac and offers magnificent panoramas from the slopes of Mount Kenya at an altitude of almost 3000 metres. Then comes the breathtaking descent to the wild and spectacular scenery of the semi-desert, with its volcanic landscape broken by high ranges of grotesquely shaped and occasionally forested hills.

**Marsabit National Reserve**

Marsabit Mountain is a sparsely populated, rarely visited massif set in the midst of an inhospitable desert. Covered with luxuriant rain forest and beautiful flowers, it is alive with a unique birdlife and remarkable denizens. This was the home of Ahmed, one of the world's largest elephants, until his death in 1974. Carrying tusks estimated at 77 kilos each, he was the only wild animal in the world ever to have been given protection under a Presidential Decree.

The mountain is a complex of old craters, none very deep, but each with its own fascination. The attractive **Lake Paradise** crater, discovered and named by Osa and Martin Johnson, is visited by numerous herds of buffalo and elephant, and the lake itself is the home of many water birds. **Gof Redo**, a lonely, circular crater about 200 metres deep has a clear grassy bottom and dense groups of euphorbia trees growing inside. Visitors may walk to the bottom of the crater, where greater kudu are frequently seen. Marsabit is also interesting for the varied peoples who come to its springs. At Oolanoola Wells come the jolly Rendille people with their long camel trains. The Gabbra tribe bring their cattle to a spring nearer to Marsabit village. These Borans and Somalis are of striking beauty. In the high volcanic plateau, the climate is cold with thick morning mists and heavy dews which contrast to the desert country below. Marsabit contains the greatest number of scenic contrasts of any of the parks or reserves in Kenya.

Although the Nairobi-Addis Ababa highway has been completed, the 560-km journey from the capital to Marsabit should not be taken lightly. Marsabit is sometimes included on camel trekking circuits to Lake Turkana, and aerial safaris conducted from Nanyuki offer splendid views of long, rugged, barren mountains and trackless desert, as well as several hours at the wells amongst the nomads.

**Lake Turkana**

Mysterious, remote and forbidding, its crocodile-infested waters subject to perilous and unpredictable squalls, Lake Turkana has been described as 'a sinister jade sea set in black, purple and blood-red lava'. Yet this desert oasis which has hardly changed its ways for over a thousand years is becoming Kenya's newest and most exciting tourist attraction. Lake Turkana was once connected with the Nile and is today one of the most scenic and rewarding fishing areas in the world. Apart from giant Nile perch, of which the record so far is 108 kilos, there are fighting tigerfish and rare golden perch.

The lake is reached from Nairobi in three hours' flying time or about eight to nine hours' driving in dry weather. The normal route from Nairobi to the west side of the lake is about 760 kms and goes via Eldoret, Kitale and alongside the Cherengani Hills to Amudat and Lodwar. The road is used by saloon cars, but before setting out enquiries should be made with the Automobile Association.

**The Turkana**

The picturesque Nilo-Hamitic Turkana extend west of the lake in Uganda and Sudan. These are a proud, independant cattle people, who venerate animals, regarding them as intermediaries between their souls and those of their ancestors. With their heavy metal ankle, arm and head bands, their ostrich-shell adorned belts, they are characterised by rich ceremonials such as the initiation to manhood at which the youth is required to kill a bull with his spear. Dancing and chanting is gay, even frenetic. The Turkana differ from other Nilo-Hamitics in that they do not circumcise, and from the Bantu and Nilotic tribes in the high status they accord women in their society.

At the oasis of **Loiyangalani**, on the eastern side of the lake, where hot springs run down from Mount Kulal, there is a good airstrip and a Catholic mission, and a popular tourist lodge. Close by, on inhospitable shores of bare lava rock, live the El Molo, who must number among the smallest tribes in the world. Little is known of their origins, but anthropologists believe they may be survivals of the primitive race which peopled East Africa long before the arrival of the Nilo-Hamitic and Bantu groups.

**The El Molo tribe**

Sixty-five kms north of Loiyangalani, **Mount Porr** rises 330 metres above the level of the lake. Ascent is arduous due to the high temperature, but worthwhile for the magnificent panorama. At the summit are mysterious circles, arrows and animals carved into the broken rock.

**Richard Leakey's Australopithecus find**

But what really focused world attention on Lake Turkana was the spectacular discovery in 1969 by Richard Leakey of a splendid Australopithicus skull on the northeastern shore of the lake, near the boundary with Ethiopia – just ten years after his parents made their renowned 1.75 million year old find at Olduvai in Tanzania. What may be the richest Pliocene-Pleistocene fossil area in Africa was located. Tools found may date back 2.6 million years, making them the oldest stone implement find in the world. Also unearthed were another humanoid skull and remains of extinct pigs and elephants possibly more than four million years old.

In 1973 a new national park, **Siboloi**, was gazetted on the northern part of the eastern shore of the lake. It comprises three widely differing ecological zones (lake, shore and desert) and includes some of the prehistoric sites of early man.

### The Northern Frontier District

This area is still commonly referred to by its old colonial administrative name, and known familiarly as the NFD, although it now embraces parts of four provinces. It comprises all the arid northern section of Kenya, including the Tana River, Marsabit, Samburu and Lake Turkana areas. For the venturesome traveller with adequate equipment and experience, it offers a chance to get off the beaten track to places where visitors are rarely seen and Western influence is negligible.

**Routes** A route which can be completed without undue haste in a week passes from Nanyuki or Nakuru to Maralal (where it is worthwhile detouring to the Losiolo viewpoint over the Rift Valley), Baragoi and South Horr in the shadow of Mount Nyiru, to Loiyangalani on the shore of Lake Turkana west of Mount Kulal. Thence through the Chalbi or Koroli Deserts, with their mirages and dust devils, to the trading posts of Maikona or Kargi, and on to Marsabit and Isiolo. A special Turkana Bus departs weekly on this route, offering the excitement of a rugged adventure without the problems of having to organise it yourself.

A more easterly circuit, which can be joined to the previous one and which again takes a week or so, passes from Isiolo to the crenellated whitewashed town of Wajir, on to the *Beau Geste* pink fort of El Wak and up the Kenya-Somalia border to Mandera (1000 kms from Nairobi), where it is possible to cross the palm-fringed River Daua by raft (pedestrians only) and set foot in Ethiopia. The route continues along the river to Ramu, thence to Takaba and Moyale, the hilly frontier post where there is a road crossing to Ethiopia, and back to Marsabit. In all it is a 2400 kms round trip from Nairobi.

Other areas of interest to the intrepid include the virtually untrodden Mathews Range to the west of the Isiolo-Marsabit road, the hills of West Pokot and Turkana districts, and the Lamu/Tana River hinterland. In all these areas it is advisable, although not mandatory, to travel with a minimum of two vehicles, at least one being four-wheel drive, and to leave details of intended itineraries with the authorities. Trekking safaris in the Northern Frontier can be arranged using camels and local guides.

### Towards Uganda

From Nakuru, the Kenya-Uganda highway passes near **Molo**, its farms famous for the tender lamb much

**The Dorobo: Kenya's oldest inhabitants**

sought after by Kenyan restaurateurs. Further on, in the Mau Forest, are the Dorobo or Wanderoo people, Kenya's oldest inhabitants, thought to be related to the Kalahari Bushmen of South Africa. Dressing in skins and living close to nature, the Dorobo have an intimate knowledge of animal life. A Masai legend says that a Dorobo gave birth to a boy, from whose shin bone issued a girl, and they became the ancestors of the human race.

Approximately 80 kms north of Nakuru is **Lake Bogoria** (formerly Hannington), reached through Kampi ya Moto and Mogotio by a road which is well signposted once the turn-off in Nakuru has been located – turn north toward Marigat at the roundabout in the middle of the town, by the KFA headquarters. The lake and its shores, which recently became a national reserve, is the home of greater kudu and greater and lesser flamingoes, and has hot springs and geysers. Treat the water with respect; it is boiling and sometimes flows under solid-looking grass; it is an uncomfortable trip back with scalded feet to the nearest proper medical facilities in Nakuru. Camping is permitted at the lake shore (no facilities); for a pleasant site, turn left at the end of the track. Otherwise the nearest accommodation is at Nakuru or Lake Baringo.

To the north west of Nakuru, reached by road or rail and climbing to 3000 metres over the eastern wall of the Rift, are the farming centres of **Eldoret** and **Kitale**. They are set amidst a great area of maize and wheat fields, dominated by the 4660-metre Mount Elgon, whose eastern (Kenyan) side comprises the **Mount Elgon National Park**, for which the nearest tourist accommodation may be found at the Mount Elgon Lodge or in Kitale town. The summit is actually in Uganda. A museum has recently been opened in Kitale, featuring a large collection of butterflies, and displays of artefacts from this area.

**The Suk tribe**

North of Kitale is the Nilo-Hamitic Suk or Pokot tribe. Culturally similar to the Turkana, they have remained untouched by Western society and their chief diet still consists of milk, blood and meat. The men wear conical ivory lip plugs, often a metal nose plate and the traditional pigtail of red ochre and mud; a ball of ostrich feathers fixed to the base of the neck reaches down to the waist.

**Tea estates**

Branching southwest from the highway at Mau Summit, you come to **Kericho**, centre of Kenya's great tea estates, situated 1330 metres above sea level. Here you will find accommodation, tennis, golf, trout fishing, and interesting visits to the estates.

**Kisumu**, Kenya's port on **Lake Victoria** and commercial centre of the expanding Nyanza province, lies 1240 metres above sea level. Kenya Railways provide a local service on the lake (in ships with second and third class sitting accommodation only) between Kisumu pier, Homa Bay, Karunga and the Mfangano and Rusinga Islands. The Nilotic Luo people, whose most famous member was the cabinet minister Tom Mboya, live on *shambas* (farms) along the Nyanza shores of the lake. Tom Mboya's grave is on Rusinga Island, reached by steamer from Kisumu or Homa Bay.

**The Luo**

Forced to fight the Abaluhya, Nandi, Kipsigi and Kisii in order the establish themselves in the area, the Luo, whose name is Swahili for swamp, became renowned for their skill in warfare; they used to fight in a tight-knit phalanx, protected by a wall of huge shields and long spears thrust at the enemy. Today they engage in more peaceful occupations such as farming and fishing; they are also noted for their business astuteness. Ear rings used to denote prestige and Luo men were not qualified to wear them unless they had achieved the age of fifty, or renown as a warrior, or an abundance of wealth, wives, children, cattle or grain.

**Lambwe Valley National Reserve**, near Homa Bay, has been developed as a tourist attraction. Apart from the usual animals and birds of interest to the tourist, the more uncommon Jackson's hartebeest and the sitatunga are found here; buffaloes hide inside the forest. Many water birds are to be seen at Simbi, a volcanic lake near Homa Bay, whose deep stagnant waters have inspired legends similar to that of Sodom and Gomorrah; the nearby hot spring of the Homa volcano, 23 metres down a deep gorge called Abundu, is worth a visit. Soda ash deposits from the mountain, used locally for cattle food or for cooking vegetables, constitute an important item for barter with the neighbouring Kisii and Kipsigi. It was west of Mount Homa that Louis Leakey located his Kanam man (1935-37). Rock paintings on Mfangano Island in Homa Bay fill the locals with superstitious awe.

# PRACTICAL INFORMATION

The listings for this chapter are arranged alphabetically. For details on travel, sources of information, etc, see the *Nairobi* listings. For additional information on accommodation throughout Kenya, see the *Background* chapter. Many hotels in this section offer reduced rates during the low season, approximately 15 April to 31 July.

## AMBOSELI NATIONAL PARK

### Accommodation

**Amboseli Lodge and Safari Camp.** Tel: Radio call 2061. Reservations: PO Box 20211, Nairobi. Tel: Nairobi 338889. Telex: 22371 attention Amboseli Lodge. Facing Mount Kilimanjaro, this is a traditional-style tourist class rustic lodge offering simple accommodation in the lodge itself and yet more basic accommodation in tents. Lounge, dining room, bar, snack bar and pool. Heavily used by groups. Apply for rates, which are moderate.

**Amboseli Serena Lodge**, c/o PO Box 48690, Nairobi. Tel: Nairobi 338656. Telex: 22377 attention Amboseli. This is a modern first class lodge in the Kilimanjaro area, designed like a stockade, with Masai motifs and craftwork. It is 3 kms from the Ol Tukai-Kilaguni road. All rooms have private toilet, bath, shower and large windows facing the waterhole; there is plenty of plains game to be seen. Lounges, restaurant, bar; pool overlooking natural springs; and a sun terrace. 990/- single, 1300/- double and up, full board. Additional persons are charged from 460/- extra.

**Namanga Hotel**. Tel: Radio call 2104. Reservations: PO Box 30471, Nairobi. Tel: Nairobi 29251. All rooms with bath or shower; pool. Tourist class; apply for rates.

### Food

Both the **Amboseli Lodge** and the **Amboseli Serena** welcome casual diners; the first moderately priced, the second expensive.

## ELDORET

### Accommodation and Food

**New Wagon Wheels Hotel,** Elgeyo Road, PO Box 2753, Eldoret. Tel: Eldoret 2296. A small hotel, only two rooms with bath. The original mud and wattle walls constructed in 1917 are still standing. The restaurant is popular and inexpensive. Apply for rates, which are moderate to inexpensive.

## EMBU

### Accommodation and Food

**Isaac Walton Inn,** 1.5 kms north of Embu, PO Box 1, Embu. Tel: Embu 28. A simple, comfortable place, most rooms with bath. 275/- single, 330/- double, bed and breakfast. The restaurant is open to all-comers, moderately priced fare.

## KERICHO

### Accommodation and Food

**Tea Hotel,** PO Box 75, Kericho. Tel: Kericho 40. A mansion set amidst a tea plantation 1.5 kms from town, now a first class hotel. The rooms are spacious, with bath or shower; also there are cottages. Pool, tennis and squash courts, golf course; good fishing nearby. The bar and dining room are open to passers-by; moderately priced menu. 290/- single, 550/- double, suites 890/-, breakfast included.

## KIBOKO

### Accommodation

**Hunter's Lodge,** on the main Nairobi-Mombasa road. Tel: Radio call 2021. Reservations: PO Box 67868, Nairobi. A small place set in tree-shaded grounds, near a dam excellent for fishing. Pool and tennis court, open-air dance floor, bar and snack bar. Tourist class. 250/- single, 410/- double.

## KISII

### Accommodation

**Kisii Hotel,** PO Box 26, Kisii. Tel: Kisii 48. In the Lake Victoria area south of

Kisumu; this is a 10-room place, some with bath, inexpensive; apply for rates.

## KISUMU

### Accommodation

**Sunset Hotel,** Aput Lane, PO Box 215, Kisumu. Tel: (035) 41100. Overlooking the Nyanza Gulf of Lake Victoria at the south end of town, this is the newest hotel in Kisumu. Rooms with bath, radio, air conditioning, balcony with lake view. Restaurant and bar, outdoor pool and resident herd of hippos. 300/- single, 525/- double with breakfast; each additional person 155/-.

**New Kisumu Hotel,** Jomo Kenyatta Avenue, PO Box 1690, Kisumu. Tel: Kisumu 2520. An old colonial-style hotel with moderate rates; most rooms with bath.

### Food

For inexpensive light meals and snacks try the **Espresso Coffee House** on Otuma Street or the **Labella Restaurant** and the **Lido Restaurant** both on Odinga Odinga Street. Also on Odinga Odinga Street are the moderately-priced **Alfirose** and **Mona Lisa**.

**New Kisumu Hotel:** the restaurant here is open to passers-by and offers lobster and tilapia at very moderate prices.

**The Sunset Hotel's restaurant** is expensive, but the setting over the lake is marvellous and the food good. Wednesday lunches are African dishes; Sunday is the traditional day for curry and a barbeque by the pool.

## KITALE

### Accommodation

**Mount Elgon Lodge,** c/o PO Box 30471, Nairobi. Tel: 336858 Nairobi. Telex: 22033 Nairobi, attention Mount Elgon. Originally a farm house, now a small tourist class lodge in an area rich in animal, bird and plant life. All rooms with bath. Restaurant and bar. From 175/- per person, including breakfast.

## LAKE BARINGO

### Accommodation and Food

**Lake Baringo Club,** PO Box 1375, Nakuru. Reservations: PO Box 47552, Nairobi. Tel: Nairobi 22860. A bird-watching lodge on the lakeshore near Kampi ya Samaki, with its own resident ornithologist; over 400 species of bird-life have been catalogued in the area. Dining room, bar, terrace, pool; boats for hire, excursions and expeditions organised. 570/- single, 775/- double, full board.

**Baringo Island Camp,** on Ol Kokwa Island. Reservations: Thorn Tree Safaris, Esso House, Kaunda Street, PO Box 42475, Nairobi. Tel: Nairobi 25641 or 25941. Telex: 22025 Acacia, Nairobi. Sheer escapism at this beautifully-tented camp surrounded by the waters of Lake Baringo. Pool, boat trips, water sports. 460/- single, 745/- double, full board. Visitors welcome to the bar and restaurant on a high point of the island overlooking the lake where hippos, crocodiles and a vast number of birds provide the entertainment.

## LAKE TURKANA

### Accommodation

**Oasis Lodge,** Loiyangalani, on the eastern side of the lake. Tel: Nairobi 25641 or 25941. On the lakeshore amidst palm trees, a simple place, utterly relaxing. Rooms with shower; two pools, boats for hire. 635/- single, 850/- double, full board.

**Lake Turkana Fishing Lodge,** Ferguson's Gulf, on the western side of the lake. Tel: Radio call 02142. Reservations: Ivory Safari Tours, Mama Ngina Street, PO Box 74609, Nairobi. Tel: Nairobi 26623. Modern timber cabins, rooms with showers. Pool, beach, fishing, boating, game, Turkana dances. 435/- single, 690/- double, full board.

**Eliye Springs Fishing Club,** Eliye Springs, on the western side of the lake; PO Box Lodwar. Tel: Radio call 2064. Reservations: PO Box 43047, Nairobi. Tel: Nairobi 28951. Accommodation in bandas, and so slightly cheaper than the

Lake Turkana Fishing Lodge to the north.

**Food**
Particularly recommended is the makuti-roofed restaurant overlooking the lake at the **Oasis Lodge**. Expensive. Closed in May.

## MARALAL

### Accommodation and Food

**Maralal Safari Lodge,** 3 kms from town in the Maralal Game Sanctuary. Double rooms in twin-roomed chalets, decorated in Samburu style. Natural water hole and salt lick attract zebras and elands; they lick outside, passers-by are welcome to dine inside. 460/- single, 730/- double, full board. Reservations: Thorn Tree Safaris, Esso House, Kaunda Street, PO Box 42475, Nairobi. Tel: Nairobi 25641 or 25941.

## MARSABIT NATIONAL RESERVE

### Accommodation

**Marsabit Lodge,** c/o PO Box 30471, Nairobi. Tel: Nairobi 336858. Telex: 22033 Nairobi. A small game lodge in the most remote of Kenya's major game parks, on the edge of a lush volcanic crater – two hours by light plane from Nairobi. Comfortable units, all with bath. Dining room and bar; pool. Occasional gathering place of nomadic tribesmen and their camel caravans. Game viewing, including rare Abdul elephants and Kudir antelopes. 300/- single, 525/- double, with breakfast.

## MASAI MARA NATIONAL RESERVE

### Accommodation

**Fig Tree Camp,** at a secluded site on the north bank of the Talek River just outside the reserve. Tel: Radio call 3725. Reservations: PO Box 67868, Nairobi. Tel: Nairobi 20592. Rustic tented site. 515/- single, 800/- double.

**Governors' Camp,** c/o PO Box 48217, Nairobi. Tel: Nairobi 331871/2. Luxury tented camp. Game viewing, river trips. Little Governors' Camp across the river for even greater solitude. Rates all-inclusive except drinks. 1030/- single, 1600/- double.

**Keekorok Game Lodge,** in the reserve. Tel: Radio call 2178. Reservations: PO Box 40075, Nairobi. Tel: Nairobi 22860. Telex: 22146 Nairobi. Stone and cedar cottages or tents, all rooms with bath or shower. Dining room, bar, terrace; outdoor pool, hot-air balloon rides, Land Rovers available. 690/- single, 990/- double, full board.

**Mara River Camp,** c/o Bookings Limited, near New Stanley Hotel, PO Box 20106, Nairobi. Tel: Nairobi 25255. Telex: 22071 Nairobi. Simple but adequate facilities genuinely reminiscent of the old hunting camps. Tented accommodation. Apply for rates.

**Mara Sara Camp,** on the western bank of the Mara River just north of the reserve. Reservations: PO Box 43230, Nairobi. Tel: Nairobi 21716. Rondavel-style camp. 480/- single, 800/- double.

**Mara Serena Lodge,** on a high plateau overlooking the rolling plains and distant mountains of the reserve. Tel: Radio call 3757. Reservations: PO Box 48690, Nairobi. Tel: Nairobi 338659. Telex: 22878 Nairobi. An imaginatively architectured lodge incorporating Masai craftwork, set within the reserve. All rooms with bath, shower, toilet. Public areas, in domed units, include a restaurant and bar. Pool, sun terrace, supply shop. 925/- single, 1225/- double, full board.

**Food**
If travelling around the reserve, the best places to pause for a meal are the **Fig Tree Camp, Governors' Camp** (Cordon Bleu cooks, lunchtime buffet) and the **Keekorok Lodge** (lunchtime buffet). All are expensive.

## MERU

### Accommodation

**Pig and Whistle Hotel,** Mwendantu Street, PO Box 99, Meru. Tel: Meru 288. A small place, 19 rooms, all with bath or shower. 225/- single, 305/- double, with breakfast.

**Meru Mulika Lodge,** in the national park. Reservations: PO Box 30471, Nairobi. Tel: Nairobi 336858. Telex: 22033 Nairobi. Built in African style, with illuminated water hole to attract day and night herds of game. Rondavels with bath and verandah. Dining room and bar; pool. Occasional sight of rare white rhinos. 615/- single, 750/- double, with breakfast.

**Food**
The **Pig and Whistle** is a good place to stop in at. The cosy atmosphere of a small hotel, simple menu including traditional African dishes as well as curries and grills. Moderately priced.

## MOLO

**Accommodation and Food**
**Highland Hotel,** 4 kms north of Molo on the Molo-Mau Summit road, PO Box 142, Molo. Tel: Molo 50. Overlooking the Rift Valley. Nine-hole golf (at 2530 metres, the highest course in the Commonwealth), tennis, skittles, squash, riding. All rooms with bath. Tourist class; apply for rates. The restaurant is open to passers-by, good fare.

## MOUNT KENYA

**Accommodation**
**Mount Kenya Safari Club,** PO Box 35, Nanyuki. Tel: Nanyuki 2141. Telex: 28120 Nanyuki. Reservations also through the Inter-Continental Hotel, Nairobi. An exclusive retreat halfway up Mount Kenya. Accommodation is in small suites, single and double rooms, and private cottages with their own garden terraces and two double bedrooms. Three dining rooms (one outdoors), lounges, reading and writing room, heated pool, sauna, plus nine-hole golf course, tennis, riding and fishing. 695/- single, 1200/- double, with breakfast.
**Mountain Lodge,** PO Box 113, Kiganjo. Tel: Kiganjo 3622. Telex: 22033. East of Kiganjo on the slopes of Mount Kenya, 29 kms from the main Nairobi-Nanyuki road. Signposted from Karatina, also from the main Kiganjo-Nanyuki road. This is the closest of the tree-lodges to Nairobi, and can be reached in two and a half hours, the last part of the journey along a scenic mountain track. 600/- single, 960/-double, full board.
**Naro Moru River Lodge,** on the Nairobi-Nanyuki road at 170 kms, PO Box 18, Naro Moru. Tel: Naro Moru 23. Double rooms, bandas, self-service cottages; also a camping site available. The air is fresh and at night brisk here at 2130 metres up the side of Mount Kenya. Mountain climbing, riding, birdwatching and game viewing are the activities. 345/- single, 460/- double, full board. Reservations can also be made through Alliance Hotels, PO Box 14287, Nairobi. Tel: Nairobi 742272. Telex: 22591.

**Food**
Meals at the **Mount Kenya Safari Club** are famous, the lunchtime buffets ludicrously overwhelming, the evening menu runs to five courses, and the bill is in keeping. Not quite so expensive are the meals at the **Mountain Lodge** where the standard of cooking is consistently high. In the moderate range is the **Naro Moru River Lodge** where fresh trout is a specialty.

## SAMBURU NATIONAL RESERVE

**Accommodation and Food**
**Samburu Game Lodge,** in the reserve. Reservations: PO Box 47557, Nairobi. Tel: Nairobi 22860. Telex: 22146 Nairobi. Built of local stone and mountain cedar to blend in with the landscape, the lodge and cottages are far off the beaten track, though you still get electric light, bath and shower, constant hot water in your room, plus use of deep freezers, bottle coolers and swimming pool. 12 tents also available. 690/- single, 990/- double, full board. Part of the complex and slightly cheaper is **River Lodge** on the Buffalo Springs side of the river. Meals served to passers-through at either lodge, both expensive, River Lodge's cuisine possibly better.

## TAITA HILLS

**Accommodation and Food**
**Taita Hills Lodge,** in the Ponderosa

Game Sanctuary which adjoins Tsavo National Park. Tel: Radio call 2011. Reservations through the Nairobi Hilton Hotel. All rooms with tub shower/bath and balcony. Restaurant, bar, lounge, terrace cafe, shops, pool, tennis – highly sophisticated facilities generally. Camel riding tours and safaris can be arranged. Private game and bird viewing sanctuary. 690/- single, 850/- double, full board.

**Salt Lick Lodge**, near Tsavo National Park, in private sanctuary 10 kms from Taita Hills Lodge, whose facilities it complements. Tel: Radio call 2011. Reservations through the Nairobi Hilton Hotel. Built like a village on stilts with interconnecting walkways; viewing platform for observing animals at the water holes and the floodlit salt lick. All rooms with bathroom and specially-constructed 'close-up view' windows. Restaurant, bar, newsstand, souvenir shop. Children under 8 not accepted. 860/- single, 1060/- double, 1480/- triple, full board.

## TANA RIVER GAME RESERVE

### Accommodation

**Baomo Lodge,** 160 kms north of Malindi (35-minute flight, two and a half hours by car, but roads often impassable mid-April to mid-July). Reservations: Tana River Camp Limited, PO Box 33, Malindi. Tel: Malindi 270 or radio call 3704. Rooms, bandas and tents, all with bathroom annexes, hot and cold running water. Bar and verandah restaurant: European cuisine with Italian specialities. Foot safaris in the Tana Gallery forest with experienced and armed escorts; a paradise for birdwatchers, botonists and game viewers; river canoe trips to see hippos, crocodiles and birdlife. 630/- single, 760/- double, full board.

## TSAVO NATIONAL PARK

### Accommodation

**Crocodile Tented Lodge,** just outside Saba gate of Tsavo East, on the road to Malindi. Reservations: World Travel Bureau, PO Box 41178, Nairobi. Tel: Nairobi 27930. Swimming pool, crocodile feeding by floodlights every night. 460/- single, 690/- double, full board.

**Kilaguni Lodge,** 32 kms from the Nairobi-Mombasa road, inside Tsavo West. Reservations: PO Box 30471, Nairobi. Tel: Nairobi 336858. Telex: 22033 Nairobi, attention Kilaguni. Renowned game lodge, built to blend into the surrounding country. Bath or shower in all rooms, plus verandah. Pool; dining room and bar overlook floodlit water holes. 720/- single, 1000/- double, full board.

**Ngulia Safari Lodge,** inside Tsavo West, reservations as for Kilaguni Lodge except that telex should be for the attention of Ngulia. On the edge of the Ndawe Escarpment at 900 metres with panoramic views. Similar facilities and game viewing opportunities as at Kilaguni, and identical prices. The big difference: Ngulia is heavily booked by groups.

**Voi Safari Lodge,** just off the Nairobi-Mombasa highway at the eastern entrance to Tsavo East, PO Box Voi. Tel: Voi 17. Also reservations as for Kilaguni and Ngulia lodges. Beautifully designed in a dramatic site, all bedrooms have bath and fine views. Bar, lounge, terrace, dining room, pool, game lookout near waterhole. Easy access by rail: 11 kms from Voi station. 660/- single, 845/- double, full board.

### Food

All three of the above lodges serve passers-by; the view from the Ngulia Safari Lodge restaurant over 80 kms of open country is magnificent. All are in the expensive category.

# THE KENYA COAST

A tropical paradise, Kenya's coast offers long white beaches shaded by palm trees, refreshed by trade winds and protected by a continuous coral reef running within a mile of the shore. The reef, which is broken only at Mombasa and Malindi, creates a series of blue lagoons perfect for safe swimming and goggling.

There is plenty of excitement for those who venture on the Indian Ocean – scudding over a lagoon on water skis, sweeping before the blustering monsoon on a graceful yacht, exploring the wonderlands of the warm coral pools abundant in tropical fish and delicate underwater flora, or battling with a giant of the deep at the end of a fishing line. Usually the fish you catch are for you to dispose of – a catch which you cannot eat in a whacking great meal can be sold at a local auction. All sporting equipment and facilities are provided at most of the coastal resorts, and interesting side trips can be made to see the dances of the colourful African tribes inhabiting the hinterland.

The coast offers the fascination of ancient civilisations – Greek, Arab, Persian and Chinese. Its forests are the haunt of many wild animals, and regular safaris operate from the coast to the Tana River Game Reserve, Tsavo National Park and to the game sanctuaries beneath the snowy dome of Kilimanjaro.

**Climate**

The climate is warm and equable, the mean maximum temperature being 30°C, the minimum 23°C. The warmest months are February to March, the coolest June to July, and the most pleasant September to October. The mean humidity is 75 percent and the rains fall during April, May and November. As the sun is much hotter than in Europe or other temperate zones, you should, at least until you become acclimatised, wear dark glasses and expose your skin only for short periods. Clothing should consist mainly of cool cottons and linens, although woollen sweaters may be needed for the early morning. When appearing in public outside your hotel, you should be careful to respect the Moslem proprieties and be reasonably covered up. Plenty of the hotel boutiques and town shops sell attractive short or long locally-styled dresses and skirts which are quite inexpensive. Dress in the evening is sometimes formal. Malaria is now rare, but when coming to the coast you should take a reliable prophylactic before arriving in Kenya, and continue taking it after your departure (your doctor will advise).

### Travelling to and along the Coast

**By sea and air** The busy port of Mombasa is the most important in East Africa, serving not only Kenya but countries as far afield as Zaire, Sudan and Ethiopia. Cargo liners from all corners of the world call here regularly, although today very few carry passengers. Kenya Airways operates frequent flights between Nairobi, Mombasa and Malindi, and smaller companies connect these three points with the Afro-Arabic island of Lamu. Mombasa's Moi Airport is at Chamgamwe on the northwest mainland, about 13 kms from the city centre. This new international airport can accommodate jumbo jets, and international charter flights from Europe are increasingly landing direct at Mombasa.

**Rail** Two trains leave Nairobi every evening for Mombasa, and vice versa, arriving the following morning. These comfortable overnight trains are well served by sleeping cars and restaurants, and you may be lucky enough to spot a lion or two as the train passes through Tsavo National Park.

**Roads** The 490-km Nairobi-Mombasa highway can be covered in about six hours and there is a tarmac road between Mombasa and Malindi, driving time about one and a half hours. Buses and taxis ply frequently between the two cities. North of Malindi an unsurfaced road runs for 200 kms to the Lamu ferry. It then travels north to Garissa, where it meets the road to Somalia. These roads are sometimes closed by heavy rains and you should check at Malindi before proceeding. From Mombasa a surfaced road runs along the south coast to Tanga and Dar es Salaam, but the border post at Lunga Lunga is for the time being closed.

### Mombasa

**History** Named by the Arabs the Island of War because of its stormy history, Mombasa is Kenya's second city and the largest port on the eastern side of Africa north of Durban. It is in fact connected to the mainland by the

Makupa Causeway, a land bridge for the main road and railway to Nairobi. It was the opening of the railway in 1901 that revived Mombasa's fortunes, making it the gateway to East Africa. Its history goes back at least to 500 BC when it was known to Phoenician sailors, and identified as Tonike it appeared on Alexandrian maps of the 1st C AD. Vasco da Gama was the first European to land, in 1498, but was soon driven off to Malindi by hostile Arabs. The port continued to be contested by the Arabs and Portuguese during the next two centuries, and eventually became part of the empire of the Sultan of Muscat. Mombasa languished during most of the 19th C after the Sultan transferred his court to Zanzibar.

**The old town**

Mombasa is really two towns and two ports. The most fascinating part of the city is the old **Arab town** that lies between Makadara Road and the old harbour, a warren of twisting narrow streets filled with an air of intrigue between high houses decorated with intricately carved balconies. Here goldsmiths ply their craft side by side with silk dealers, perfume makers and spice merchants. The **old harbour** is still used by Arab dhows, graceful sailing craft built to a traditional pattern that evokes the age of Sinbad, when they carried slaves, spices and ivory. Most spectacular are the large, ocean-going dhows which navigate with the trade winds across thousands of miles of open sea without the aid of radio or radar. From December to April, when they arrive from Persia, Arabia and India, you can hire a rowing boat out to visit them. Their bearded captains (*nahoda*) may even offer you a cup of sharp bitter coffee from a beak-spouted copper pot. The nahoda sell fine carpets, ex-bond, in the **Old Customs House**, open daily from 8am to noon and 2pm to 4pm.

You reach the old harbour by walking down Nkrumah Road, past the old Treasury Square, Fort Jesus and into Government Square with the Customs House and numerous shops selling perfumes, brassware and carvings. Pink-walled **Fort Jesus** rises above the old harbour, and was built in 1593 by the Portuguese as a stronghold against the rebellious Arabs. In 1696 it suffered the great 33-month siege which ended with the Arabs storming the fort and killing the 12 remaining defenders. Today the fort houses a comprehensive **museum**, open daily between 9am and 6pm, with historical, architectural and cultural relics, and

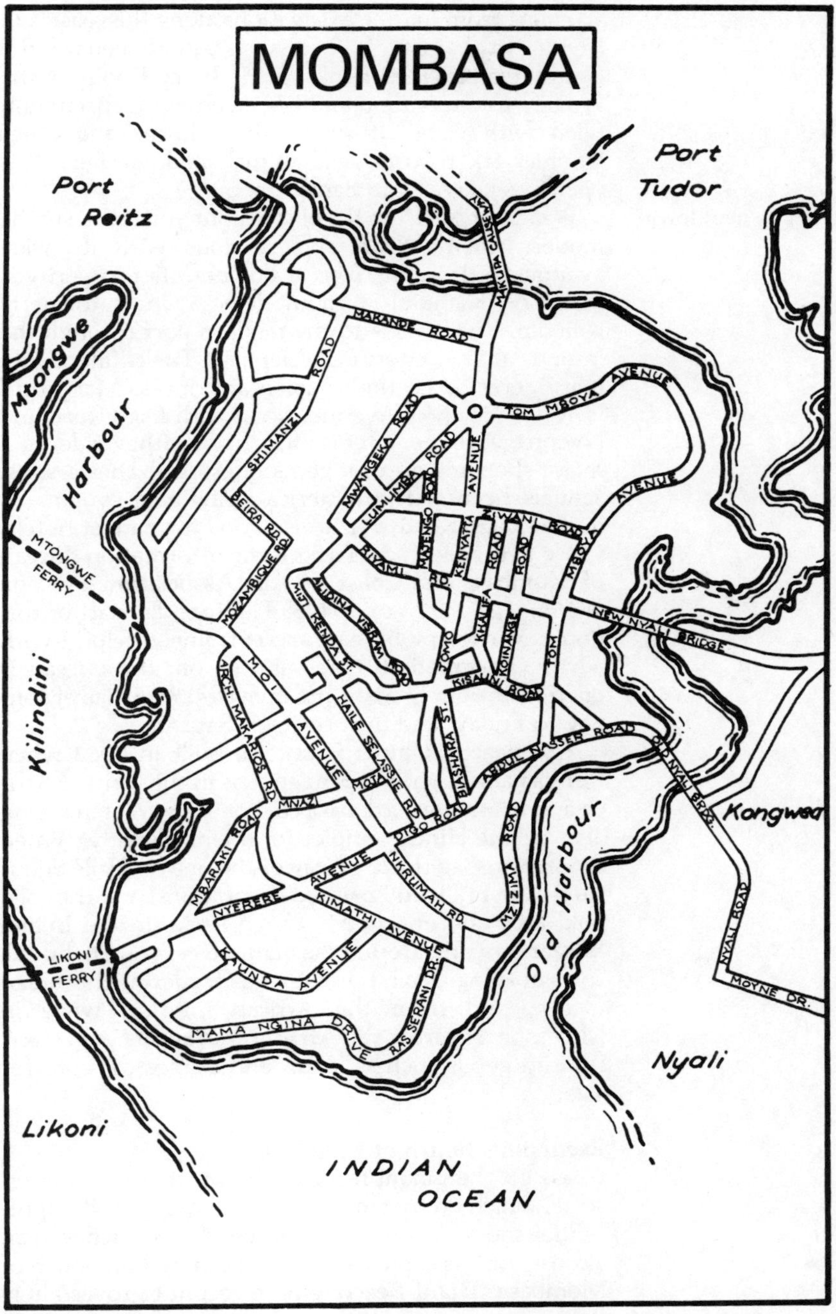
MOMBASA
Port Reitz
Port Tudor
Mtongwe
Harbour
MTONGWE FERRY
Kilindini
MAKURA CAUSEWAY
MAKANDE ROAD
SHIMANZI ROAD
TOM MBOYA AVENUE
MWANGEKA ROAD
LUMUMBA ROAD
ABDEL AVENUE
BEIRA RD.
MOZAMBIQUE RD.
RIYAMI RD.
MASENGO ROAD
KENYATTA AVENUE
DIWANI ROAD
KHALIFA ROAD
KOINANGE ROAD
TOM MBOYA AVENUE
NEW NYALI BRIDGE
ALIDINA VISRAM ROAD
KENDA ST.
JOMO
KISAUNI ROAD
MOI AVENUE
ARCH. MAKARIOS RD.
HAILE SELASSIE RD.
BIASHARA ST.
ABDUL NASSER ROAD
OLD NYALI BRDG.
Kongwea
MNAZI
MOTA
DIGO ROAD
MBARAKI ROAD
NYERERE AVENUE
NKRUMAH RD.
KIMATHI AVENUE
MZIZIMA ROAD
Old Harbour
NYALI ROAD
MOYNE DR.
LIKONI FERRY
KAUNDA AVENUE
RAS SERANI DR.
MAMA NGINA DRIVE
Nyali
Likoni
INDIAN OCEAN

artefacts from marine excavations along the coast. On Mvita Road, just off Treasury Square behind the Kenya Commercial Bank, is the **Ivory Room** of the Wildlife Conservation and Management Department, filled with elephant tusks, rhino horns and other trophies taken from dead animals and poachers. It is open weekdays from 8am to noon.

**The new town**

Walking back from the old harbour you return to the **modern town**, clean and spacious with its wide avenues and bright tropical flowers. Its prosperity is based on Kilindini Harbour; Moi Avenue (formerly Kilindini Road) leads to the modern port through the famous arch of enormous **Elephant Tusks** (metal, not ivory), erected on the occasion of Princess Margaret's visit in 1956. Moi Avenue, along with Digo Road and Nyerere Avenue intersecting from either side, is a major shopping area for gemstones, Arab chests, saris, sandals, herbs, African fabrics, straw hats – you name it. The Digo Road area is also good for budget hotels. Close to the Elephant Tusks is the **Information Bureau of Mombasa and Coast Tourist Association**, PO Box 99596; Tel: 24173 or 25428. The friendly staff of this non-government bureau are extremely helpful with advice, information, maps and so on; the bureau is open from 8am to noon and 2pm to 4.30pm daily Monday to Friday, and 8am to noon Saturdays.

The nearby **Uhuru Fountain**, built in 1963 when Kenya gained her independence, is in the form of Africa and bears the Mombasa coat of arms. Worth seeing also are the **Hindu temples** for their brilliantly painted decorations (eg the doorway of the one on Haile Selassie Road), brilliantly painted decorations, and the solid gold atop the one in Mwagogo Road. In the **Indian Bazaar** centring around Biashara Street you can buy all sorts of things from the countries bordering the Indian Ocean, and from the African interior, while in Mwembe Tayari is the **African Market** where typical African goods such as kikois and beaded caps are for sale.

### Excursions South of Mombasa

Cross on the Likoni ferry to the southern coastal resorts, which are noted for their tranquility and unpretentiousness. A series of silver beaches stretches in an almost uninterrupted strip for about 60 kms south of Mombasa. **Diani Beach**, where coconut groves alternate with charming local settlements, and which also has a casino, is the most attractive. Hotels offer facilities for fishing and all water sports, as well as the novel sport of parasailing, the participant harnessed to a parachute attached by a long line to a Land Rover.

The road from Likoni runs parallel to the coast, passing through banana, sisal, palm and sugar plantations. Ten kilometres south of the Likoni ferry, on the right, is the turn-off to Tanga and the Tanzanian border. Kwale, about 20 kms after the turn-off, offers fine views. This is the area of the **Shimba Hills Nature Reserve**, the only place in Kenya where the increasingly rare sable and roan antelope are to be seen. In the fine forest of immense trees there are also elephant, leopard, buffalo, pythons and a wide variety of bird life. Sixty-five kilometres south of Mombasa, at the quaint village of **Shimoni**, is the Pemba Channel Fishing Club, base for some of East Africa's best big game fishing, with an outstanding record for striped marlin. There is a restaurant on Wasini Island off Shimoni, and some 8 kms offshore a marine park, **Kisiti Mpunguti**, has been established. The park area includes three islands, Kisiti, Mpunguti ya Chini and Mpunguti ya Juu, all of which are rich in birdlife. At various places along Kenya's south coast, there are ruins of Arabic origin.

**Excursions North of Mombasa**

If you cross the Nyali toll bridge you can reach Malindi after crossing over Mtwapa Creek by toll bridge and Kilifi Creek by ferry on a 150-km journey through land cultivated with sisal, cashew nuts, coconut palms and capok trees. The coast north of Mombasa is more varied than that to the south. At **Nyali** on a hillock not far from the shops and just past the cement silo stands a monument to Dr Ludwig Krapf, the great missionary explorer and the first recorded European to see Mount Kenya; his family is buried in a small enclosure nearby. Turning left immediately after crossing the Nyali Bridge, you will come to the village of **Freretown**, established in 1874 by Sir Bartle Frere for slaves liberated from Arab dhows by the Royal Navy. Here too is the grave of one of the bearers who carried Livingstone's body to the coast. Many species of birds are to be seen in this area.

At **Bamburi** there are beach cottages, self-help apartments and several fine hotels and restaurants.

Follow the signs to the small privately run **Kipepeo Aquarium** where hundreds of specimens of tiny beautifully coloured and strange shaped tropical fish are displayed in aerated tanks. Then on through the Giriama country where the women in their topless white kilts, usually with an infant slung over their shoulder and a burden on their head, are an integral feature of the coastal scene. You will then pass the access roads to the Shanzu Beach hotels and soon reach **Mtwapa Creek**. Once traversed by a hand-hauled 'singing ferry', it now has a permanent bridge. On the north bank of the creek there is a restaurant overlooking the water, and two deep sea fishing establishments. There are hotels between Mtwapa and Kilifi Creek which is 55 kms north of Mombasa. At nearby Mnarani overlooking the Indian Ocean and the creek, hotels offer facilities for deep sea fishing and water sports.

**Giriama country**

### To Watamu

Beyond Kilifi the road cuts through the bush and in less than half an hour you will reach the turn-off to Watamu, 16 kms south of Malindi. This area is fast developing as a resort in its own right, with several hotels, a marine national park, and the nearby, mysterious, ruined city of **Gedi**.

**Ruined city**

Believed to have been founded in the 13th C, Gedi was mysteriously deserted some time during the 17th C, overgrown with jungle and only rediscovered in the 1920s. It is possible that Gedi was abandoned after an attack by marauding Galla tribesmen who used to raid the coast from Somaliland. Another theory is that the wells dried up, causing the inhabitants to leave. To be seen today are several mosques including the Grand Mosque which had 17 columns, the Sultan's Palace, a prison, several giant pillar tombs, houses made of coral rag and faced with plaster and dressed stone, numerous wells and a conduit system for water. Four skeletons were found at the bottom of the largest well. Ming dynasty porcelain and stoneware from China, glazed earthenware and glass from Persia, and cornelian beads from India have been found on the site and can be seen in the nearby museum. A good map-guide to Gedi is available at the entrance.

**Marine parks**

The road continues past Gedi, leading to the beach

*Fishing boats off Malindi*

and to the **Watamu Marine National Park**. Both here and at the **Malindi Marine National Park**, glass-bottomed boats may be hired, fully equipped with snorkels, goggles and flippers, for the exploration of these wonderlands of fish and coral. Spearing the fish is prohibited and they will therefore feed from your hand.

At **Watamu** the Blue Lagoon and Turtle Bay have hotels with fine white beaches where swimming is unrestricted by the tide, and there are facilities for deep sea fishing, inshore and creek fishing, reef goggling and glass-panelled boat trips to the Marine Park. Mida Creek, adjoining Turtle Bay, is a staging post for migratory birds.

### Malindi

'Far Malindi' of *Paradise Lost* is one of Kenya's most popular tourist spots. This delightful little resort, with its palm-thatched houses and old Arab dhows, began to attract the attention of big game fishermen after the last war, and has now developed into Kenya's playground, offering all the amenities of the Mediterranean Rivieras at a lower cost.

Malindi has long enjoyed a reputation for hos-

**Vasco da Gama**

pitality. In 1498, when Vasco da Gama called here, in contrast to – and probably because of – his hostile reception at Mombasa, he was royally and exotically entertained by the local ruler. He spoke of the well-being of the people and of their tall, white-washed houses with many windows. There are still tall, white houses with big windows, but now a tarmac road runs by them. And out beyond the old fishing village, where the 15th C coral pillar commemorating da Gama's visit still stands, is a European holiday resort with modern hotels.

The main attraction of Malindi is the blue Indian Ocean which rolls through a break in the coral reef to allow excellent surfing at certain times of the year in the bay where the principal hotels are situated. The rest of the Malindi coast offers goggling, sailing and water skiing. Spear fishing is not permitted due to the proximity of the marine parks.

**Big game fishing**

From November to April big game fishing is excellent (and inexpensive) and Malindi is building an international reputation for its unlimited reservoir of marlin, sailfish, barracuda, kingfish and tunny. In October or November fishing contests are held as part of the annual Malindi Sea Festival; in late January the International Bill-Fish Competition takes place. There are several sea fishing clubs in Malindi, and a scuba diving centre at Silversands. Other attractions include a snake park, demonstrations of snake catching, bird watching trips, and excursions to Gedi.

The Malindi Golf Club, which accepts temporary members, has a nine-hole course and a tennis court. All the major hotels have swimming pools and some games rooms. Horses are available for exhilarating rides along the beach, and in the evening dances and cinema shows are held under the stars. Those interested in local traditions will enjoy the exhibitions of Giriama dancing held in a nearby village. A travelling discotheque frequently visits the four main hotels which are all situated within walking distance of the town. Here modern shops provide nearly all the tourist's requirements.

### Lamu

North of Malindi and a few kilometres offshore lies the Lamu archipelago, best known for the Afro-Arab town of Lamu which has maintained its mediaeval character almost intact. It shares the same cultural heritage with Zanzibar, but whereas the old part of Zanzibar is barely alive and fast giving way to modern architecture and life styles, the old town of Lamu bubbles with traditional life.

**The old Afro-Arab town**

The town stands on the northeastern shore of **Lamu island**. It is characterised by overhanging houses, dark alleys, exquisitely carved doors and picturesque mosques. Part of the **Pwani Mosque** dates back to 1370, the **Friday Mosque** to 1511, but the majority of Lamu's buildings were constructed at the end of the 18th C. During the last one and a half centuries the people of Lamu have changed little in their customs, pastimes, dress and means of living. The visitor will still see Bajuni fishermen at work, women entirely covered by black cloaks, old men sipping thick black coffee on their doorsteps, street vendors peddling their wares and children sleeping in the dug-out canoes. Donkeys remain virtually the only means of transport.

Fine examples of traditional coastal craftsmanship are displayed at the **Lamu Museum**: wooden doors, jewellery, costumes and two house rooms furnished in 19th C style. The museum also has an interesting dhow gallery.

Lamu's history abounds in colourful personalities. In the 1880s the British Vice-Consul here was J G Haggard, brother of H Rider Haggard. The island was the site of the first attempted communist state on the continent. In 1894 a group of Austrian, Scandinavian, German and British free-thinkers arrived in the *SS Reichstag* with the intention of establishing an African 'Freeland' based at Lamu. Described by the *Kenya Weekly News* as a 'crowd of unpractical idealists and downright scoundrels', they left after their exploratory attempts up the Tana River failed and their liquor supplies ran out.

**Getting to the Lamu archipelago**

The other islands, of which the largest are **Manda** and **Pate**, have some fascinating old ruins, wildlife (sometimes including lions and leopards, which swim across from the mainland) and excellent fishing. They are, however, difficult to get to: arrangements must be negotiated with boatmen in Lamu town.

Lamu can be reached by dhow (dhow safaris are organised to and from Malindi), bus or car – which have to be abandoned at Mokowe on the mainland from where travellers are transported by ferry to the carless island. Light aircraft charter companies in Malindi carry passengers to and from Lamu via the airstrip on Manda Island where boats wait to carry passengers across the channel to Lamu.

Small and traditional, Lamu provides a surprising amount of varied accommodation: local houses of all standards, small hotels where teachers of the Koran may board and two luxury and expensive international standard hotels.

# PRACTICAL INFORMATION

The listings for this chapter cover Mombasa first, and then the rest of the Kenya coast alphabetically. For details on travel, sources of information, etc, see the *Mombasa* and the *Nairobi* listings. For additional information on accommodation throughout Kenya, see the *Background* chapter. The low season along the coast is from May through June and from September to mid-December, when hotel rates are usually considerably reduced.

**Warning**: Robbery with violence is now quite common in Mombasa. Do not walk the streets or along the beaches alone at night. Also avoid carrying a bag which can be snatched. And do not try to sleep out on the beaches.

## MOMBASA

### Accommodation

**Oceanic Hotel,** Mbuyuni Road, PO Box 90371. Tel: 26191. Large hotel with swimming pool and casino. 565/- single, 605/- double, with breakfast.

**Outrigger Hotel**, Ras Liwatoni, PO Box 82345. Tel: 20822. Telex: 21215. Comfortable businessman's hotel overlooking Kilindini Harbour. Rooms air-conditioned with bath and balcony. Restaurant, pool and patio bar. 290/- single, 415/- double, with breakfast.

**Manor Hotel**, Nyerere Avenue, PO Box 84851. Tel: 21822. Long established tourist class hotel in the middle of the island, opposite the cathedral, on the road leading to the Likoni ferry. Comfortable rooms with bath, some air-conditioned. 205/- single, 310/- double.

**Castle Hotel**, Moi Avenue, PO Box 84231. Tel: 21683. Telex: 21249. 205/- single, 300/- double, with breakfast.

**New Carlton Hotel**, Moi Avenue, PO Box 86779. Tel: 23776. 175/- single, 250/- double, with breakfast.

**Hotel Splendid**, Msanifu Kombo Street, PO Box 90482. Tel: 20967. 185/- single, 250/- double, with breakfast.

**Cosy Guest House**, Haile Selassie Road, PO Box 83011. No meals. 46/-single, 69/- double.

**YMCA/YWCA**, PO Box 96009, Likoni, Mombasa. 92/- per person, full board.

**Hydro Hotel**, Digo Road near the market.Tel: 23784. Popular place for shoestring travellers, and good for meeting people travelling along the coast. No single rooms. 24/- dorm or on the roof, 65/- double room.

### Food

Of course you can eat at your hotel, but to get the flavour of Mombasa you should wander about the streets where every cafe fills up with locals eating Swahili foods – curries, beans in coconut milk and puffy mandazi. Street food is prepared on tiny jikos whose charcoal fires light up the dark lanes. If you would like to try the varied tastes of Mombasa, start on Abdul Nasser Road. Stop in at the Khayam Hotel for mkato nyamo, or the New People's for mushkaki. Elias is good for curries throughout the day and night, while the Abbasi Tea Room offers over 30 fresh fruit juices for the thirsty.

**Abbasi Tea Room**, Abdul Nasser Road. Apart from the 30 or so juices (including watermelon and tamarind), there are snacks of kebab, mushkaki, parotha and prawn curry. Moderately priced.

**Capri Restaurant**, Ambalal House, Nkrumah Road. Tel: 311156. Elegant, with excellent food and service. Seafood and grills. And the Hunter's Bar for quick meals, snacks and drinks. Expensive.

**Hydro Hotel**, Digo Road near the market. Tel: 23784. Due to limited space, the tables are sometimes jammed into the bedrooms. Indian cuisine amidst well-made beds. The place and the food are basic, but also incredibly cheap.

**Mistral**, Moi Avenue. Tel: 24911. A family-style French restaurant and cocktail lounge. Expensive to moderately priced seafood and steaks.

**Singh Restaurant**, Mwembe Tayari Road, off Kenyatta Avenue. The decor is dull but the food is good and the place is popular. Moderately to inexpensive Indian cuisine.

### Shopping

Apart from visiting the **markets** (see text), the following might also serve your purposes.

**Gemstones of Africa**, Moi Avenue, PO Box 83877. Tel: 21942. Superior quality and design.

**Sonia Arts,** City House, Moi Avenue, PO Box 84963. Tel: 20781. Local fabrics and dresses, jewellery, handicrafts and souvenirs.

**Coast Drapers and Curios**, Moi Avenue, PO Box 84026. Tel: 24281. Wakamba wood carvings, Makonde sculptures, Zanzibar chests, batiks, khangas, maridadi fabrics, meerschaum pipes, semi-precious stone jewellery, underwater and goggling equipment.

**Huseini Stationary Mart**, Digo Road (Regal Cinema Building), PO Box 90162. Tel: 25908. English, German, Italian and French books and newspapers, maps, guide books, postcards.

**Mombasa Chemists**, Digo Road, PO Box 81356. Tel: 23662 or 26969.

### Information

The **Tourist Information Bureau**, Moi Avenue, near the Elephant Tusks, PO Box 99596. Tel: 24173 or 25428. Open Monday to Friday, 8am to noon, 2pm to 6pm, and on Saturdays 8am to noon. Extremely helpful with advice and information; sells national park and road maps, postcards and other publications on the coast.

Major **hotels**, **travel agents** such as American Express and your **consular representative** can all be valuable sources of varied information.

### Travel

Some useful addresses and phone numbers:

**Kenya Airways**, Moi Avenue, PO Box 90671. Tel: 21251.

**Moi Mombasa International Airport**. Tel: 433211.

**American Express**, Express Kenya Limited, Nkrumah Road, PO Box 90631. Tel: 24461.

**Automobile Association**, Moi Avenue, PO Box 83001. Tel: 26778.

**Kenya Rent A Car** (agents for Avis), Moi Avenue, PO Box 84868. Tel: 23048.

**United Touring Company**, Moi Avenue, PO Box 84782. Tel: 316333. Agents for Hertz; also safari operators.

**Archers Group of Companies**, Moi Avenue near Agip garage, PO Box 84616. Offers a wide range of travel services. Tel: 25362 for tours and car hire.

**Coast Bus Service**, opposite Mwembe Tayari, Jomo Kenyatta Avenue, PO Box 82414. Tel: 20916. Buses to Nairobi and along the coast. Also safari buses for hire.

**Kenya Bus Service**, Jomo Kenyatta Avenue, PO Box 90380.

The **railway station** is at the far end of Haile Selassie Road, away from Digo Road.

**Other Things**
**Central Post Office**, Digo Road. Open 8am-noon and 2pm-4.30pm Monday to Friday; Saturdays 8am to noon; Sundays 9am to 1pm.
**Hospitals**: Mombasa Hospital (Tel: 312191), Aga Khan (Tel: 312953), Pandya Clinic (Tel: 311010).
**Emergencies:** Dial 999 or call the operator.
**Inoculations**: Enquire at the Municipal Medical Office. Tel: 26791.
**Immigration Department**, Nkrumah Road beyond Treasury Square on the left, PO Box 90284. Tel: 311745.
**Consular representatives**: A few countries have honorary consuls in Mombasa; the United States does not. British consul, Mr W James, PO Box 90590. Tel: 23076. Mornings only.

## THE REST OF THE KENYA COAST

**BAMBURI** (10 kms north of Mombasa)
**Accommodation**
**Bamburi Beach Hotel**, c/o PO Box 83966, Mombasa. Tel: Mombasa 485611. Informal beach hotel. All rooms with air conditioning, shower and balcony with sea view. Grill room, beach bar, freshwater pool. Activities include watersports, golf, tennis, and riding. A good family hotel. 515/- single, 690/- double, full board.
**Whitesands Hotel**, c/o PO Box 90173, Mombasa. Tel: Mombasa 485926. Telex: 21175 Mombasa, attention Whitesand. Also Tel: Bamburi 252. First class beach hotel. Rooms with bath, air conditioning and balcony. Restaurant, bar, shops, freshwater pool. 660/-single, 965/- double, full board.

**DIANI** (30 kms south of Mombasa)
**Accommodation**
**Africana Sea Lodge**, c/o PO Box 84616, Mombasa. Tel: Mombasa 742272 or Diani 2021. Telex: 21189 Mombasa, attention Africana. On the beach, accommodation in individual air-conditioned rondavels set in a tropical garden. Restaurant, grill room, bar, lounge, disco and pool. Water sports, diving, tennis and squash. 585/- single, 850/- double, full board.
**Robinson Baobab Hotel**, c/o PO Box 84792, Mombasa. Tel: Diani (01261) 2026. Telex: 21132 Robaobab. A popular tourist class beach resort set atop high cliffs overlooking the Indian Ocean. Air-conditioned rooms with shower or cool makuti-roofed bungalows. Restaurant, nightclub, pool, sports and watersports, and children's activities. 565/- single, 920/- double.
**Trade Winds Hotel**, c/o PO Box Ukunda, Mombasa. Tel: Diani 2016. Telex: 21139. Tourist class hotel with Arabian-style architecture, on the beach and near the Shimba Hills Game Reserve. All rooms with air conditioning, bath, shower, and verandah. Pool, barbecue, restaurant. Watersports. Pleasant ambience. 605/- single, 845/- double, full board.
**Two Fishes Hotel**, PO Box 23, Ukunda via Mombasa. Tel: Diani 2101. Telex: 21162. Informal first class African-style hotel, 5 kms from Ukunda village. Air-conditioned rooms with bath or shower and verandah. Dining room, three bars, pool. Activities include deepsea fishing, goggling and sailing. 625/-single, 890/- double, full board.
**Nomad Beach Tented Hotel**, PO Box 1, Ukunda via Mombasa. 195/- single, 345/- double.

**Food**
**Nomad**, near Ukundi and Diani Beach. Tel: Diani 2155. Rustic restaurant under a high makuti roof; its specialities are spaghetti and seafood. This is an opportunity to get out of the tourist hotels and mix with the locals among whom it is a favourite; very popular with young travellers despite being moderate to expensive.

**KIKAMBALA** (26 kms north of Mombasa)
**Accommodation**
**Whispering Palms Hotel**, PO Box Kikambala. Tel: Kikambala 6. Telex: 22033 attention Whispering Palms. Tourist class hotel right on the beach

amidst, yes, a forest of palms. All rooms air-conditioned, many with shower or bath and verandah. Two pools, barbecue patio, games room, disco, plus watersports and fishing. 440/- single, 695/- double, full board.
**Kikambala Beach Cottages**, c/o PO Box 83344, Mombasa. 83/- per two-bed cottage, 276/- per eight-bed cottage.

**Food**
**Le Pichet**. One of the finest restaurants in Kenya, and expensive. Sublime seafood and desserts: try Prawns Piri Piri, Crab Mousseline, Tilapia au Beurre and Glace Grand Marnier.

**KILIFI** (60 kms north of Mombasa, midway to Malindi)
**Accommodation**
**Mnarani Club**, PO Box 14, Kilifi. Tel: Kilifi 18. Telex: 22033. Popular sports club and base for big game fishing and scuba diving. Comfortable rooms with bath, some with balconies. All the usual facilities, including pool, open-air dance floor with bar overlooking the creek and Indian Ocean. Scuba diving school. 555/- single, 780/- double, full board.

**LAMU ISLAND** (180 kms north of Malindi)
**Accommodation**
**Peponi Hotel**, PO Box 24, Shella, Lamu. Tel: Lamu 29. On the outskirts of Shella village with its Omani character and mosques, and at the entrance to Lamu harbour, this is an informal first class beach hotel of white cottages with ceiling fans and verandahs. A dining room and bar are in the main building. A 13-km beach starts outside your door, and deepsea fishing and powerboat hire are available. 472/- single, 673/- double, suite 1455/-, full board.
**Petley's Inn**, PO Box 4, Lamu. Tel: Lamu 48. Telex: 21153 Lamu. On the waterfront overlooking the dhow quays, this famous inn dating back to the 1800s is now a tourist class hotel, renovated, but still in Swahili style. Rooms with four-poster beds, bath or shower, shuttered windows, ceiling fans. This is the centre of local acitivity, an island landmark, with the museum next door. Also pool and disco, to bring things up to date. 440/- single, 760/- double, with breakfast.
Also there are numerous very cheap places to sack out on this island once known as 'the Kathmandu of Africa':

**Castle Lodge**, just behind and to the left of the prison in the market square, costs 11/- on the roof with a mattress, 22/- for a single inside, 65/- for a double; at similar prices are the **New Century**, **Bahari Lodge** and **Amu Lodging**; while for half that price you can stay at the **Karibuni Lodge**, very clean, with showers and friendly management; or get a double for 95/- at **New Maharus**.

**Food**
Both **Petley's Inn** and the **Peponi Hotel** are good, moderately-priced places to have a meal, the Peponi with the bonus of its marvellous view over the water.
**S K Ghai's**, on the waterfront, should be tried for its lobster thermidor, crab, sweet and sour prawns and home-made ice cream. Moderately priced.

The **Olympic Hotel's restaurant**, on the waterfront south of Petley's, is stark and cheap, but the food is good.

**Of Interest**
The *Moulid el Beni* or **Prophet's birthday** is celebrated in Mohammed's honour throughout the Islamic world on the 12th day of the third month of *Rabei el Awal*. (The Islamic calendar is lunar and advances 11 days against the Western calendar each year. In 1983, for example, the Moulid el Beni would begin on the evening of 15 December; in 1984 on the evening of 4 December.) During this week Moslems from all over East Africa and the Arabian Gulf converge on Lamu for one of the greatest celebrations of traditional pomp anywhere in the Islamic world. The island population doubles, rooms can be impossible to get unless booked in advance, but if you can manage to be here then, you can enjoy the carnival atmosphere of dancing,

drumming, singing and music played on flutes and tambourines.

**LIKONI** (5 kms south of Mombasa)
**Accommodation**
**Shelly Beach Hotel**, PO Box 96030, Nairobi. Tel: Nairobi 451221. Tourist class hotel on the south mainland, just 3 kms from the Likoni ferry with minibus service into Mombasa. Air conditioning and bath or shower in main rooms or cottages, simply furnished, pool and private beach. Activities included glass-bottomed boat and sailing. 375/- single, 575/- double, full board.

**MALINDI** (120 kms north of Mombasa)
**Accommodation**
**Blue Marlin Hotel**, PO Box 54, Malindi. Tel: Malindi 4 or 306. Telex: 21153. Atmospheric tourist class beach hotel dating back to 1931 and a favourite of Ernest Hemingway's when he went deepsea fishing. All rooms with bath or shower; air conditioning in the newer wing. Grill room specialises in seafood. Pool and sauna. 425/- single, 750/- double, full board.
**Eden Roc Hotel**, Lamu Road, PO Box 350, Malindi. Tel: Malindi 8 or 91. Telex: 21225. First class hotel on clifftop overlooking private beach, with fine views of the bay. All rooms with bath or shower, balcony or terrace. Restaurant, bar, grill and disco; pool, games room, tennis. The main buildings and bungalows are set in extensive tropical gardens. 430/- single, 630/- double, half board.
**Lawfords Hotel**, PO Box 20, Malindi. Tel: Malindi 6. Telex: 21153. Like the Blue Marlin, an atmospheric 1930s tourist class hotel, but without Hemingway. The hotel is on the seafront, just outside of town. The rooms have bath or shower, and air conditioning is available. Dining rooms and bars, one bar alongside one of the two pools. Games room, disco, goggling. 455/- single, 805/- double, full board.
**Sindbad Hotel**, Lamu Road, PO Box 30, Malindi. Tel: Malindi 7. Telex: 21023 attention Sindbad. Arabic-style tourist hotel sloping down towards the sea, a popular place arranged as main building and cottage accommodation. Rooms with bath or shower and air conditioning. Restaurant, bar, pool. 435/- single, 735/- double, full board.
Apart from these standard resort hotels, there are plenty of places to stay in Malindi very cheaply. The **Metro Hotel** on the seafront, Tel: 31, costs 80/- double. The **New Safari Hotel**, next to the bus station, costs 70/- double and serves as a convenient brothel as well. The **Malindi Rest House**, opposite the market, is owned by the bakery two doors along. A dorm bed will cost 20/-
There is also a **Youth Hostel**, about 25/- per person, or more expensive doubles, with cooking facilities available. Also cheap and very popular is **Gilani's Boarding House**, Vasco da Gama Road; Tel: 307.

**Food**
The **Umande** is just outside town (follow the signs). Tel: Malindi 220. This is a beautiful outdoor restaurant under a huge makuti roof. The view over the sea is splendid, and the seafood is too – haute cuisine and expensive.
The **Metro Hotel** on the seafront runs a simple little restaurant on the verandah where the food is moderately priced and good – curries, kuku paka (chicken in coconut sauce), vegetarian dishes and ample birianis.
**Giliani's Boarding House**, Vasco da Gama Road, is open to all-comers for its wide variety of curries and masala at very low prices.
**Bawaly and Sons**, Odinga Street, is the place to stop for halva and a small cup of black spiced coffee.

**NYALI** (7 kms north of Mombasa)
**Accommodation**
**Nyali Beach Hotel**, c/o PO Box 90581, Mombasa. Tel: Mombasa 471551. Telex: 21241. A 1940s colonial-style first class hotel on the oceanfront; accommodation in main building and cottages. All rooms with air conditioning and bath, most with balcony and mini-

bar. Restaurant, grill, bar. Pool, private beach, watersports on tap. 605/- single, 965/- double, full board.

**Reef Hotel**, Mwamba Drive, c/o PO Box 82234, Mombasa. Tel: 471771. Telex: 21199. Hotel and thatched cottages with nearly 1 km of private beach. All accommodation with air conditioning, bath and balcony. Restaurant, three bars, pool, tennis, mini-golf, fishing and riding. 600/- single, 750/- double, full board.

**SHANZU** (20 kms north of Mombasa)
**Accommodation**
**Serena Beach Hotel**, c/o PO Box 90352, Mombasa. Tel: Mombasa 485721. Telex: 21220 Mombasa. Arab village-style cluster in tropical gardens, this is a modern first class complex right on the beach. All rooms with bath, shower, balcony and air conditioning. Dining room, three bars, disco, pool, tennis, deepsea fishing, watersports and inland safaris. 885/- single, 1080/- double, full board.

**WATAMU/TURTLE BAY** (98 kms north of Mombasa)
**Accommodation**
**Seafarers Hotel**, PO Box 274, Malindi. Tel: Watamu 6 or Malindi 6. Telex: 21153 attention Seafarers. Informal beach hotel with aqua club; simply furnished rooms and family cottages, most with shower. Restaurant, bars, grill, disco. Freshwater pool, white sand beach, watersports. 425/- single, 745/- double, full board.
**Turtle Bay Beach Hotel**, PO Box 457, Malindi. Tel: Watamu 3. Telex: 265933. Informal modern hotel on the beach, all rooms with balcony overlooking the sea, bath or shower, air conditioning available. Restaurant, bar. Pool, watersports, glass bottom boats. From 265/- single, 355/- double, full board.

# TANZANIA BACKGROUND

## Basic Facts

Tanzania is a united republic (Tanganyika and Zanzibar) within the Commonwealth. Its mainland area is 928,000 sq kms, of which 53,000 sq kms is inland water; including the Indian Ocean islands of Zanzibar, Pemba and Mafia the area of the country is 930,700 sq kms. Tanzania's mainland coastline stretches for 804 kms along the Indian Ocean.

The population of the country was 17.5 million at the 1978 census. Dar es Salaam is the largest city (population 757,000 on current estimate) and capital, though it is proposed to transfer the capital to Dodoma. Other major urban populations, currently estimated, are Mwanza (110,600), Tanga (103,500), Tabora (67,400), Iringa (57,200), Arusha (55,300), Moshi (52,300), Mtwara (48,500) and Dodoma (45,700).

Swahili is the official language but English is widely spoken, and some German, French and Italian is also spoken in tourist areas. See the *Kenya Background* chapter for a vocabulary of useful Swahili words and phrases.

## Country

Situated just south of the equator, Tanzania stretches from the Indian Ocean 1100 kms west to Lake Tanganyika. It boasts 800 kms of virtually untouched, palm-fringed coastline along the Indian Ocean. The interior forms part of the vast highlands extending from Ethiopia to South Africa which is split by the Great Rift Valley.

**Regions**

The narrow low-lying eastern coastal zone is characterised by lush green rows of the world's biggest sisal crops. Beyond these extends a vast miombo woodland, home of great herds of elephant, buffalo and other game. There is high rolling plateau in the west central region, and scattered mountainous zones consisting of green forest, high altitude moorland, snow and blue glacier ice. In the north the Masai Steppe, 213 to 1967 metres above sea level, is semi-arid with small hills and occasional mountains. The major river system is the Rufiji which flows into the Indian Ocean south of Dar es Salaam.

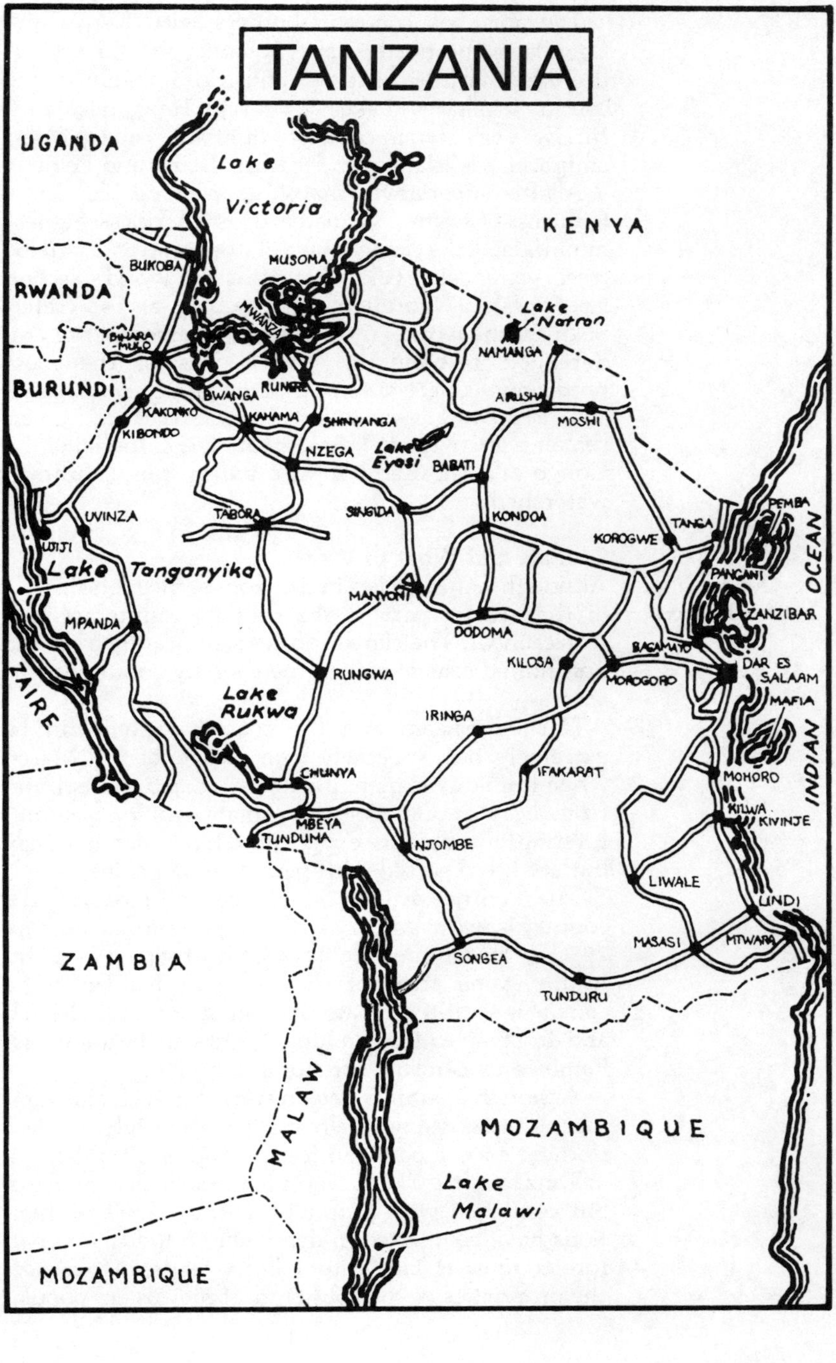
TANZANIA
UGANDA
Lake Victoria
KENYA
RWANDA
BURUNDI
BUKOBA
MUSOMA
MWANZA
BIHARA -MULO
BWANGA
RUNERE
KAKONKO
KIBONDO
KAHAMA
SHINYANGA
NZEGA
Lake Natron
NAMANGA
ARUSHA
MOSHI
Lake Eyasi
BABATI
SINGIDA
TABORA
UVINZA
UJIJI
Lake Tanganyika
KONDOA
KOROGWE
TANGA
PEMBA
PANGANI
ZANZIBAR
OCEAN
MANYONI
DODOMA
MPANDA
KILOSA
MOROGORO
BAGAMAYO
DAR ES SALAAM
MAFIA
INDIAN
ZAIRE
RUNGWA
Lake Rukwa
IRINGA
IFAKARAT
CHUNYA
MBEYA
TUNDUMA
NJOMBE
MOHORO
KILWA KIVINJE
LIWALE
LINDI
MASASI
MTWARA
SONGEA
TUNDURU
ZAMBIA
MALAWI
MOZAMBIQUE
Lake Malawi
MOZAMBIQUE

Tanzania has common borders with Kenya and Uganda in the north; Zaire, Rwanda and Burundi in the west; Zambia, Malawi and Mozambique in the south. It shares Lakes Victoria, Tanganyika and Malawi with certain of these countries. Tanzania also embraces the islands of Zanzibar, Mafia and Pemba.

All the superlatives may be applied to Tanzania's features: Mount Kilimanjaro is Africa's highest mountain, Lake Tanganyika its deepest and longest fresh water lake. Lake Victoria is the world's second largest lake, Ngorongoro its second largest crater. Selous is the world's most extensive game reserve, and Serengeti resounds to the hooves of the most prodigious congregation of plains game. *Zinjanthropus (Australopithecus) bosei* is amongst the earliest of human remains discovered. Three great rivers, the Nile, the Congo and the Zambezi, are fed by the Tanzanian watershed.

**Outstanding natural features**

### Climate and What to Wear

Although Tanzania lies in the tropics, the high altitude of the greater part of the country counteracts the tropical heat. The climate varies significantly from the hot, humid coastal belt to the cool invigorating highlands.

Dar es Salaam and the coastal regions can be extremely hot, especially from December to March when humidity is high. Evenings are usually cool, and from May to October the climate is very pleasant. Intermittent rains are experienced from March to May but are interspersed with periods of sunshine.

The central plateau which covers most of the country is warm and dry with temperatures averaging 27°C in the daytime and invariably dropping at night. In the game areas of the northern highlands the climate is semi-temperate, averaging 18°–21° in March and dropping to 15.5° in June. Nights can be quite cold. Pemba and Zanzibar are hot and humid.

Although Tanzania has no winter as such and summer clothing will normally suffice, some light woollen clothing should be taken for the higher altitudes.

Tanzania has a reputation for informality in dress, but combined with propriety. Former dress prohibitions have been lifted in deference to the customs of foreign tourists, but visitors should take care to respect the proprieties of the country's large Moslem population. Away from the beaches, keep cool but covered. See-through dresses or very short ones offend the local people, and on the island of Zanzibar they are strictly forbidden.

Women should pack light cotton wear for the daytime and cocktail or long skirts for formal evening entertainment. The Tanzanian-made kanga and kitenge prints, colourful, comfortable and suitable for all occasions, are worthwhile buying.

For men open-neck shirts and light trousers are recommended for daytime wear, and long-sleeve shirts with neckties for evening. Inexpensive locally made safari suits, lightly buttoned with collars and pockets, are popular with visitors.

Good sunglasses, wide-rimmed hats, suntan oil and insect repellants are advised both for the coast and up country. These are available locally. For appropriate dress on safari and in the game parks, see the *Safari in Tanzania* section, following.

## History

**Origins of man**

The unearthing by Louis Leakey at Olduvai Gorge of *Zinjanthropus* and *Homo Habilis,* which are amongst the oldest human fossils ever found, indicate that Tanzania has been the scene of human habitation since the very dawn of mankind. Over a thousand rock paintings discovered in the Kondoa district prove the existence of Stone Age hunters in the highlands to the south.

**African migrations**

During the first millenium AD there were large-scale migrations from lands to the north with pockets of Bushman-like inhabitants surviving until two or three centuries ago. Bantu immigrants brought with them iron working and pottery making skills, absorbing the hunters and nomads into more settled communities.

**Colonisation**

Active colonisation began in the 8th C AD in Kilwa and Zanzibar with the Arabs from Oman. Two centuries later the Persians arrived on the coast building prosperous stone cities of which remnants are still visible. Vigorous development along the coast from the 11th to the 16th C saw the evolution of the Swahili language from the intermarriage of African, Arabian and Persian. The early coastal inhabitants were known as the Zenj, a negroid people famous for their oratory and for their fighting qualities. Their name is preserved in 'Zanzibar'.

Trade quickly developed in ivory, rhinoceros horn and coconut oil, and routes into the interior were pioneered. By the 13th C Kilwa had surpassed all other towns, gaining control of the gold trade from Zimbabwe. With the transitory settlements formed by the Turks and Portuguese in the 16th and 17th C commercial trade declined. It was revived in the 19th C, however, with copper and gold from the interior and with the notorious slave trade. The Arabs opened up trade routes and established commercial depots at places like Tabora and Ujiji where the local rulers exchanged ivory and slaves for guns and cloth.

**The slave trade**

Zanzibar had always been the jumping-off spot for the mainland. Indeed at the height of the Arab and Shirazi (Persian) domination it was the commercial trading centre for the whole of East Africa and especially for the slave trade. Some slaves were put to work locally, but most were exported to Arabia, Persia, Egypt, Turkey and even further afield. In the early 19th C the Imam of Oman, Sayyid Said, introduced the clove plantations for which the island is still famous and in 1840 made Zanzibar his capital. Reports from the early European explorers and missionaries led to increasing efforts to suppress the slave trade and Sultan Barghash of Zanzibar was finally forced to outlaw it entirely in 1873. Along the coastal region, however, it was continued illegally until colonial times.

**The Germans and British**

German influence in the area began in 1884 when Dr Karl Peters negotiated with the tribal chiefs for their land. Six years later the coastal strip was acquired by Germany on payment of £200,000 to the Sultan of Zanzibar. The mainland territory was declared the protectorate of German East Africa, but Zanzibar became a British protectorate. After the First World War the Germans were expelled from Tanzania, and most of German East Africa came under a League of Nations mandate to the British, who renamed it Tanganyika.

**Independence**

In 1961 Tanganyika became the first East African country to achieve independence, with Dr Julius K Nyerere, leader of the Tanganyika African National Union (TANU), as Prime Minister. The following year the country was proclaimed a Republic within the Commonwealth and Nyerere became its President. In 1963 Zanzibar was granted independence. Its Sultan was subsequently overthrown by the Afro-Shirazi Party (ASP) representing the African majority. In 1965 the island signed an Act of Union with Tanganyika, creating the United Republic of Tanzania with Nyerere its President.

The President's policy has been essentially one of agrarian socialism. He has emerged as a statesman with acknowledged moral integrity and respected international standing. Tanzania is a frontline state and has taken a strong line in favour of liberation movements, particularly in southern Africa.

### Government

When Zanzibar and Tanganyika united, the two entities retained separate administrations except for the military and diplomatic services. They also kept their singular parties until February 1977 when TANU and ASP merged to form a combined ruling party, the Chama cha Mapinduzi (CCM). The National Assembly, led by the Prime Minister, has both appointed and elected members. Of the latter, 96 are elected by the mainland and 10 by the islands. There is a Constitutional Court with an equal number of judges from both entities.

### People and Religion

**Tribes**

Over 120 different peoples make up Tanzania's African population, which constitutes 98.5 percent of the whole. They are mostly of Bantu origin but there is no dominant tribe. Only the Wasu Kuma number more than one million. Amongst the others the best known are the Nyamwezi, pioneers of the early trade routes into the interior; the Ha; the Makonde, renowned for their sculpture and their stilt-walking; the Chagga; and the Wahehe, the famous warriors who resisted the Germans. A small proportion is made up of peoples of Nilotic origin, of which the best known are the elaborately coiffured and red ochred spear-carrying Masai.

**Arabs and Asians**

The national language is Swahili, but many tribes have their own dialects, customs and culture. Arab immigrants, who have been arriving into the country over the past thousand years, have virtually been assimilated into the African population through intermarriage. Peoples of Indian and Pakistani origin who migrated into Tanzania during the last three centuries today number about 50,000, and Europeans 20,000. The inhabitants of Zanzibar and Pemba are mainly a mixture of Shirazis (descendants of the early settlers from Persia), Arabs from the Gulf countries, and Comorians.

**Animism, Islam and Christianity**

The original inhabitants, basically animistic, believed in ancestor worship and the unity of the dead and the living. Islam arrived with the first Arab traders and now has about three million adherents. The first Christian missionaries, arriving in the mid-19th C, have succeeded in attracting 2,600,000 followers. The Asian population is divided between the Hindu and Moslem faiths.

## Visitors Information

**The northern circuit**

Tanzania's tourist attractions can be divided up geographically. There is the northern circuit taking in Mount Kilimanjaro, Serengeti National Park with its renowned wildlife migrations, Selous Game Reserve (the largest in Africa), Ngorongoro Crater Reserve, Lake Manyara National Park, and about 20 lesser parks and reserves containing the world's most prodigious and varied concentration of wildlife. Safaris along this circuit include hunting, fishing, game viewing, photographic and mountaineering.

**The coastal circuit**

The coastal circuit takes in 800 kms of unspoilt tropical shoreline with sandy palm-fringed beaches along the clear Indian Ocean, all of it ideal for scuba diving, snorkelling, shell collecting and exploring the coral reefs – plus visits to exotic Zanzibar and Mafia island for big game fishing.

Also there is the Rift Valley, Lake Victoria and Lake Tanganyika, with explorations of historic and prehistoric sites like Olduvai Gorge (earliest human fossil remains), the discovery of Makonde art, and the rich folklore of friendly, hospitable people everywhere.

The best season for visiting the north and game reserves elsewhere is all year except for the rainy seasons in April, May and November. The coast is best from May to October.

For further information, contact the Tanzania Tourist Corporation, 3rd floor, IPS Building, PO Box 2485, Dar es Salaam. Tel: 27671. Telex: 41961. Or get in touch with Tanzania Tourist Offices abroad: London, New York, Frankfurt, Milan and Stockholm.

## Entry and Exit Formalities

Tanzania makes it very difficult to enter direct from

Kenya (see the *Kenya Background* chapter). It is a bit easier, however, to go from Tanzania to Kenya: you still have to get permission from the Commissioner of Police in Dar es Salaam and must write to the Kenya authorities – with luck this procedure takes a week or so. Admission and transit are prohibited to nationals and alien residents of South Africa, although they may be permitted to transit by the same aircraft within six hours provided they do not leave the airport. Non-South Africans with a South African stamp in their passports might also find themselves refused entry to Tanzania. Moderation in dress is advisable, especially when entering the country.

**Visas**

Visas are required for all visitors in advance except the following: British citizens if not of Asian descent with passport numbers prefixed with C or D, and nationals of Australia, the Bahamas, Bangla Desh, Barbados, Botswana, Canada, Cyprus, Denmark, Fiji, Finland, Gambia, Ghana, Greneda, Guyana, Iceland, India, the Irish Republic, Jamaica, Kenya, Lesotho, Malawi, Malaysia, Malta, Mauritius, Nauru, New Zealand, Nigeria, Norway, Papua New Guinea, Samoa (Western), the Seychelles, Sierra Leone, Singapore, Soloman Islands, Sri Lanka, Swaziland, Sweden, Tonga, Trinidad and Tobago, Uganda and Zambia. Also, visas are not required of holders of a Tanzanian re-entry pass, or those transiting Tanzania to a third country by the same or first connecting aircraft on the same day if not leaving the airport. Visas may be issued on arrival to visitors from countries where Tanzania has no representation, or in emergency cases by the Principal Immigration Officer, PO Box 512, Dar es Salaam.

Note that a refundable deposit of 5000/- may be required from visitors who have no onward or return tickets.

In addition to the above requirements, all temporary visitors other than members of the diplomatic corps and their dependants must hold a visitor's pass which can be obtained free of charge upon arrival or from a Tanzanian diplomatic mission abroad.

Normally there are no vaccination requirements, but see the *Health* section, following.

**Customs regulations**

Customs regulations permit the free import by persons over 16 of 200 cigarettes or 50 cigars or 250 grams of tobacco, one bottle of alcoholic beverage and half a litre of perfume. A permit should be obtained in advance from the police for the import of firearms. Visitors buying skin articles, Makonde carvings or other local handicrafts or valuable gems must keep cash sale receipts for presentation to customs officials on departure.

## Travel to and within Tanzania

**The Tanzania-Kenya border**

The break-up of the East African Community and the closure of the border with Kenya changed the whole pattern of Tanzanian communications. Previously the main air, rail and road links all lay between Dar es Salaam and Nairobi. For information on how to travel between the two countries, see the *Kenya Background* chapter.

**International flights**

**Air**. Tanzania is served internationally by numerous airlines including Aeroflot, Air Comores, Air France, Air India, Air Madagascar, Air Tanzania, Air Zaire, Alitalia, British Airways, Egyptair, Ethiopian Airlines, KLM, Lufthansa, Pan Am, PIA, Sabena, SAS, Somalia Airways, Swissair and Zambia Airways. There are international airports at Dar es Salaam, Kilimanjaro, Zanzibar and Mtwara.

Air Tanzania Corporation, the national carrier, was launched in 1977 following the collapse of East African Airways. Air Tanzania's international services operate to Addis Ababa, Blantyre, Comoro, Djibouti, Entebbe, Harare, Lusaka, Mauritius, Muscat and the Seychelles.

**Domestic flights**

The airline's domestic services cover Arusha, Bukoba, Dar es Salaam, Dodoma, Kigoma, Kilwa, Lindi, Mafia, Masasi, Mtwara, Musoma, Mwanza, Nachingwea, Pemba, Songea, Tabora, Tanga and Zanzibar.

Additionally, there are several domestic air charter companies, such as Tanzanair, Tanzania Aviation and Flight Services International, which operate flights for safaris, business tours, aerial photography, etc., from Dar es Salaam, Arusha and Mwanza.

Dar es Salaam International Airport is the main gateway to the country, though Kilimanjaro International Airport, on the Sanya Juu plains between Moshi and Arusha, is also capable of handling wide-bodied jets, and caters for travellers wishing to fly directly to Tanzania's wildlife zone. There is a magnificent view of snow-capped Mount Kilimanjaro on arrival or takeoff. There are also international airports at Zanzibar and Mtwara.

There is an airport tax of 40/- levied on all passengers embarking at any airport on mainland Tanzania whether for international or domestic destinations.

**Sea.** The principal seaports are Dar es Salaam, Tanga and Zanzibar, though as with Mombasa international passenger services are virtually a thing of the past.

**Island and coastal services**

There are regular ferries from Dar es Salaam to Zanzibar. The more adventurous way is to go by Arab dhow. If you cannot find one that is going to Zanzibar from Dar es Salaam, take a dhow to Bagamoyo up the coast and directly opposite Zanzibar, and try from there. Bring your own food and water when sailing on dhows.

The Tanzania Coastal Shipping Line, City Drive, Dar es Salaam (Tel: 25329) operates passenger ships from Dar es Salaam to Kilindoni (Mafia island), Kilwa, Lindi and Mtwara. They sail once every two or three weeks.

**Lake services**

A boat runs the entire length of Lake Tanganyika, sailing from Bujumbura via Kalemi and Uvira in Zaire. Also there is a Lake Victoria steamer plying between Mwanza and Bukoba, but it is always very crowded.

**Land transport**. There are buses, trucks, taxis and matatus (shared taxis), all affected by petrol shortages, while the buses break down often and it is seldom possible to make advance bookings on them. For long distances, rail travel is the best bet.

**Rail**

There are three rail routes. The Central Line, built by the Germans between 1905 and 1914 through rugged and inhospitable country bisects the whole of Tanzania. It runs from Dar es Salaam almost due west to Kigoma on Lake Tanganyika where it picks up traffic from Zaire, Burundi and other countries of Central Africa. It has a branch line to Mwanza on Lake Victoria. The Tanga Line, built by the British, connects Tanga with Moshi and Arusha. Both of these lines are operated by Tanzania Railways. Then there is the Tanzam (Tanzania-Zambia) or Uhuru Railway, a magnificent feat of engineering financed and built by the Chinese, which became fully operational in 1977. This is operated by the Tanzania Zambia Railway Authority (Tazara).

Services are slow, spartan and crowded. Sleeping accommodation is available, and on Tanzania Railways there are restaurant or buffet cars offering limited refreshments. On Tanzam it may be necessary, however, for you to take food and drink with you.

Student reductions of 50 percent are obtainable on the railways if you have both an International Student Identity Card and a confirmatory letter from the university specified on the card – you must have both.

**Roads and motoring.** Tarmac roads connect Tanzania with Kenya and Zambia, though the border with Kenya is virtually closed (see *Entry and Exit Formalities* in the Kenya and Tanzania *Background* chapters). From Lusaka and Zambia the Great North Road is tarmac all the way to Dar es Salaam. The 500-km main road link to Rwanda is being improved , as also is the 650-metre Unity Bridge which, together with a 100-km road line, will connect Tanzania with Mozambique across the Ruvuma River.

From Dar es Salaam an all-weather road leads west through Mikumi National Park to Iringa where lesser grade roads branch north via Dodoma and Kondoa to the northern game areas (from Dodoma to Mwanza and Bukoba on Lake Victoria), and south to Mbeya and the southern highlands. Some all-weather roads are suitable for saloon cars except during the long rains in April and May.

**Difficult road conditions**

Note that despite Tanzania's vast area of 884,000 sq kms, there are only 34,000 kms of roads. More than 70 percent of these are earth roads which are frequently impassable in the rains, 14 percent are engineered gravel roads and only eight percent bitumenised. Clearly the road network is inadequate to meet even domestic needs.

Driving in Tanzania is on the left hand side and traffic signs are international. Petrol stations are fairly frequent along the main highway, but you should make enquiries before setting out for game parks or remote areas. Highway patrol cars are yellow and black. The speed limit is 80 kms per hour on the open highways, 50 kms within the cities, and 50 kms within the parks and game reserves. Visitors may drive in Tanzania on a valid international or overseas driving licence provided they register with the Licensing Authority.

For information about road conditions and routes, contact the Automobile Association of East Africa, Cargen House, Azikiwe Street, Dar es Salaam (Tel: 21965). They have reciprocal arrangements with British and other motoring associations and offer an excellent service.

**Special note.** Petrol is in extremely short supply, though usually more readily obtainable by foreigners who must, however, pay in foreign currency. No petrol is sold from Friday night to Monday morning; stations are closed. Driving is banned from 2pm Sunday to 5am Monday. Also: There are numerous roadblocks throughout Tanzania for security. Travellers should beware of fake roadblocks – gangsters dressed up in police uniforms. These occur mainly after sunset, so avoid driving at night.

**Car hire.** The following rates are indicative only and subject to increase. All include chauffeur: Tanzanian roads are so bad that self-drive cars are almost as expensive.
Peugeot 504 saloon, maximum four passengers, 230/- per day, 7/25 per km.
Volkswagen Combi, maximum seven passengers, 230/- per day, 7/50 per km.
Land Rover, maximum seven passengers, 230/- per day, 8/85 per km.
Range Rover, maximum four passengers, 230/- per day, 11/- per km.
Ford transit, maximum 13 passengers, 460/- per day, 9/20 per km.

**Accommodation**
Tanzania's hotels, though not nearly so numerous as Kenya's, are on a par with regard to imaginative design and superb location. They are also very expensive. They are suffering, however, from lack of maintenance. Spare parts are not available and when something breaks down it may take months to repair. Most of the hotels in Dar es Salaam were recently without air conditioning for several months, and there are frequent disruptions in electricity, water and phone services. Light bulbs are at a premium and if there is one in the reading lamp over your bed you must consider yourself most fortunate. The situation is compounded

by a chronic shortage of food and beverages. The choice on menus is very limited, and bars frequently run out of beer, whiskey and konyagi, to say nothing of the much-prized Coca Cola.

But none of this prevents the city hotels from being packed throughout the year, especially in the capital. Advance confirmed reservations are essential: you should book at least one month before your visit. It is generally considered that there would be enough business in Dar es Salaam for twice the number of hotels already in existence.

**Dar es Salaam**

The leading hotels in Dar es Salaam are the Tanzanian Tourist Corporation's Kilimanjaro (luxury class) and the privately owned Motel Agip (first class), both much sought after. The first is more spacious and elegant, the second has the reputation for efficiency and cuisine. The New Africa, Motel Afrique and Twiga are more moderate in price and in service. Oyster Bay Hotel, 6 kms from the centre and attractively located on the sea, is moderate in price and excellent in service, and has an excellent seafood restaurant.

For the budget traveller there are numerous hotels in Dar es Salaam, especially near the market – though they are expensive for what you get. It is usually acceptable for two people to take a single room. Also Sikh temples will often take travellers: some make a small charge, but even at the free ones it is a good idea to make a donation.

**Beach hotels**

Of the beach hotels north of the capital, Bushtrekker's luxury Bahari Beach is a favourite with many for its traditional design and friendly service, although the Tanzanian Tourist Corporation's Kunduchi Beach is in the same category, and Africana Vacation Village, more moderate in price, is delightfully laid out. The only disadvantage at the last is that you are limited to table d'hote meals, unless you have transport. Beach hotels usually offer discos, films, Goma dancing and other evening entertainment during the high season. As they are situated around 25 kms north of Dar es Salaam, these hotels are primarily holiday resorts, but lack of rooms in the capital is forcing more people to frequent them.

**Arusha**

In Arusha, in the heart of the game park area, the prestige hotels are Bushtrekker's New Arusha, right in the centre of town, and TTC's Mount Meru, 2 kms out. The centrally located Equator and Safari, as well as TTC's Hotel 77 near Mount Meru, follow closely in standard and the last has a particularly good restaurant. There are several moderate class hotels in the city, and some cheap ones along Uhuru Road, near the railway station and near the market.

**Game lodges and camps**

Tanzania's magnificent game lodges and camps usually fare better than the city hotels in that they mostly have their own electricity and water supplies. Moreover their menus are enhanced by a variety of game meats. Here again advance bookings are essential because Tanzania's unique wildlife heritage ensures that its game lodges and camps are filled to capacity throughout the season. It is difficult to say which are the best lodges – nearly all are superbly sited and designed. Perhaps the most spectacular are the Lobo and Seronera in Serengeti, Mbuyu in Selous, Ngorongoro Crater Lodge and Ngorongoro Wildlife Lodge in Ngorongoro Crater, Lake Manyara Hotel in Lake Manyara National Park, and Mikumi Wildlife Lodge in Mikumi National Park. But there are a host of delightful smaller lodges and camps listed in this Guide.

**Camping.** It is usually forbidden to camp outside specified areas in the parks because of the danger from animals, but permission and advice can be obtained from the park warden. For information and reservations, write to Tanzania National Parks, PO Box 3134, Arusha. Camping elsewhere outside cities is unwise for foreigners without a professional guide. Apart from the danger from wild animals, there have been incidents of looting and violence in remote areas. In cities some hotels have camping sites.

**Special note.** Accommodation rates throughout this Tanzania section are exclusive of tax and service charges. A 10 to 12½ percent government tax is added to hotel bills throughout the country, the proceeds going towards tourist development. Most Tanzanian hotels offer reduced rates for children. Some hotels outside the capital and larger cities offer substantially reduced rates during the low season, usually mid-April to the end of June. Tanzania's hotels have not been officially classified, except for the deluxe and first class categories. This Guide employs its own system of classification.

Non-Tanzanian residents are required to settle hotel bills in foreign currency.

'Hotel' in Tanzania often means restaurant, so ask for 'lodgings'.

## Food and Drink

**Abundance and shortages**

The Tanzanian diet should be based on the abundant supply of fresh, wholesome food. Meat, dairy products, local vegetables and fruits such as bananas, oranges, paw paws, avocados and mangoes are excellent, to say nothing of the king-size cashew nuts. Seafood includes prawns, lobster, oysters, swordfish and marlin. There is talapia from the lakes and rainbow and brown trout from the hill country.

But the response to socialist policies has been corruption, black marketeering and disruption in supplies. Even in the cities, many Tanzanians are obliged to cultivate their own garden plots to obtain enough food (otherwise unaffordable on the blackmarket), and hotels can offer only a limited menu, with a surprisingly poor selection of fruit and vegetables, sometimes entirely running out of eggs, bread, coffee, beer, whiskey and Coca Cola.

Most hotels serve European-style cuisine and in Dar es Salaam there are restaurants serving Indian and Pakistani food. A typically Tanzanian dish you might like to try is banana meal, which consists of bananas, meat and assorted spices. Avoid uncooked vegetables and salads unless you are quite sure they have been properly prepared and handled.

**Wine and beer**

Tanzania produces two wines: Dodoma Red, variable in quality, and Dodoma Rosé, which is usually pleasant. There are no imported wines, nor imported beers. Local lager-type beer, however, such as Kilimanjaro, Ndovu (Tusker), Pilsner, Crown and Safari is quite good. Pombe, African home-brew beer, exists in many varieties.

**Spirits and water**

Konyagi, the local gin, is a purer form of alcohol than many of the so-called 'foreign' gins and whiskeys, and a lot cheaper. Except in the better hotels, water should be boiled and filtered before drinking, though water is generally safe in the main towns.

Note that especially outside the main cities meal hours are fairly rigid. Breakfast is normally from 7.30am to 9.30am, lunch from noon to 2.30pm and dinner from 7pm to 9pm.

## Health

Yellow fever vaccination is strongly recommended for all visitors travelling outside the main cities, and cholera, typhoid and paratyphoid vaccinations are also advised. Malaria risk exists all year round at all altitudes including in urban areas.

Water is generally safe in main towns and most game lodges; elsewhere water and milk should be boiled and filtered. A mosquito net is essential when camping. Swimming in lakes and rivers exposes you to the risk of bilharzia.

The Flying Doctor Service, c/o Kilimanjaro Christian Centre, PO Box 3010, Moshi, offers limited membership to visitors for a modest fee and will fly those injured or ill to the nearest urban centre for treatment. Membership is advised if you are intending to travel privately in remote areas.

## Personal Safety

In daytime it can be dangerous to walk alone in lonely places such as beaches, and at night even city centres can be unsafe. Mugging and robbery are common; thieves are sometimes armed. To protect yourself against pickpockets, carry minimal amounts of cash and other valuables. Passports and travellers cheques as well as wristwatches and cash are regularly stolen. (See also under *Accommodation*.)

## Photography

**Religious objections and spy phobia**

As a courtesy to Moslem beliefs, shared by many Tanzanians, permission should be requested before photographing people. Also note that bridges, railway stations and public buildings are regarded as security installations and should not in any circumstances be photographed. Visitors should exercise the utmost caution in using cameras away from tourist beaches and game parks.

## Culture and Entertainment

**Music and dancing**

That the African 'is born with music, lives with music and dies with music' is particularly in evidence in Tanzania where widely varying snake, stilt and ritual dances have been handed down through countless generations. Over the centuries transoceanic contacts with Arabia, India, China and later Europe have all left their mark. Throughout the country rituals, varying according to tribes, are held to celebrate birth, initiation, marriage, death, harvesting, and so on, but these are not programmed in advance and it is rare for the visitor ever to see any. However, there are two dance troupes, the National Dance Troupe and the Muungano Dance Troup, which give occasional peformances for the public, the first at Lumumba Hall in Dar es Salaam and the second at the National Village Museum at Boko, 10 kms along the Bagamoyo Road. Performances include the famous Makonde masked stilt and snake dances. (For Makonde sculpture, see under *What to Buy*, following.)

**Theatre** Theatre, concerts and musicals are presented in the capital by the National Theatre and by the Dar es Salaam Amateur Arts Society at the Little Theatre, Oyster Bay, just before the drive-in cinema. The Asian Drama Society gives presentations in the Shishi Kunji Hall two or three times a year and there is an Indo-Tanzanian Cultural Centre. Also active in Dar es Salaam are the British Council, the Alliance Francaise, the Goethe Institute and the USIS. There is a Little Theatre also in Arusha, next to Hassanalis and opposite Subzalis in Uhuru Road, where the Arusha Amateur Arts Society gives several presentations a year of theatre and music. Arusha has two cinemas, and there are several in Dar es Salaam. Most of the films shown are Asian. There is no casino in mainland Tanzania, but one is scheduled for the Bwawani Hotel on Zanzibar.

### News, Radio and Telecommunications

All media are government-controlled. The *Daily News* is published daily and the *Sunday News* weekly in English. *Kipanga, Ngurumo* and *Uhuru* appear daily in Swahili, *Mzalende* every Sunday, and there are some regional and denominational publications. Air mail editions of many British, French and German publications are available.

Radio Tanzania broadcasts mainly in Swahili, but provides regular news bulletins and entertainment programmes in English. The BBC World Service and other overseas radio services broadcast regularly to East Africa. There is no colour television service on the mainland, but it is available on the islands of Zanzibar and Pemba.

International postal, telephone and cable services

are good, and there are some telex services.

**Money Matters**

The unit of currency is the Tanzania shilling (Tshs),
**Currency** divided into 100 cents. Tshs 20 (or 20/-) equals T£1 (though currency denominations are always in shillings, not pounds). The following denominations are in circulation:

*Coins:* 5, 10 and 50 cents, and Tshs 1.
*Notes:* Tshs 10, 20 and 100.

The approximate rate of exchange is UK£1 equals
**Rates** Tshs 15, and US$1 equals Tshs 10. But rates are subject to fluctuation and should be checked.

There is no limit to the amount of foreign currency which may be brought into Tanzania, but it must be declared on arrival. Visitors without onward or return tickets may be required to pay a refundable deposit of 5000/-. Export of foreign currency by visitors is permitted up to the amount declared on arrival, but it might be necessary to show receipts for money spent during their stay. Import and export of local currency is strictly forbidden. Residents of Tanzania, Kenya or Uganda must offer for sale all foreign currency to an authorised dealer. Kenyan, Ugandan and Tanzanian currencies are not interchangeable.

The unrealistic exchange rate of the Tanzania shilling makes everything in Tanzania about twice as expensive as in Kenya, except possibly hotel rates. Meals in particular are very expensive. Not surprisingly, there is a flourishing black market; you are likely to be approached in the street with offers four or five times better than the official rate. Sometimes the Tanzanian notes offered are counterfeit; the real problem, however, is the law and the recent crackdown on corruption which was becoming a feature of Tanzanian life: if you get thrown into a local prison there will be nothing your embassy can do for you. Banks and other authorised dealers are the appropriate places to exchange cash and travellers cheques.

The acceptance of international credit cards for pay-
**Credit cards** ment of goods and services is generally still restricted to a very small number of hotels, shops, airlines, etc, mostly in Dar es Salaam. Visitors intending to pay by credit cards are advised to check in advance whether this will be acceptable to the Tanzanian concerns involved.

**Tipping discouraged or forbidden**

Tipping is officially discouraged in Tanzania, but due to Western influence it is becoming more common. Although a service charge is included in hotel and restaurant bills, tips are usually offered to waiters and barmen. Small tips are also given to other hotel staff for special services. There are set fees for porters at airports and hotels. Tips should *not* be offered in Zanzibar.

Banks are open weekdays from 8.30am to noon, Saturdays from 8.30am to 11am.

### What to Buy

Makonde art, leather articles and meerschaum pipes are the most sought after items but there are a host of others to choose from. Jewellery set with locally mined precious and semi precious stones is popular, in particular the famous tanzanite or blue zoisite for which northern Tanzania is the only source and which can cost from a few pounds to several hundred. Diamonds have increased in price but are still good buys. There are brooches of lion or leopard claw, tribal earrings and bracelets. The last, made from copper, aluminium, rhino or elephant hair entwined with gold, are worn traditionally for good luck, prestige, or protection against evil spirits, wild animals and other dangers.

Colourful beadwork armbands, headbands and belts of tribal design are available, as well as brass, copper and silver ware in the form of miniature lanterns, incense burners (*chetezo*) and rose water sprinklers (*mrashi*). The coast and the islands, particularly Zanzibar, offer superb examples of Arab-style carvings, brass-studded chests, daggers in polished wooden sheaths, in addition to the characteristic clove pomanders.

Locally woven baskets are strong and attractive, and splendid sea shells are used for necklaces and table lamps. Colourful *kanga* and *kitenge* for women are widely sold, and batiks are popular in various forms. The last is the ancient Javanese art of producing designs on cotton materials by waxing the parts which are not to be dyed. The process is repeated for each colour.

The Tanzania Handicraft Marketing Corporation controls the great national treasure of Makonde art and is its major promoter and exporter. The Corporation operates several sales emporia in Dar es Salaam and Arusha. In association with its parent body, the Small Industries Development Organisation, the Corporation has launched a programme for the restoration and development of handicrafts. Established artists are paid to train apprentices for a five-month period, after which the trainees return to their respective working groups to teach what they have learned. Some form their own cooperative societies.

The Tanzania Wildlife Corporation is a specialised manufacturer, dealer and exporter of all types of game skins, head mounts, full mounts and rug mounts. Smaller articles are offered for sale such as handbags, wallets, belts, watchstraps, hairbands, key cases, sandals, shoes, jackets, hunting spears, ceremonial drums, ivory and ivory carvings, rhino horns, hippo teeth, lamp stands, saddles, stools, ash trays, book ends and beadwork.

**Meerschaum pipes.** Meaning sea foam in German, Meerschaum is so called because it resembles this substance when floated on water. It is actually a rare mineral belonging to a group of hydrous magnesium silicates. The ancient Greeks used meerschaum as a form of soap, the North Africans used it as building blocks, and in Asia Minor deposits have been worked for 2000 years.

The mineral was discovered in Tanzania in the mid-1950s when a prospector stumbled upon what is the largest known deposit of meerschaum in the world. It was utilised for the making of smoking pipes. Meerschaum pipes carved by genuine artists are not exported and may be obtained only in Tanzania.

**Makonde art.** The most positive and uninhibited of all East African contemporary artists are the Makonde sculptors of Tanzania. Their work is a vigorous comment on the human story of life and death in a tribal setting. It is also a direct response to the artist's new suburban surroundings.

Originating in Mozambique, the Makonde migrated to the highlands of southern Tanzania around the turn of the century for reasons of employment. A proud, distinctive and highly sensitive race, they tend to isolate themselves in small groups and are regarded by other peoples with both respect and fear. The society is matrilineal and its women are distinguished by large and prestigious lip plugs made of metal. Both males and females file their teeth and adorn their faces and bodies with elaborate cicatrising. In tribal ceremonies they balance themselves on very high stilts, dancing, twisting and turning with amazing grace.

**The Makonde and their sculptures**

But the best known talent of the Makonde is seen in their ebony sculptures. Masterpieces in naturalistic style carved out of this notoriously difficult wood were used for ceremonial rites, the skill being passed on from father to son. Makonde art centred on the mother figure. It later widened to take in themes from everyday life: love and passion, good and evil, man's relationship to animals, social ways, religion and anti-religion, fears and anxieties, struggle, hardship, conflict.

The tradition goes back beyond three centuries of known art into the roots of time where fact merges with myth. In the beginning, the myth says, there was a being, not a man, who lived alone in a wild place and was lonely. One day he took a piece of wood from a tree and carved a female figure. He placed it upright in the sun by his dwelling. Night fell, and when the sun rose again the figure had come to life as a woman and became his wife. They conceived and a child was born, but in three days it died. 'Let us move from the river to a higher place where the reeds grow', said the wife. And this they did. Again they conceived and a child was born, but after three days it too died. Again she said, 'Let us move to yet higher ground where the thick bush grows'. And once more they moved. A third time they conceived and a child was born. The child lived and he was the first Makonde.

Since the 1950s a second style has evolved in Makonde art, more complex than the original naturalistic. Representing the *shetani* or spirits of their folk culture, it is sometimes grotesque or distorted in form. Elimo P Njau, Director of the Kibo Art Gallery in Moshi, states: 'Makonde sculpture speaks a spontaneous language, at once formal, dynamic and personal, as well as challenging to the sensitive art student, scholar of African art, historian, ethnologist, psychologist, clergyman and the rigid traditionalist alike. Here is a daring victory of the so-called African savage over the polite existence of the modern art-school trained artist. There is no end to the human drama and dance in movement, and to the variation in form, context and subject matter.'

Makonde art has come to be appreciated by foreigners, and in Japan a special society has been formed for lovers of the art. Unlike the masses of curios found in almost every country throughout Africa, each genuine Makonde carving is an individual work of art. Some imitation work has inevitably sprung up, but authentic pieces are still to be found in the villages, at the sales emporia of the Tanzania Handicraft Marketing Corporation or of the Tanzania Wildlife Corporation, and at reputable private establishments.

Visitors who buy Makonde carvings or any other local handicrafts should note that although export licences are not required, it is essential that cash sales receipts be retained for presentation to the customs officials on departure from the country.

**Hours of Business**

Government office hours are from 7.30am to 2.30pm weekdays, 7.30am to 12.30pm Saturday. Commercial office hours are the same, though some may close on Saturday.

Shop hours are usually from 8am to 12.30pm and from 2pm to 6pm Monday to Saturday.

Banks are open from 8.30am to noon weekdays, 8.30am to 11am Saturday.

Pharmacies are open as per shop hours, and also 9am to noon Sunday and public holidays.

Bars are usually open from 10am to 2pm and from 5pm to 11pm.

**Time and Public Holidays**

Tanzania is three hours ahead of Greenwich Mean Time. Noon GMT is 3pm in Tanzania. When quoted a departure time for transport, check that it is not Swahili time, which begins at 6am, the hour of sunrise. (See the *Swahili Vocabulary* section in the *Kenya Background* chapter for an explanation of Swahili time.)

Official public holidays are 12 January, Zanzibar Revolution Day (mass rallies and tribal dances throughout the country celebrating the overthrow of the Sultan); 5 February, CCM Day (commemorating the birth of TANU, the ruling party of Tanganyika, and of Afro-Shiraz, the ruling party of Zanzibar; the two parties united in 1977 to form the current national ruling party CCM, Chama cha Mapinduzi, or Party of the Revolution); Good Friday; Easter Monday; 26 April, Union Day; 1 May, International Workers' Day; 7 July, Peasants' Day; 9 December, Independence Day and Republic Day; and Christmas Day. In addition, Id-ul-Fitr, marking the end of Ramadan, and Id-ul-Azhar, the start of the pilgrimage to Mecca 70 days after the end of Ramadan, are Islamic holidays of variable date, as is Maulid Day, celebrating the birth of the Prophet. (See the *Practical Information* section under *Lamu* in Kenya for an explanation of the Moslem calendar.)

### Weights, Measures and Electricity

The standard domestic electricity supply is 230 volts 50 cycles AC. Lamp sockets are the bayonet type and plugs are three-pin, with round or square pins. It is useful to carry an adaptor.

The British system of weights and measures has been dropped in favour of the metric. The *Kenya Background* chapter contains a conversion table.

### The Economy

**A subsistence economy**

Tanzania is listed by the United Nations as the second poorest nation in the world after Bangla Desh. In a 1981 speech marking the twentieth anniversary of independence, President Nyerere noted that a country like Tanzania, starting out from absolute poverty and always operating on the borderline of disaster, is bound to make some mistakes and that those mistakes have much more serious consequences than they do in richer countries where there is some economic cushion.

The economy is in serious trouble. World prices for Tanzania's main exports – coffee, cotton and sisal – have collapsed, while until recently the cost of importing oil has been rising, leaving the country short on foreign exchange and unable to import raw materials and spare parts. Factories have been grinding to a halt or operating at only a fraction of their capacity. To some extent the free market – a blackmarket, as it circumvents Tanzania's laws – has made up for shortages at a price, but a new crackdown on government corruption, black marketeers, smugglers and hoarders has resulted in new shortages – and such absurdities as people being arrested for having two tubes of toothpaste in their homes.

World prices apart, two major factors contributing to the disruption of the Tanzanian economy have been the dissolution of the East African Community and the war with Uganda. Conservative estimates put the cost of the war at US$500 million, and while much of the world applauded Tanzania's struggle against Amin, scarcely any international financial aid was extended.

**Agrarian collectivism**

Since independence Tanzania's policy has been essentially one of agrarian collectivism. In his famous 1967 Arusha Declaration Nyerere announced the orientation of the state towards African socialism by the creation of *ujamaa* (community) villages. These were designed to incorporate collective production, equality of opportunity and self-reliance. Nyerere was rejecting not only Western concepts but also the traditional tribal customs of shifting agriculture. In a major rural upheaval more than 1200 ujamaa villages were established by 1970, and a staggering 11 million people were 'villagised' between 1973 and 1976. Communal ownership of property led to the early nationalisation of foreign-owned banks, insurance companies and trading houses, as well as numerous processing industries, plantations and settler farms.

**Trade**

Since independence Tanzania has switched from traditional trading partners such as Britain, Kenya and Japan to a more diffuse pattern. Imports are now dominated by the European Community, the United States and China, with food grains coming mainly from the United States and Canada. Exports are rather diversified. Trade with China is largely associated with the Tanzam railway which has yet to be paid for. Trade with Mozambique is actively encouraged and the two countries plan a free trade area. A protocol has been signed with Rwanda and Burundi to exploit the Kagera river basin. India imports large quantities of cashew nuts and is providing finance, expertise and equipment for Tanzanian projects. The closure of the border between Kenya and Tanzania in 1977 has affected the latter less in trade than in tourism.

**Agriculture and natural resources**

Almost 75 percent of Tanzania's foreign exchange comes from the export of agricultural commodities such as cotton, coffee, sisal, tea, cashew nuts, tobacco and pyrethrum. Agriculture thus provides the basis of the country's economy and will continue to do so for the foreseeable future.

Tanzania is one of the world's three biggest producers of high quality Arabica coffee, the other two being Kenya and Colombia. Tea is exported mainly to Canada, the United States and Ireland. Sugar, tobacco and sisal are important industries but the last has declined since nationalisation due largely to increased competition from synthetic fibres and to labour shortage. In view of the alternate booms and slumps in the sisal market, large sisal plantations have been uprooted and the land given over to more reliable produce such as cattle ranches and food crops.

Tanzania's production of cashew nuts, the second largest in the world, is mostly exported raw to India. Oil nuts, oil seeds and pyrethrum feature amongst the mainland's more important secondary products, and Zanzibar is of course famous for its cloves. Tanzania's livestock herd, the second largest in Africa, is grazed extensively over 40 percent of the country, which is tsetse free.

A joint UNDP-Tanzanian programme is underway to develop the hitherto virtually unexploited fisheries of Lake Tanganyika which are reportedly amongst the richest in East and Central Africa. Norway is assisting in the improvement of fishing techniques and facilities in Lake Victoria and along the Indian Ocean.

Exploration for minerals is being intensified in an attempt to reduce the country's heavy dependence on cash crops. Sixteen African countries have come together to form the East and Central Africa Mineral Research Centre which is based at Dodoma. There are plans for a second Tanzanian university to be set up near the Centre to offer advanced scientific advice on geological, geophysical and hydro-geological prospecting and exploration.

The existing diamond and gold mines were for years a major source of foreign exchange, but production is now fast declining. Salt has shown an increase in production, but gemstones, tin and mica have dropped. Coal and iron reserves are being investigated by China, West Germany and Romania. Oil exploration is being continued with Agip but so far only natural gas has been found in economic quantities on Songo Songo Island 190 kms south of Dar es Salaam.

**Industry** Textiles, food, beverages, tobacco, footwear, chemicals, paper, printing and construction constitute the basic industries. This sector, however, is running at about 50 percent efficiency in terms of capacity, with certain key industries such as cement, fertilisers and steel rolling even below that figure. Growth has been hampered by shortages of water and power in the major towns; administrative difficulties in paying for imported raw materials, machinery, spare parts; lack of skilled personnel, particularly engineers, technicians and accountants; and excessive bureaucracy. All these factors have been aggravated by the general absence of effective incentives in the economy.

The objective of the industrial strategy is to build up key industries using local materials to form the basis of an integrated industrial economy. The core is to be the iron and steel complex at Mbeya which will probably be financed by China.

## Tourism

**Tanzania vs Kenya** The 1977 closure of the Kenya-Tanzania border suddenly and forcefully made the Tanzanian authorities aware of the extent to which their country's invaluable tourist assets had hitherto been exploited by its neighbours. Tanzania's tourist drive had been overshadowed by Kenya's ambiguous worldwide publicity. This had often given the impression that certain of Tanzania's game parks were situated in Kenya or at least were mere excursions to be made from Kenya.

In fact in terms of tourist attractions Tanzania can more than hold its own with its northern neighbour. The border closure has resulted in a much more positive attitude on the part of Tanzanian officials to the potential of tourism as a foreign exchange earner and the need for an intensified campaign abroad to promote Tanzania as a self-contained destination.

The Tanzania Tourist Corporation (TTC) has embarked on a policy to preserve the country's unique wildlife heritage and to combine it with other less celebrated but very real tourist assets. The splendid Tanzanian coast with its limitless tropical beaches, surprisingly little exploited, is now being developed as a tourist attraction in its own right.

Two major tourist circuits are being evolved with strategically placed hotels and lodges throughout the already popular northern circuit comprising the great game areas (Serengeti, Ngorongoro, Tarangire and Manyara National Park), and the coastal circuit covering Dar es Salaam, Mafia Island, Zanzibar and Mikumi National Park.

The two circuits are linked by Kilimanjaro International Airport at Sanya Juu, between Moshi and Arusha, and by a good tarmac road between the capital and Arusha. The reintroduction of hunting safaris has proved a major foreign exchange earner in addition to the game viewing, photographic, trekking, mountaineering and sea safaris. Package tours are being offered to include the wildlife areas of the north and the beach resorts of the Indian Ocean.

These tours are offered by the State Travel Service (STS), a TTC subsidiary and the largest tour and transport operator in the country. It runs a fleet of 260 vehicles including Volkswagen Combis, Land Rovers, Range Rovers, Peugeot 504s and Ford Transits.

TTC began with the concept of area planning giving priority to the building of tourist hotels to serve the cities of Dar es Salaam, Arusha and Mwanza, Kunduchi Beach, Mafia Island and the national parks. It is significant that all the hotels and lodges are designed to conform with the country's existing environment and culture without marring the natural scenic beauty, and no beach hotel is permitted to be taller than the coconut tree. TTC today has 15 hotels providing more than 3000 tourist beds. Furthermore, it actively encourages and assists hotel building by the private sector.

The tourist industry has already grown over the last decade from a position of obscurity to the eighth most important source of foreign exchange, in addition to becoming a valuable engine of employment. It is TTC's intention to become Tanzania's third most important source of revenue after coffee and sisal.

## Safari in Tanzania

**Hunting safaris**

In Tanzania it is still possible to take a hunting safari in the grand old style – complete with bearers, trackers, skinners, drivers, cooks, hot baths and iced drinks. Tanzania is in fact one of the very few countries left in the world where big game hunting still exists. Within the total area of 930,000 sq kms are found some of the

*Sleeping lion*

world's most exciting varieties of wildlife. More than 60 species may be hunted across magnificent, almost virgin terrain than can tax hunting skills to the maximum.

The species range from the big five (elephant, rhino, lion, leopard and buffalo), which are found in most parts of the country, to the rare oryx, gerenuk and the gazelle, generally referred to as the northern species; and the puku, sable antelope and southern reedbuck, known as the southern species. Sub-species of main species are also obtainable, such as the Livingstone and East African (or Roosevelt) sable.

Hunting safaris are fully in line with Tanzania's role as leader in wildlife conservation. It has been proven that selective hunting is conservation, but in September 1973 when it was realised that illegal hunting and poaching were endangering certain species, hunting was completely banned for a five-year period. During this time the national parks reinforced their patrols and anti-poaching squads, resulting in a significant increase in the wildlife's population. The authorities were thus able to re-introduce carefully controlled hunting from 1 July to 1 December each year. Maximum emphasis is placed on conservation and maintenance of the ecological balance of the various species.

Hunting quotas are determined by experts in the Game Division and are strictly supervised by the Tanzania Wildlife Corporation. This Corporation, which is primarily concerned with the overall welfare and preservation of wildlife, is the sole authority empowered to issue hunting licences. Its activities include cropping, catching of live animals, trapping of birds, photographic safaris and hunting expeditions.

Hunters may choose between continental hunting in the cool north and big game or bird hunting in the challenging south. Continental hunting, where the hunter stays in hide waiting for an animal to appear, is possible only in the Mount Meru Wildlife Project on the eastern slopes of the mountain. Covering 20,000 hectares, it is well equipped with roads and stalking paths, as well as superbly sited tree hides and view points. A photo hut and two fully furnished hunting houses are provided for guests, and there is safari accommodation at a lodge reasonably close to the hunting area.

More popular by far is the renowned big game hunting safari, consisting of luxury mobile camps, four-wheel drive vehicles, and accompanied by at least one professional hunter.

Bird shooting has long been associated with big game hunting, but in response to demand it has now been made into a self-contained safari.

The Tanzania Wildlife Corporation ensures that for those who like killing animals it will hurt the hunter nearly as much as it hurts his prey: two hunters, for example, with the services of one professional hunter, can expect to pay US$575 per day each, with a minimum of 15 hunting days for boring animals like buffalo, 30 days for lion – that is anything from US$8625 to US$17,250 per person. And that is just the basic cost: park entrance fees, hire of transport, game licences, taxidermy, etc, are all extras. A game licence for a buffalo will set you back 1265/-, for a lion 6900/-, and for an elephant 11,500/-.

For information on hunting safaris, and to make bookings, contact the Tanzania Wildlife Corporation, PO Box 1144, Arusha. Tel: 2828. Telex: 4280 Tawico. This is a subsidiary of the Tanzania Tourist Corporation which has tourist offices abroad (New York, London, Milan, Frankfurt and Stockholm), and with a head office in Dar es Salaam: 3rd floor, IPS Building, PO Box 2485. Tel: 26680. Telex: 41061.

### Tips on what to wear, and photography

See the *Safari in Kenya* section for tips on what to take and wear on safari, and on photographic technique and equipment. Of course as an alternative to going on a hunting safari in Tanzania, you can choose merely to shoot animals through your lens, as in Kenya – plenty of purely photographic safaris are offered by operators in Tanzania.

**Fishing safaris**

Tanzania offers some of the world's finest big game fishing, both offshore and inland, but notably from Mafia Island. Fascinating species abound on the fringes of the coral shelf off the coast and with the northeast monsoon between October and March come the big migratory fish, marlin, sailfish, tunny and an occasional swordfish. During the southeast monsoon from May to October the bigger varieties of the local fish are caught. Mafia Island Fishing Lodge is te renowned base for offshore big game fishing.

Good tiger fish, Nile perch, tilapia and yellow belly are plentiful in Lake Tanganyika, and black bass in crater Lake Duluti near Arusha. Mounts Kilimanjaro and Meru, the northern and southern highlands regions and the Pare and Usumbara Mountains in the west are criss-crossed with innumerable cold, clear forest streams, many of which have been stocked with rainbow and brown trout. In the northern region the streams are within easy reach of comfortable modern hotels, and in the southern highlands there are fishing camps on the more popular rivers.

**Water sports**

The Indian Ocean coast of Tanzania offers unparalleled opportunities for swimming, snorkeling, scuba diving and all sea sports.The conchologist will delight in the infinite variety of sea shells, some unique to the area. Fringed with coral reefs, the shoreline hosts a superb selection of fish and crustacea. Swimming is possible in these tropical waters throughout the whole year, and even during the monsoons from April to October you can swim inside the protective reef. In the calm season try scuba diving on the outer edge of the reef and view enormous blue crayfish, striped lionfish, starfish, damsel fish, clownfish and a dozen other varieties, all to a background of fantastic coral formations. Tanzania's coastal attractions are as yet little exploited, the main centres being Kunduchi Beach, Bahari Beach and the offshore Mbudya, centre for water skiing. Visitors are advised to bring their own gear and equipment, especially for scuba diving.

**Mountaineering**

Although only three degrees south of the equator, the summit of Mount Kilimanjaro is perpetually snow-capped, offering romance and challenge to the most seasoned mountaineers as well as to non-skilled climbers. Mawenzi, the lower peak (5660 metres) provides a difficult and exciting climb for anyone with alpine experience; the higher peak, Kibo (6447 metres) offers only a long hard walk. Arusha's Mount Meru is Tanzania's second climbing attraction, and in the Rift Valley north of Lake Manyara the active volcano Mount Lengwai (3147 metres) may be tackled. The southern highlands, one of the most beautiful regions in the country, offer Mount Rungwe (3237 metres), as well as the majestic Livingstone and Bundule mountain ranges.

## National Parks and Game Reserves

Fully recognising the value of its unique concentration of wildlife and the responsibilities which it involves, Tanzania has taken a leading role amongst the nations of the world in terms of active conservation. Fourteen percent of the mainland area has been set aside for the effective protection of wildlife and their habitats. When independence was achieved in 1961 the country had only one national park, the Serengeti. Today there are 11, in addition to 16 game reserves and 57 game controlled areas. Although Tanzania is amongst the poorest nations of the world, it spends more per capita on conservation than do most of the world's richest states.

**Preserving wildlife**

The *Arusha Manifesto*, promulgated in 1961 on the eve of independence, set the stage upon which future Tanzanian wildlife policies would be based. In solemn acceptance of the country's commitment to preserve wildlife at all costs, it was decided to establish a College of African Wildlife Management at Mweka in the north of the country to train personnel for the parks and reserves.

**How to view game**

The early mornings and later evenings are the best time to observe animals and birds. During the heat of the day many of the animals retire to rest under cover. You should set out early and drive slowly. Although the official speed limit within the parks is 50 kms per hour, you have much more chance of spotting wildlife if you drive at 25 kms per hour. Blowing of car horns is forbidden, as also is the playing of radios, as these noises unnecessarily disturb and frighten the animals. No driving is permitted between 7pm and 6am.

It is wise to employ the services of a guide who will be familiar with animal movements and conditions and will increase your chances of spotting them. Follow his advice with regard to safety rules and do not lean out of car windows. Under no circumstances should you feed game animals. Nor is it safe to stroll around outside park lodges in the evening hours without a professional escort. It should be borne in mind that the big cats are the most dangerous of all animals because they can see you in the car, whereas the others can only see the vehicle. Domestic pets are forbidden in game parks, as also are firearms.

Look under trees and bushes for the prick ears of

some animals raising their head, and keep a watch out in the trees for the dangling tail of a leopard lying on a branch. Observe movements of the plains animals which may appear to be disturbed for no apparent reason – they may have sensed a lion nearby. Tick brids may indicate the presence of rhino or buffalo in bush country, and vultures circling can mean a kill in the vicinity. When photographing it is better to start at a fairly long range and gradually work closer, then to drive straight up and frighten the animals off.

National park entry fees help to meet the cost of maintaining the animal sanctuaries and are valid 24 hours from the time of issue. The National Parks Authorities have published a series of small books giving descriptions of each park, illustrations and suggestions for tours. These can be obtained from the Director, National Park Authorities, PO Box 3134, Arusha.

**Fees**

There are charges for persons and vehicles entering national parks and for camping at established sites. The following are the rates for foreigners (Tanzanians are charged less) per 24-hour period:

Entry permit for persons 16 or older: 40/-.
Entry permit for persons 4 to 15: 20/-.
Entry permit for persons 3 or under: free.
Entry permit for vehicles up to 2000 kilos,
 a) private: 100/-.
 b) commercial: 200/-.
Entry permit for vehicles over 2000 kilos,
 a) private: 400/-.
 b) commercial: 800/-.
Camping permit, 16 or older: 40/-.
Camping permit, 4 to 15: 20/-.
Camping permit, 3 or under: free.
Camping permit, servants: 10/-.

The services of a guide cost 50/- per day, though 125/- per day is payable if the guide is asked to go beyond his normal route.

Note that all the above charges may have to be paid in foreign currency.

# DAR ES SALAAM

**Low-key capital**

Informal and relaxed, Dar es Salaam is beautifully situated on the shores of a palm-fringed bay midway along the Tanzanian coast. Present capital and main port of the country, it is far from being a modern metropolis, despite the gradual appearance of a few skyscrapers. Colour and sound mingle in the harbour area of this century-old town where narrow winding streets and low buildings date back to the Arab period. Squat two-storey buildings from German times with high ceilings and surrounding verandahs are practical in the tropical heat, and elsewhere fine architecture reflects an intriguing mixture of African, British and oriental influences.

Freighters, trading vessels, passenger liners and the occasional Arab dhow are to be seen in the charming and nearly landlocked harbour, as well as the fast *ngalawas* or dug-out canoes which bring in their daily catch to the open-air fish market. The capital has a profusion of tropical flora and is beautiful even in the December heat, when all the flame trees and frangipanis are in bloom, not to mention the Indian laburnum, a spectacular flower with cascades of yellow blossoms.

Independence Avenue, the main street in the new quarter of the town, is lined with government buildings, embassies, banks, airline offices, travel agencies, shops and curio stores. Fine materials and saris are to be found in the Indian Bazaar running between India and Market Streets. Tanzania's famous Makonde art is on sales display at the Art Gallery Arcade in the IPS Building where the head office of the Tanzania Tourist Corporation (TTC) is also located.

Dar es Salaam is the centre of Tanzania's magnificent coastal circuit for tourists, as is Arusha for the northern circuit covering the main game parks and reserves.

**History**

The modern history of Dar es Salaam dates from 1857 when the Sultan of Zanzibar decided to turn the inland creek just south of Mzizima into a safe port and trading centre. The town was fittingly called Dar es Salaam, meaning Haven of Peace. It achieved its early importance with the advent of the steamship which rendered the former port of Bagamoyo impractible. In

1891 the German High Commissioner transferred the seat of his government from Bagamoyo to Dar es Salaam, and in 1902 a floating dock was made operational. The importance of the port was subsequently enhanced by the construction of the Central Railway to Lake Tanganyika. Today Dar es Salaam is the terminal also of the new Tanzam Railway which enables it to handle trade from both Tanzania and Zambia. The capital is scheduled to be transferred to the more central location of Dodoma.

**Points of Interest in Dar es Salaam**

The **National Museum**, situated in the Botanical Gardens, has as its outstanding attraction the 'Hall of Man' where Dr Leakey's first finds from Olduvai Gorge, including the skull of Nut-cracker Man (*Zinjanthropus Bosei*) and other human fossils are displayed, and where the stages of Man's development over the last two million years are clearly traced and illustrated. There is a major ethnographical collection with handicrafts, witchcraft paraphernalia, dancing masks and traditional musical instruments. Fine models of dhows and other local craft are well displayed, as also is the collection of Tanzania's gold-bearing ores. The history of the coast is portrayed with Chinese porcelain, glazed Persian pottery, 'trade wind' beads from India, and a notable series of copper coins of the Sultans of Kilwa. The museum is housed in a spacious, well-lit building open from 9.30am to 7pm. Admission is free.

The **State House**, whose architecture shows traces of Arab influence, is the official residence of the President. Located in extensvie grounds near the harbour entrance, it was, in colonial days, the Governor's house. The gardens now boast a private zoo which was founded by the President. It is forbidden to photograph any part of the State House.

In the peaceful waters of **Kurasini Harbour**, bordered with mangroves and palms, graceful dhows unchanged throughout the centuries mingle with modern ships. The *jahazi* and *mashua*, locally made native craft, ply between Mafia Island and Lamu, sometimes venturing as far as Mogadishu. During the northeast monsoons from December to March, the larger *bateels* and *badane*, splendid examples of oriental ship building, arrive from India, Arabia and the Persian Gulf, bringing carpets, silver, brassware and salted

*Dar es Salaam: Haven of Peace*

fish. When the wind changes direction they sail back with cargoes of salt, mangrove poles, matting, copra, ivory and rhino horns, the last believed to be an aphrodisiac. The bearded and turbaned crews remain impervious to the hustle and pressure of this modern age. Launch tours of the harbour may be arranged.

Superbly laid out amidst lawns and gardens, the **University of Dar es Salaam** is a skyscraper township on Observation Hill at the outskirts of the city and has accommodation for a student population of over one thousand at its present stage. It is reached via either Morogoro or Bagamoyo Road.

**Kariakoo Market**, where an interesting diversity of peoples congregate, is the capital's main market. Here you will find colourful local atmosphere as well as exotic fruits, fresh fish, spices and other Tanzanian produce.

**Mnazi-Mmoja Park** is near Jamhuri and Uhuru Streets in the hub of the city. On one side there are a fish pond, a bandstand and the Uhuru Torch Monument erected to symbolise the Freedom Torch placed on the peak of Mount Kilimanjaro at Tanzania's attainment of independence. The Republic Fountain on the other side of the park commemorates the foundation of the Republic in 1962.

The **Village Museum**, 10 kms along the Bagamoyo Road, is a spectacular project which you should not miss. Consisting of a collection of traditional, authentically constructed dwellings of various Tanzanian tribes, it displays several distinct architectural styles with building materials ranging from sand, grass and poles to mud and rope. Villagers demonstrate their ancient skills of carving and weaving and offer their products for sale. A restaurant has been built in attractive local style. The museum is open daily from 9.30am to 7pm.

At **Msasani Village**, 8 kms north along the coast, you can see the village life and habits of local fishermen who chisel their *ngalawa* boats out of logs. Tombs and pillars date from the 17th to the 19th C.

# PRACTICAL INFORMATION

## ACCOMMODATION IN DAR ES SALAAM

See the *Tanzanian Background* chapter for general information on accommodation throughout the country. Note that a 10 to 12½ percent tax must be added to all rates shown here, and that non-Tanzanian residents are required to settle their hotel bills in foreign currency. Most hotels offer reduced rates for children. Hotels in Dar es Salaam, in all categories, are heavily booked throughout the year and it is essential to reserve in advance.

*Deluxe:*

**Kilimanjaro Hotel**, overlooking the harbour between City Drive and Kikuvoni Front, PO Box 9574. Tel: 21281. Telex: 41021. In the city centre, near Parliament and government buildings, this TTC hotel is one of the best in the country. Luxury rooms with bath and shower, verandah, radio and air conditioning. Summit rooftop restaurant and Simba restaurant with dinner dance and nightclub; also bars and Bruncherie selfservice snacks. Shopping arcade with bank and airline offices, and large outdoor swimming pool. 575/- single, 760/- double, suites 1250/- to 1520/-, with breakfast.

*First Class:*

**Motel Agip**, on City Drive overlooking the harbour, PO Box 529. Tel: 23511. Telex: 41276 Motagi. Situated in the heart of the business and shopping district, near the air terminal, it is greatly in demand by businessmen and reservations are particularly essential. It is not really a motel. All rooms with shower and air conditioning. The ground floor bar is a popular rendezvous, and the restaurant is one of the best in town (Crab Mornay, steak and Chicken Maryland particularly recommended). 515/- single, 725/- double, with breakfast.

**Oyster Bay Hotel**, 6 kms from city centre, Toure Drive, PO Box 2261. Tel: 68631. In an area of embassies and luxury residences, but no shuttle bus to town (taxi 60/-). All rooms with bath, air

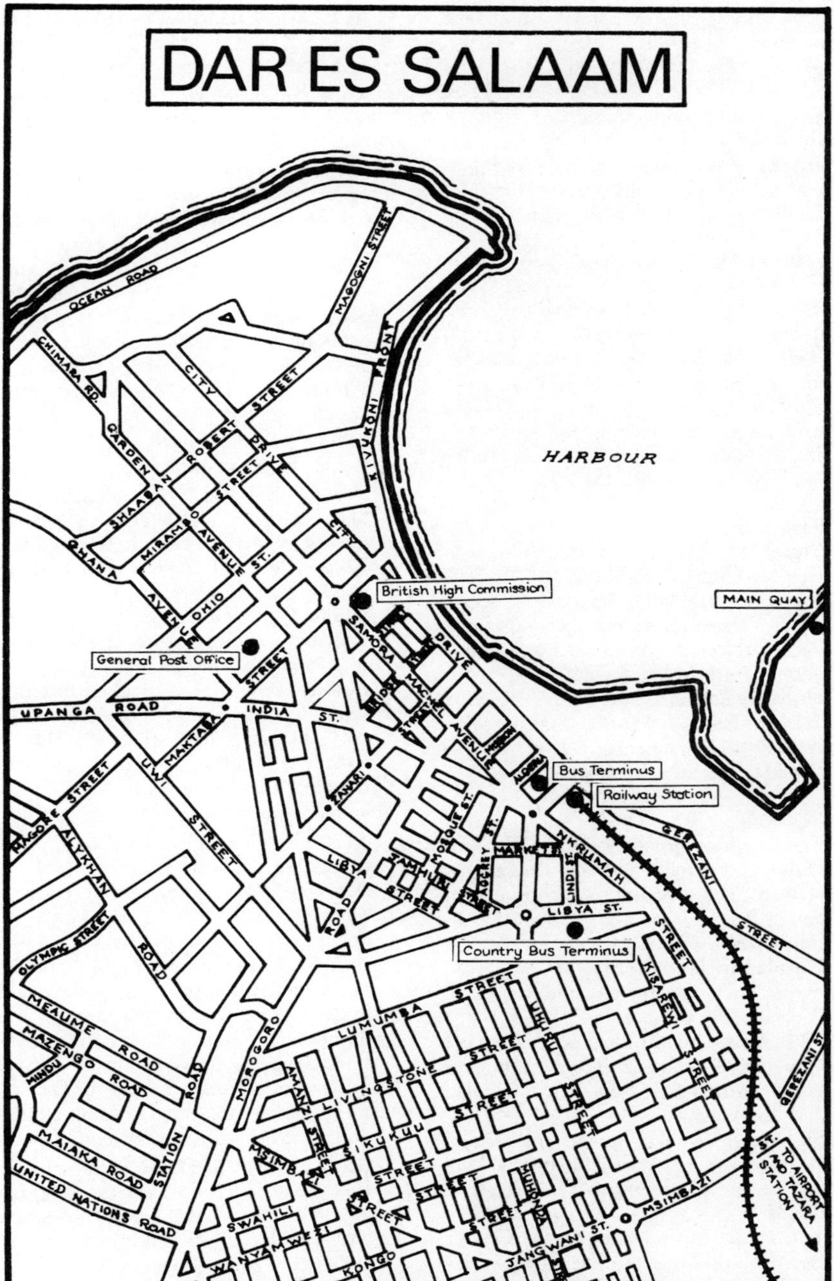
DAR ES SALAAM
HARBOUR
MAIN QUAY
OCEAN ROAD
MAGOGNI STREET
CHIMARA RD.
CITY STREET
KIVUKONI FRONT
GARDEN
ROBERT
DRIVE
SHAABAN
STREET
MIRAMBO
AVENUE
CITY
GHANA
ST.
OHIO
AVENUE
British High Commission
General Post Office
STREET
SAMORA
DRIVE
MACHEL
AVENUE
UPANGA ROAD
INDIA ST.
MAKTABA
UWI
STREET
ZANAKI
Bus Terminus
Railway Station
MAGORE STREET
ALYKHAN
STREET
MOSQUE ST.
LIBYA
JAMHURI
STREET
MARKET
NKRUMAH
LINDI ST.
LIBYA ST.
GEREZANI
STREET
ROAD
Country Bus Terminus
OLYMPIC STREET
ROAD
MEAUME
MAZENGO
ROAD
ROAD
LUMUMBA
STREET
KISAREWE
STREET
MOROGORO
ROAD
LIVINGSTONE
AMANI
STREET
STREET
GEREZANI ST.
MAIAKA ROAD
STATION
SIKUKUU
MSIMBAZI
STREET
UNITED NATIONS ROAD
SWAHILI
STREET
STREET
MSIMBAZI
TO AIRPORT AND TAZARA STATION
WANYAMWEZI
KONGO
JANGWANI ST.

conditioning and verandah. Excellent open-air restaurant facing the sea, fresh seafood the speciality; also bars and snack bar. Spacious grounds and tropical palm-fringed beach in front of the hotel, ideal for swimming. Informal atmosphere; a good choice for families. 360/- to 415/- single, 530/- to 570/- double, single suite 675/-, double suite 835/-, with breakfast.

**New Africa Hotel**, Azikwe Street, overlooking the harbour, PO Box 9314. Tel: 29611. Telex: 41061. Rooms of varied quality, all with air conditioning and bath or shower. Restaurant, cocktail lounge, coffee shop, grill and patio bar. Gift shop. Hunting, fishing and island excursions arranged. 430/- to 505/- single, 655/- double, 800/- triple, suites 790/- to 1260/-, with breakfast.

*Tourist class:*

**Motel Afrique**, corner of Bridge and Kaluta Streets, PO Box 2572. Tel: 31034. Central but quiet location, above supermarket, all rooms air conditioned with bath or shower. 325/- single, 440/- double, with breakfast.

**Skyways Hotel**, City Drive, PO Box 21248. Tel: 27061. All rooms with shower. 325/- single, 440/- double, with breakfast.

*Inexpensive:*

The **Clocktower Hotel** and the **Windsor Hotel**, both similar and near the railway station and bus terminus at the western end of City Drive, charge about 170/- single, 285/- double.

**Florida Inn**, Jamhuri Street near Zanaki Street, costs 80/- for bed and breakfast. A clean, simple place.

**YMCA**, behind the new post office off City Drive, is like a decent hotel, and takes women too. Pool. 100/- for bed and breakfast.

**Sikh temples** takes guests for around 20/-; reputed best is the one at the corner of Nkrumah and Livingstone Roads.

You could also try **camping** at Oyster Bay, but this can be risky – robberies have occurred.

## ACCOMMODATION ALONG THE COAST NORTH OF DAR ES SALAAM

**Kunduchi Beach Hotel**, 24 kms north of the city, PO Box 9313, Dar es Salaam. Tel: Dar es Salaam 47621. Telex: 41061 attention Kunduchi. Built in Arabic style beside a lagoon and villages this is one of Tanzania's finest hotels, though rather formal for a beach hotel. Split-level rooms with bath, air conditioning and ocean view balcony. Tropical gardens, swimming pool, usual dining and drinking facilities. The beach is broad and sandy; seafari trips to nearby Mbudya island. 530/- single, 690/- double, 820/- triple, suites 925/- to 1390/-, with breakfast.

**Bahari Beach Hotel**, 26 kms north of the city, PO Box 9312, Dar es Salaam. Tel: Dar es Salaam 47101. Telex: 41185. Extensive resort in the style of an African Village, ie coral chalets with thatched roofs, each containing four air-conditioned double rooms. Freshwater pool, beach, jetty for sea sports, sailings to Mbudya island. An attractive Bushtrekker hotel (private chain) with a relaxed atmosphere. Excellent cuisine and service. Shuttle service to Dar es Salaam and airport. 495/- single, 610/- double, 760/- single suite, 990/- double suite, with breakfast.

**Africana Vacation Village**, near Kunduchi, 24 kms from the city, PO Box 60172, Dar es Salaam. Tel: Dar es Salaam 4721. Telex: 41114. Cheapest and most informal of the large beach complexes, extremely pleasant. Its disadvantage is that the only food available is their table d'hote menu for lunch or dinner – no other eateries in the vicinity. Banda-type rooms with bath or shower, no airconditioning. Shuttle to Dar and the airport. 345/- to 460/- single, 565/- double, 690/- suites, with breakfast.

**Rungwe Oceanic Hotel**, Kunduchi, PO Box 5659, Dar es Salaam. Tel: Dar 47185. Telex: 41055 Teer. 315/- single, 540/- double in air-conditioned rooms, full board. 260/- single, 505/- double in rooms with ceiling fans, full board. Also

**camping** facilities, 10/- per person per night. Meals available at the hotel.

## FOOD

The best restaurants are found in the hotels, with the exception of the **Bushtrekker Restaurant** in the TFDL Building at the junction of Upanga and Ohio Streets (Tel: 31957). Considered the leading restaurant in Dar, the atmosphere is elegant, the air conditioned, the bar pleasant, the prices stiff. Open for lunch and dinner.

There are a number of Indian restaurants around town – the **Paradise, Sheesh Mahal, Amrabali, Zahir, Royal** – serving good curries at reasonable prices.

And on Samora Machel Avenue there are two or three modern coffee/snack bars; try the **Cappucino** next to the Extelcom Building. Everywhere samosas are sold by street vendors.

## SHOPPING

The **Tanzania Handicrafts Marketing Corporation** (Handico), Samora Machel Avenue, PO Box 9363 (Tel: 26993), control's the sale of Makonde and other local crafts. Its sales emporia are: **Handico Art Gallery**, IPS Building Arcade, Samora Machel Avenue (Tel: 25113); and **Tausi Handicrafts Shop**, NBC Investment House, Samora Machel Avenue (Tel: 29231).

Most of the good shops are near the intersection of Maktaba Street and Samora Machel Avenue, including an excellent **bookshop**, several **chemists**, airline offices and banks.

## RECREATION AND ENTERTAINMENT

Dar es Salaam offers a wide variety of recreational opportunities. The **Gymkhana Club**, open to all including temporary members, has a challenging 18-hole golf course, more than a dozen tennis courts, and offers rugby, cricket, football, hockey and table tennis.

Horses can be hired at the **Riding School**, and the **Motor Sports Club** organises frequent rallies, including the famous Tanzania Thousand. There is a thriving **Yacht Club**, and most of the big game fish can be caught off the coast near the capital. The Dar es Salaam **Swimming Club**, delightfully situated at the harbour entrance, is open to visitors, and there is an **Aqua Sports Club** at the Kilimanjaro Hotel.

The capital's many unspoilt, sandy **beaches**, notably at Oyster Bay, Leopard's Cove, Masani, Mbwa Maji, Mvua, Mjimwema and Kunduchi, are ideal for swimming, skin diving, goggling and shell collecting: cones, scorpions, olivads, murex and tower shells abound, and there are giant shells living on the deep coral reefs. **Honeymoon Island** near the harbour entrance, and **Sinda Island** some 15 kms off the coast, offer the same opportunities.

The only **nightclub** is the Simba at the Kilimanjaro Hotel. For **cinemas**, see the daily press.

## INFORMATION

**Tanzania Tourist Corporation,** 3rd floor, IPS Building, Samora Machel Avenue, PO Box 2485; Tel: 26680 or 27671; Telex 41061.

Your **hotel desk** or those of the leading hotels, as well as your **embassy**, can be valuable sources of varied information.

## TRAVEL

**Dar es Salaam International Airport** is 13 kms from the city. Facilities include a restaurant, bar, post and telecommunications, agencies of the National Bank of Commerce open at arrival and departure times of international flights, and a duty-free shop for departing passengers. A taxi into town will cost 175/- to 230/-, but there is also an airport shuttle bus to the New Africa Hotel costing 45/-, and the ordinary 67 bus costing a few shillings. A taxi to the beach hotels will cost around 460/- to 575/-.

There is an **airport departure tax** on all flights, domestic and international, of 40/-.

**Airline offices** will be found in the

major hotels, eg the Kilimanjaro, and near the intersection of Samora Machel Avenue and Maktaba Street.

**British Airways**, Coronation House, Samora Machel Avenue, Tel: 20322.

**Air Tanzania**, Airways Terminal, Tancot House, City Drive, Tel: 21251.

**National Tours Limited**, Jamhuri Street and Upanga Road, PO Box 9233 (Tel: 20681; Telex: 41025) operates shuttle services using 14-seat Ford Transits:

New Africa Hotel to airport, linking with all domestic and international flights, 45/-.

New Africa Hotel to beach hotels, every two hours from 9am to 5pm, 45/-.

Beach hotels to airport in high season.

There are **taxi stations** at the New Africa Hotel and the Kilimanjaro Hotel; these taxis offer their services at fixed and reasonable charges:

To airport, 175/- to 230/-.

To beach hotels, 230/- to 290/-.

To Oyster Bay, 70/-.

Additionally, there are numerous private taxis cruising round town whose fares are negotiable, and these should be established in advance. Expect to pay 35/- to 45/- minimum within Dar.

**City buses** within Dar cost 1/- to 1/50.

Some **car-hire** firms, offering both chauffeur and self-drive services, are:

**Tanzania Taxi and Tour Services**, New Africa Hotel, Tel: 21028.

**Co-Cabs**, Kilimanjaro Hotel, Tel: 32828.

**Valji and Allibhai Limited**, Bridge Street, Tel: 20522 or 26537.

**White Cabs**, corner of Jamhuri and Zanaki Streets, Tel: 23078 or 33450.

The **Tanzania Automobile Association**, Maktaba Street (Tel: 21965), provides a useful route-advisory service. Reciprocal membership with the British AA and other national automobile associations.

The **train and intercity bus stations** are near one another at the southwest end of City Drive.

The **bus** journey from Dar to Arusha takes 12 hours due to the poor state of the road and the near-inevitability that the bus will break down along the way; it will cost 120/-. The duration and cost of other long-distance journeys can be calculated from this example.

There is a daily **train** departing Dar at 3.30pm for Moshi, arriving 9.30am, ie 18 hours, and which then continues on to Arusha. The Dar-Moshi fare is 260/- first class, 118/- second class, plus 25/- for bedding and about 50/- for a meal aboard. Again, this can serve as an example for other journey times and fares.

The **air** fare from Dar to Arusha is 750/- one way, and there is a round trip excursion fare of 1150/- provided you do not stay longer than four days. The one-way air fare to Zanzibar is 460/-. Note that both domestic and international services can be disrupted by lack of fuel. Apart from flying on **Air Tanzania's** scheduled flights, you can also charter aircraft from **Tanzanair**, PO Box 364, Dar es Salaam. Tel: 30232. Telex: 41341.

There are no regular **dhow** services to anywhere, but sailings are frequent, especially to Zanzibar – carrying cargo. Go down to the harbour and ask the captain if he will take you aboard, negotiating the price on the spot.

There are numerous **safari** operators; here are some of the best – all are reliable and can arrange budget safaris:

**Bushtrekker Safaris**, PO Box 5350. Tel: 31957. Telex: 41178.

**Kearsley Travel and Tours**, Kearsley House, Makunganya Street, PO Box 801. Tel: 20607. Telex: 41014.

**State Travel Service**, PO Box 5023. Tel: 2921. Telex: 41060. A subsidiary of TTC and the largest operator in Tanzania.

**Subzali Tours and Safaris**, PO Box 3121. Tel: 25907. For headquarters, see Arusha listings.

## OTHER THINGS

The **General Post Office** is on City Drive at Maktaba Street and offers **postal, telephone, telegraphic** and **telex** services. There is also a telex service available to the public (cost plus 50 percent) at the Kilimanjaro Hotel. Stamps can be purchased at hotels.

The only authorised commercial **bank** in Tanzania is the National Bank of Commerce; look in major hotels (eg Kilimanjaro) and along Samora Machel Avenue for branches.

There is a **hospital** and **dental centre** at the northeast end of Samora Machel Avenue, near the Indian Ocean, and **pharmacies** near the intersection of Samora Machel Avenue and Maktaba Street. For more information, enquire at your hotel or embassy.

Your **embassy** can assist you in a number of ways, possibly acting as a mail drop, certainly by advising on emergency medical and financial problems – though they will not lend you money.

**Australian High Commission**, Investment House, Samora Machel Avenue, PO Box 2996. Tel: 20244.

**British High Commission**, corner of Maktaba Street and Samora Machel Avenue, PO Box 9112. Tel: 29601. Telex: 41004 a/b UKREP.

**United States Embassy**, National Bank of Commerce House, 4th floor, City Drive, PO Box 9123. Tel: 22775.

# TANZANIA'S COAST AND ISLANDS

**Unexploited coast**

Tanzania's 800-km Indian Ocean coastline remains one of the great undiscovered pleasures – its sandy beaches and undersea coral gardens, its big game fishing and watersports potential, almost entirely unexploited. Only recently has the coastal circuit been promoted, and here and there the development of tourist facilities has begun. Kunduchi and Bahari Beaches, 24 kms north of Dar es Salaam, are examples of new resorts (see *Dar es Salaam* listings); near the fishing village of Kunduchi are ruins of Persian tombs and mosques dating back to the 13th C, reminders that in addition to its natural attractions the coast and islands offer historical interest.

## Bagamoyo

**Memories of the slave trade and early explorations**

The name of this historic port 72 kms north of Dar es Salaam means 'lay down the burden of your heart', reminiscent of its role as export terminus of the slave caravan route from Lake Tanganyika. Old stone pens, shackle rings and other relics of the trade can still be seen. There are reminders also of the early explorers, notably at the museum, the memorial to Burton and Speke, the house where Stanley lived and the chapel where Livingstone's body was laid before being taken to Zanzibar and thence to Westminster Abbey. The story of Susi and Chuma, devoted followers who carried the strange burden over 1600 kms on an 11-month journey from Chitambo (now in Zambia) back to the coast through treacherous terrain and hostile tribes, remains one of the most moving in the history of African exploration. Bagamoyo was once the capital of German East Africa, and still standing is the first German-built church (1880) in the country. Five kms south, at Kaole, there are ruins of 14th C mosques and tombs.

## Tanga and Lushoto

Founded by the German traveller Herman von Wissman, **Tanga** lies toward the Kenya border. It is the second town and port of Tanzania, as well as the centre of the important sisal industry. The sisal estates roundabout can be visited. A tarmac road connects Tanga to Dar es Salaam (252 kms) and to Arusha (435 kms), and

*Carved door in Bagamoyo; the town shares Arab influences with Zanzibar across the straits*

an all-weather road leads to Mombasa (but the border with Kenya is now closed).

Excursions can be made to the three beautiful **Amboni Limestone Caves** and to the hot sulphur springs at **Galanos** for the baths. Ninety-six kms from Tanga is the **Mkomazi Game Reserve** with plentiful wildlife adjoining Kenya's Tsavo National Park, but as yet closed to tourists.

**Lushoto**, 175 kms inland from Tanga, a former German hill station, is today a bracing holiday resort set high in the magnificent forest-clad Usumbara Mountains. In this region you can visit fine farms and coffee and tea estates, go trout fishing or riding, or simply enjoy a scenic drive, all enhanced by the crisp mountain air. Lushoto's Sunday market is worth attending.

### Kilwa, Lindi and Mtwara

**Kilwa** is Quiloa of Milton's *Paradise Lost*. On the coast 320 kms south of Dar es Salaam, it encompasses extensive ruins of Arab palaces, a walled town and several important mosques. This thriving port, which once had its own Sultan and minted its own coinage, was one of the major trading centres on the coast. Toward the Mozambique border the old port of **Lindi** and the modern one of **Mtwara**, with its splendid natural harbour, offer good swimming. In the interior highlands live the Makonde people, noted for their almost surrealistic carving and their peculiar stilt dances (see the *Tanzania Background* chapter).

### Zanzibar

Few places evoke such romance and sorrow as does this 85-km segment of coralline reef in the Indian Ocean, 35 kms from the mainland. Steeped in history, the old town is a maze of narrow streets with whitewashed houses and magnificently carved brass-studded teak doors, curious shops and bazaars.

**Looking around Zanzibar town**

In the main square is the former **British Consulate** (1841–74), now used for commercial offices, where such great names in African exploration as Burton, Speke, Grant and Livingstone were received. The former **Sultan's palace** (now the People's Palace) is set amidst gardens on the seafront, and nearby are the old **Arab fort** with its round stone towers and the **Beit el Ajaib** (House of Wonders), the tallest building in Zanzibar town. It entrance is guarded by two bronze cannon, one bearing the Portuguese royal arms; the Arab doors are beautifully carved and bear Koranic inscriptions, while inside the marble floors and silver decorations were imported from Europe.

A tour should include the **clove market** and the street of the **Indian bazaar**, the several **mosques** in the town, and the site of the great **slave market**, closed forcibly only in 1873. The following year the present **Anglican cathedral** made from ground coral and cement was built over the market, and the first service was held on Christmas Day, 1877. The altar stands exactly where the whipping block was located. Captured deep within the interior and driven 1000 kms or more to the coast, those Africans who survived were sold here, as many as 600 in a day. Dr Livingstone described the trade as 'the open sore of the world'. Here the sore has been healed and sanctified, if not forgotten.

The **Dhow Harbour** is where the slaves arrived, and still standing here are **Burton's house and Livingstone's**. The **Zanzibar Museum** contains portraits of the Sultans, and documents and relics of the explorers, as well as local arts and crafts.

**North of town**

About 7 kms north of the town is the **Marahubi Palace**, built for the harem of Sultan Bargash (ruled 1870–88). It stands in gardens of mango trees off the main road, its walls and domed bathhouse, its pillars which once supported now vanished balconies, overgrown with creepers and reduced to ruin by the African climate. Further on at **Bububu** is the unexpected sight of a railway station and platforms. The tracks have long since been taken up, but this was once the terminus of one of the world's shortest (15 kms) railways, which ran out from Zanzibar town. It was opened in 1906 after an enterprising American convinced the Sultan that to be up to date he must have one. Not far beyond Bububu a track leads off to the right through a coconut plantation and after 2 kms comes to the well-preserved **Kidichi Baths** beneath a series of domes, built in the early 19th C by Sultan Sayyid Said for his Persian wife. At 153 metres this is the highest spot on the island. In a small bay near **Mangapwani** village is one of the infamous slave pits from which dhows picked up slaves after the trade was declared illegal.

**South of town** Near Pete, 35 kms along the main road south of Zanzibar town, is the small primeval forest of **Jozani**, home to leopards and monkeys. Further along and forking right at 55 kms the way leads to the ruined walled city of **Kizimkazi** with its recently renovated 12th C Shirazi mosque which bears the longest kufic inscription in East Africa: 'Ordered by Sheikh es Sayyid Abu Amran bin Mussa bin Hassan Ibn Mohammed. May Allah grant him long life and destroy his enemy'. Who the enemy was is a mystery, but there is a story that when the eponymous King Kizi was faced with his invaders and had nowhere to go, he prayed for supernatural concealment. The cliffs along the shore opened up and enclosed him, and the invaders retired disappointed. The spot were Kizi disappeared is marked today.

Historical mementoes apart, the pleasure of venturing beyond Zanzibar town lies in the lush and fragrant **plantations** for which the island is famous. Zanzibar supplies 75 percent of the world's cloves, and also grows coconuts, cinnamon bark, elephant leaf, lemon grass, rice, coffee, kapok, tapioca, jack fruit, bread fruit, cocoa beans and pepper trees. And there is the attraction of the island's white sandy **beaches**, the best being Mangapwani (15 kms from town), Uroa (40 kms), Nungwi (48 kms), and Makunduchi, Jambilani and Kizimkazi (65 kms). Swimming and goggling are popular all year round, and there is good fishing from mid-October to February.

**Beaches**

### Pemba and Mafia Islands

**Pemba** lies to the north of Zanzibar with which it shares certain similarities – a history of Portuguese and Arab domination, and geologically part of the same coralline reef that runs north along the coast from Mafia. The beaches are even better than Zanzibar's and the game fishing is superb. But there are no hotels on Pemba and permission to visit the island is only rarely granted.

**Mafia** is far more accessible, only 30 minutes flying time south of Dar es Salaam with landing strips for scheduled and small aircraft. Formerly a site for Arab plantations, in the First World War the island became a British base from which the German destroyer *Königsberg* was destroyed. The wreck still lies in the estuary of the Rufiji River over on the mainland.

But the island remains unspoilt and is one of East Africa's finest bases for big game fishing, as well as spear, surf and reef fishing. The best season for fishing is from October to March, when marlin, sailfish, kingfish, dolphin, shark, tunny, barracuda, base mackerel and wahoo are the catch.

Just off Mafia lie **Tutis Reef**, a paradise for snorkeling, **Jiwani** with extensive ruins of the 15th C Persian city of Kua, and **Kibondo**, known for its traditional boat building industry.

# PRACTICAL INFORMATION

Note that the accommodation rates given below do not include the government tax.

In addition to looking through the listings here, review the *Accommodation, Travel* and other sections in the *Tanzania Background* chapter, where, for example, you will find information on sailings to the islands, and to Kilwa, Lindi and Mtwara.

The place listings that follow are arranged alphabetically.

## LUSHOTO

### Accommodation

**Lawns Hotel,** PO Box 33. Tel: Lushoto 5.

**Oaklands Hotel**, PO Box 41.

## MAFIA ISLAND

### Accommodation

**Mafia Island Lodge**, PO Box 2, Mafia Island. Tel: Radio calls 6008. Telex: 41061. The lodge stands on the sandy beach of a bay almost entirely enclosed by coral islands and reefs. With its jetty and private fleet, it is an ideal base for fishing and for swimming, goggling, shelling, sailing and water skiing. The rooms are air-conditioned with bath, and there is a restaurant, bar and swimming pool. 530/- single, 690/- double, 820/- triple, suites from 925/- to 1390/-, with breakfast.

## MTWARA

### Accommodation

**Southern Cross Hotel**, PO Box 182.

## PEMBA ISLAND

### Accommodation

A hotel is under construction at Chake Chake.

### Travel

As the island is only seldom open to visitors, you should not set off without first consulting the Tanzania Tourist Corporation in Dar es Salaam or the Friendship Tourist Bureau in Zanzibar.

There is an airstrip at Chake Chake near the centre of the island, but it may be difficult to obtain transport when you get there. Probably your best bet is to take a steamer roundtrip from Zanzibar.

## TANGA

### Accommodation

**Mkonge Hotel**, PO Box 1544. Tel: Tanga 40711. Telex: 45020. Overlooking the bay, one of the Bushtrekker chain of hotels through whom reservations should be made: PO Box 88, Arusha. Tel: Arusha 3241. Telex: 42145. Or PO Box 5350, Dar es Salaam. Tel: Dar 31957. Telex: 41178. Disco, tennis court. 345/- single, 480/- double.

**Palm Court Hotel**, PO Box 783. Tel:

Tanga 3162. There is a free **campsite** next door.
The **Sikh temple** will accommodate travellers.

## ZANZIBAR ISLAND

### Accommodation

**Oberoi Ya Bwawani Hotel**, PO Box 670, Zanzibar. Tel: Zanzibar 2041 or 2043. Telex: 57157 Bwawani. A modern first class hotel overlooking the Indian Ocean, its large rooms come with air conditioning, bath, colour TV and balcony. There is a rooftop restaurant, coffee shop, two bars, a disco, and a casino is planned. Salt water pool, also water sports on tap. 485/- single, 620/- double, with breakfast.
**Victoria House**, Victoria Street, PO Box 149. A guest house.
**Zanzibar Hotel** and **Africa House**, next to one another, are both good value at 100/- per person. Book through the Friendship Tourist Bureau (see below).

### Travel

See *Background* chapter and *Dar es Salaam* listings.
To look round the island you can hire a taxi or a tour organised by the Friendship Tourist Bureau.

### Information

**Friendship Tourist Bureau**, PO Box 216. Tel: Zanzibar 2344.
All visitors must report to the Principal Immigration Officer or to the Friendship Tourist Bureau. The strict rules of Moslem dress must be adhered to on the island.

# THE NORTHERN CIRCUIT

Tanzania's northern circuit, the most popular with tourists in search of wildlife, contains such immortal names as Serengeti, Kilimanjaro, Ngorongoro and Olduvai, apart from a score of lesser known sites. The circuit is served by the modern Kilimanjaro International Airport, which is located on the Sanya Juu plains between Arusha and Moshi, tarmac roads connecting it to both towns. A number of international airlines fly directly to Kilimanjaro from points in Europe, and there are daily services to and from Dar es Salaam.

## Arusha

**Safari centre**

The lovely town of Arusha on the slopes of Mount Meru is the point of departure for all safaris in the northern circuit. Formerly an old trading post, it is today the administrative centre of the important area producing coffee, wheat, sisal, pyrethrum, sugar, textiles and dairy products. It was from Arusha that President Nyerere proclaimed his famous *Arusha Manifesto* committing Tanzania to the conservation of wildlife. The town boasts fine hotels with over two thousand beds of first class standard. Its altitude of 1540 metres ensures an almost temperate climate throughout the year. Arusha's position on the Great North Road halfway between Cape Town and Cairo is marked by a plaque near the New Arusha Hotel.

Visitors will be intrigued to see Wa Arusha warriors strolling amidst modern shops while the colourful womenfolk make their way to the markets. Of interest too are the older buildings of the town which show evidence of former colonial influence. Arusha is 649 kms northwest of Dar es Salaam.

Numerous sporting facilities exist in and around Arusha. The Gymkhana Club, which has a nine-hole golf course, and the Gun, Rifle and Aqua Sports Clubs all welcome temporary members. There are sailing, swimming, water skiing, fishing and yachting at the crater lake of **Duluti**, 13 kms along the road to Moshi. Here too are numerous varieties of water birds, as well as land species coming down from the forests to drink amongst the reeds.

Beautiful **Mount Meru**, 4993 metres high, can be

climbed in two days, or one if you motor to the highest point of the mountain road. Both the experienced and the amateur mountaineer will find routes to their taste. An extinct volcano, its forested lower slopes are thickly inhabited by leopard, rhino, elephant and many birds.

**Arusha National Park**

Described by Sir Julian Huxley as a 'gem amongst parks', the tiny 117 sq km Arusha National Park lies between the peaks of Kilimanjaro and Meru. Situated 32 kms east of Arusha at an altitude of 1540 metres it consists of three distinct areas: the five **Momella Lakes** with their prolific birdlife, **Mount Meru** with its concentration of wildlife (see above), and the enchanting miniature **Ngurdoto Crater**. The floor of the crater has been set aside as a reserve within a reserve, 'where there shall be no interference whatsoever from man'. Visitors may view the wildlife only from look-out points on the crater rim.

The park is exceptional in that it has no lions, but there is a wealth of buffalo, elephant, rhino, giraffe, warthog, bushpig, waterbuck, bushbuck and colobus monkey. There are certain places within the park where you can leave your car and walk around with impunity. The best time to visit is from July to March with December the best month of all.

**Moshi**

Situated 890 metres above sea level in lush and fertile volcanic country, fast growing Moshi lies at the foot of mighty Kilimanjaro. The snow-capped peaks of the mountain appear to dominate town life and can be seen from every part. Centre of the coffee trade, Moshi also has large plantations of sugar and sisal, as well as many mixed farms, predominantly wheat, which contribute to its commercial prosperity. The Wa Chagga, a colourful and gay people whose women are noted for their beauty, have their headquarters here. Worth visiting are the **Mwariko Art Gallery** on Mafutu Street, where exbititions by local artists are held, and the **Djamat Khan Mosque** on Mawenzi Road.

**Mount Kilimanjaro**

**The snow mountain**

When German missionary Johan Rebmann announced in 1848 that he had travelled inland from the East

African coast and sighted, at the level of the equator, a vast mountain capped in snow, his report was greeted with ridicule by the Royal Geographical Society in London. Nonetheless, majestic and mysterious Kilimanjaro, Africa's highest, most renowned and most beautiful mountain, does stand three degrees south of the equator, and its summit *is* permanently snowclad.

An extinct volcano, it has two peaks: Mawenzi (5600 metres), which was first conquered in 1912, provides a difficult and exciting climb for experienced alpinists; Kibo, the higher peak (6447 metres) offers an opportunity for any normally fit person even without mountaineering experience to visit some of Africa's equatorial snow fields and glaciers.

**Climbing Kilimanjaro**

Kilimanjaro can be climbed in almost any month, except during the long rains in April and May, but the best months are January to mid-March and mid-July to September when cloud cover is very rare. A minimum of five days is required and solo climbs without porters are definitely *not* advised. Accommodation should be reserved well in advance and all intending climbers should first contact the Kilimanjaro Mountain Club, PO Box 66, Moshi, which will arrange for guides, porters, food, cooking and lighting equipment, sleeping bags, etc.

The starting point for the ascent of Kilimanjaro is **Marangu**, 120 kms from Arusha, where there is a hotel. Worth visiting are the Kibo Art Gallery, the Kinukamori waterfalls, and, in Ashira, Tanzania's oldest Lutheran church.

From the coffee, maize and banana plantations of Marangu, the first day's march leads through flower-dotted alpine meadows and forests to Mandara Hut (formerly called Bismarck, 2967 metres, accommodating 24 climbers, water and firewood available). The area is a game reserve frequented by elephant, buffalo, duiker, eland, leopard, colobus and blue monkeys, as well as colourful birds.

The second day's journey is a short steep walk from the forest into the moorland to Horombo Hut (formerly Peter's, 4167 metres, accommodating 31, water available, but firewood scarce) on an open hillside of giant groundsel and lobelia peculiar to Africa's mountains. From here either peak can be attempted.

Kibo climbers carry on over rough moorland to the bare, boulder-strewn saddle between the peaks to Kibo

Hut (5713 metres, accommodating 18, no water or firewood available) at the base of the peak itself. The final assault, arduous and slow, is made early in the morning on the fourth day while the scree is still frozen. Hans Meyer Cave, half-way up the scree slope, is named after the first European to reach the summit, in 1892. From Kibo Hut it takes at least four hours to reach the crater edge of Johannes Notch where there is a breathtaking view of scintillating ice walls set off by rugged rocks to the left, the central ash cone with its dome-like glacier, and the ice chasms of the crater floor.

**The summit**

Gillman's Point at 6212 metres is recognised as the top, although the highest point is Uhuru (Freedom) Point, formerly Kaiser Wilhelm Spitz, 235 metres higher and 2 kms further around the crater rim. Descent is made rapidly down the scree slopes on the return journey with occasional rests to allow for change of altitude.

Uhuru Point is so called because of the torch planted there at midnight on 8 December 1961 by Lieutenant Alex Nyirenda of the Tanganyika Rifles as symbol of Tanzania's attainment of independence. 'We, the people of Tanganyika', had said Mwalimu Nyerere, 'would like to light a candle and put it on the top of Mount Kilimanjaro which would shine beyond our borders giving hope where there was despair, love where there was hate, and dignity where there was only humiliation'.

### Tarangire National Park

Most spectacular in the dry season from June to October when several thousands of animals migrate from the waterless southern Masailand to the last remaining pools of the Tarangire river, this park covers 26,000 sq kms at an altitude of around 1100 metres. A special feature is the presence of the greater kudu, but the dense wildlife population also includes black rhino, elephant, buffalo, lion, oryx, eland, lesser kudu, gerenuk and large numbers of impala. Of the birdlife outstanding are the bateleur eagle, secretary bird, Masai ostrich, buff crested bustard, beautiful sunbird, red bishop and paradise whydah.

Tarangire has nine distinct vegetation areas, of which the Acacia Tortilis parklands are the most attractive, and where the fringe-eared oryx and the sly antelope are to be spotted. The park is heavily infested with the tsetse fly to which the wildlife is immune, but domestic animals and man are not. Easily accessible from both the north and the south, Tarangire is 128 kms from Arusha by tarmac road and 8 kms from the Cape to Cairo road.

At Kolo just south of Tarangire, guides may be obtained for visits to the famous **Kondoa Irangi rock paintings** from the last stage of the Stone Age hunting cultures which flourished in the region between two and seven thousand years ago. Painted on the walls of natural rock shelters, they depict hunting scenes with stylised human figures and animals in red, brown, purple and black.

### Ngorongoro Crater and Olduvai Gorge

**One of the wonders of the world**

'It is impossible to give a fair description of the size and beauty of the Crater', writes Dr Bernhard Grimzek, 'for there is nothing with which to compare it. It is one of the Wonders of the World'. **Ngorongoro Crater** is indisputably one of Africa's most beautiful areas of wildlife and certainly one of the most spectacular settings of scenic splendour anywhere.

With no break whatsoever in its 67-metre wall, this is the largest intact crater in existence, exceeded in magnitude only by five damaged ones. Some eight million years ago Ngorongoro was an active volcano whose cone collapsed leaving a crater, or more properly a caldera, some 20 kms in diameter. The crater rim, where the hotels and lodges are superbly sited 2286 metres above sea level, rises high over the Serengeti plain.

Only four-wheel drive vehicles are permitted to make the 610-metre descent from the rim to the crater floor. Covering 160 sq kms, this is the home of over 30,000 animals, notably the 'big five', 3000 gazelle and 15,000 wildebeest. In addition, pastoral Masai herd about 100 head of cattle here. The perennial swamps are an important migratory point for flamingo which form a shimmering pink haze during the spring months.

The Ngorongoro Conservation Area was established as a separate multiple land use area allowing continued inhabitation by the pastoral Masai together with environmental protection. Natural phenomena include deep crater lakes (**Embagai**); waterfalls

(**Munge**); active volcanoes (**Oldonya Lengai** meaning 'Mountain of God'), which is worshipped by the Masai, and shifting sands. Some of the earliest archaeological finds in East Africa, neolithic graves and rock workings, have been discovered under the Ngorongoro burial mounds.

The 180-km drive from Arusha to Ngorongoro takes just over three hours through spectacular scenery: the base of the Great Rift Valley Wall, the entrance to Manyara National Park, the Mbulu Plateau, the Karatu and Oldeani wheat and coffee farms, and finally through the temperate forest zone up to the crater rim. Magnificently located right on this rim are two rural lodges, both equipped with modern facilities: Ngorongoro Wildlife Lodge operated by TTC, and the long established Ngorongoro Crater Lodge.

From Ngorongoro you can visit the renowned **Olduvai Gorge** which, under the direction of the late Dr Louis Leakey, has yielded abundant material dating back at least two million years and possibly much longer. The remains of prehistoric elephant, giant horned sheep and enormous ostriches have been found in this Stone Age site, and, more recently, the

**Earliest man**

very early human remains of the Nutcracker Man or *Zinjanthropus Bosei*, whose skull is now in the National Museum at Dar es Salaam. At this site also, Dr Leakey's wife Mary, an anthropologist in her own right, uncovered in 1969 the most intact *habilis* skull ever found, thought to date from around 1.75 million years ago. Just after this find, the Leakeys' son Richard made an equally spectacular discovery on the western shore of Lake Turkana, in Kenya, where he unearthed a splended *Australopithecus* skull.

At **Laetoli**, 45 kms south of Olduvai, one of the most important discoveries in the study of human evolution has been made in recent years. In 1974 fossil teeth of zebra and antelope were dug out of a river bed, followed later by a hominid tooth. Intensified exploration yielded, in 1977, fossilised footprints on the surface of a fine grained volcanic ash. These were animal tracks and included prints of rhinoceros, elephant, three different species of giraffe, baboon, hare and birds. All of these species are now extinct, but some of the living representations are to be seen on the Serengeti today. In 1978 three hominid trails were discovered giving Laetoli world renown. The prints are believed to have been of a family, a male followed by a female who trod in his footsteps, with one or other leading a child on the left. These trails demonstrate without doubt that our Pliocene ancestors walked fully upright with a free striding bipedal gait similar to, if not identical with ours. The footprints are at present buried for protection under sand and rock, but it is planned to erect a permanent building over the site so that visitors can witness this amazing find.

North of Ngorongoro is **Engaruka**, where the stone ruins of a great village once built on several terraces and whose origins are still open to archaeological investigation tell a story of violence and battle. This is hunting country where rhinoceros and many varieties of gazelle may be found including the rare oryx and gerenuk.

### Lake Manyara National Park

Nestling under the wall of the Great Rift Valley, this enchanting park is only 325 sq kms in area, of which 75 percent is taken up by the lake itself. There are five distinct vegetation zones: ground-water forest with towering mahogany and fig trees, extensive marshland and reeds; plains of open grassland; parklands scattered with acacia trees; and the characteristic scrubland on the precipitous face of Africa's **Great Rift Valley**. The last is the most dramatic portion of a huge earth crack that stretches 6000 kms from Turkey to the Zambezi River. This region of the Rift is the most linguistically diverse and complex in all of Africa. It is the only place on the continent containing all four major African language families: Bantu, Click, Cushitic and Nilotic.

**The Rift Valley wall**

Manyara is famous for its tree-climbing lions, its numerous buffalo and its herds of over 4000 elephant. The last are resident all year round and during the dry season come down to drink at the Endbash River. The lion keep up with the various herds of wildebeest, but take time out to recline on the limbs of the acacia trees, 3 to 7 metres above the ground, so keep a look out in the trees along the lake shore. Leopard and rhino have been seen in almost every section of the park, normally in the early morning or late afternoon. Visitors may get out of their cars at marked picnic sites, but bear in mind that dangerous animals may be nearby, especially if there is thick cover. Do not attempt to walk in the bush itself as you will certainly frighten the animals, and they often enough will frighten you.

The birds of Manyara are as spectacular as the animals. There are over 200 species, the most profuse and lovely being the flamingo, which, at certain seasons, form a solid line of pink stretching for many kilometres down the lake. Along the lake edge are various species of duck, heron, waders, jacanas, egrets, ibises and storks. Within the acacia woodlands and along the open grasslands are kingfishers, various plovers, larks and wagtails. Birds of prey are represented by the palm nut vulture, the crowned hawk eagle and the bateleur eagle. The fish eagle is common, and the colourful selection of smaller birds is quite remakable.

Lake Manyara is 128 kms southwest of Arusha on an all-weather road, which is part tarmac, through the stark landscape of the Masai steppe. The best way to spend a day in the park is to enter in the early morning and drive slowly down the main all-weather track until it reaches the hot sulphur springs called **Maji Moto** at the southern end of the park. Here you may see klipspringer standing at the rock outcrops, and reedbuck in the marshes. The springs are also a favourite feeding ground for water birds. After lunch drive back by way of some of the circuit tracks branching off from the main one and leading into the principal game areas, but note that these tracks may be closed in wet weather.

### Serengeti National Park

Symbol of African wildlife and primeval beauty, Serengeti has been immortalised by Dr Bernard and Michael Grzimek in their classic *Serengeti Shall Not Die*. The book has been filmed, and translated into 24 languages. In area 14,700 sq kms, Serengeti is Tanzania's largest park. It is also the oldest and celebrated its Diamond Jubilee in 1981.

**The great annual migration**

Serengeti contains all the 'big five' but its fame lies in its three million plains game animals, the greatest and most spectacular concentration anywhere in the world. Here you can see the unique phenomenon of the annual Serengeti migration, when thousands upon thousands of wildebeest and zebra move massively westward from the central plains to the permanent waters of the park corridor.

*Serengeti dawn*

The never-ending broad stream of these vast herds provides easy prey and it is not unusual to see up to forty lions in one day, in addition to numerous leopard, hyena and cheetah. Unrivalled photographic opportunities arise for those fortunate enough to witness the great three-day trek which usually takes place in May or June.

After moving westward, the migration breaks into two parts, one group turning northeast and the other due north to the Masai Mara Reserve in Kenya. Here the groups join again and remain until the coming of the short rains in November. They then head back in columns south again to the central plains of Serengeti.

During the rest of the year the best time for viewing the estimated half million wildebeest and over two hundred thousand zebra is during the dry months from June to September when they are massed like an army on the short-grass plains in the south of the park. They share the grazing with over half a million gazelle, attendant lion, cheetah, hunting dog and hyena, while vultures soar overhead. Serengeti's famous lion, which number 2000 and include the black-maned species, are of two types: the sedentary which stay around the central plains, and the migratory which follow the herds on their great trek. In all there are more than 35 species of plains animals and a wealth of birdlife.

Habitat changes from the vast treeless central plains and savannah-type stretches which are dotted with acacia trees and interspersed with magnificent rock outcrops, to riverine bush, thick scrub and forest in the north and along the Mara river. Streams, rivers, swamps and small lakes enhance the general beauty. Altitude varies from 200 to 900 metres. Temperatures average around 27°C at noon but drop sharply to 16°C at night when warm clothing is essential. The driest period is during the latter half of the year. Heavy rain storms may be encountered in April and May.

**Prehistoric find**

A unique historical find was revealed accidentally during building excavations in the park: two oval bowls of exquisitely carved soapstone and two of lava which were used for ancient burial rites. This find links with burial sites discovered at Njoro, Nakuru, Naivasha and Ngorongoro, and also with the Naro Sura settlement site of a people dating from 1000 to 100 BC who have been classified as the Stone Bowl Culture. Cattle bones unearthed at the various sites indicate that these people were herdsmen, while discoveries at the Njoro cave show that they wore skin clothing and adorned themselves with beads of stone, seeds and animal bones.

# PRACTICAL INFORMATION

Note that accommodation rates do not include government tax. In addition to looking through the listings here, review the *Accommodation*, *Travel* and other sections in the *Tanzania Background* chapter.

The place listings that follow are arranged alphabetically.

**ARUSHA**
**Accommodation**
*First class:*
**Mount Meru Hotel**, one km outside Arusha at the foot of Mount Meru, PO Box 877. Tel: Arusha 2712. Telex: 42065 Meruhotel. All rooms with radio, air conditioning, bath. Restaurant (Saturday dinner dance), bar and snackbar. Shops, heated pool, children's pool, adjacent to golf course, squash and tennis courts. 575/- single, 760/- double, 905/- triple, suites from 1250/- to 1520/-, with breakfast.

**New Arusha Hotel**, in the centre of town, PO Box 88. Tel: Arusha 324114. Telex: 42034 Centre. Bar, coffee bar, restaurant, grill room, disco, shops, pool and gardens. Built in 1933 and full of at-

**Mountain Club of Tanzania**, PO Box 66. All-inclusive arrangements for mountain expeditions, accommodation, equipment, guides, etc.

## MOUNT KILIMANJARO

### Accommodation

**Kibo Hotel**, c/o PO Box 102 Marangu. Tel: Marangu 4. On the slopes of Kilimanjaro, 49 kms from Moshi and 130 kms from Arusha, this is a country house-style mountain resort (built 1910) amidst a tropical forest, waterfalls and trout rivers. Restaurant, bar, garden, sunbathing lawns, terraces and outdoor pool. Mountain trips arranged. 460/- double, with breakfast.

### Climbing Kilimanjaro

Contact the Park Warden, Kilimanjaro National Park, PO Box 96, Marangu. Tel: Marangu 50. In addition to the usual park entrance fee, there are hut fees of 75/- per person per night, or campsite fees of 50/-. A guide for the five-day climb will cost 390/-, inclusive of his salary and hut fees; a porter costing a bit less. You can arrange an all-inclusive climb (entrance and hut fees, guide and porter plus their hut fees, and all meals) for 2150/- per person. Reservations are essential, 20 percent deposit required. All fees and services in the park must be paid in foreign currency. All equipment can be hired on the spot, eg sleeping bag 40/-, rucksack 50/-, boots 65/-, thick jacket 40/- – these prices are for five days. Remember that in climbing the mountain you will be passing within a short time from the tropical base climate to the arctic climate of the summit and must be properly clothed and equipped.

## NGORONGORO CRATER

### Accommodation

**Ngorongoro Wildlife Lodge**, c/o PO Box 310, Arusha. Tel: Ngorongoro 15. Telex: 41061. On the crater rim, all rooms with bath, central heating and panoramic view of the crater. Restaurant, bar, shop, wildlife viewing terrace with telescope. Trips to crater floor available. 530/- single, 690/- double, full board.

**Ngorongoro Wildlife Lodge**, c/o PO Box 310, Arusha. Tel: Ngorongoro 15. Telex: 41061. On the crater rim, all rooms with bath, central heating and panoramic view of the crater. Restaurant, bar, shop, wildlife viewing terrace with telescope. Trips to crater floor available. 530/- single, 690/- double, 820/- triple, suites 925/- to 1390/-, with breakfast.

**Camping** is prohibited inside the crater, but permitted in the conservation area. Campers must be self-reliant and self-sufficient. There is no tsetse fly at the higher levels and no mosquitoes.

### Visiting the crater floor

The hire of a Land Rover is 865/- for a half-day crater tour, and 1150/- for a full-day crater tour.

## SERENGETI NATIONAL PARK

### Accommodation

**Lobo Wildlife Lodge,** c/o PO Box 3100, Arusha. Tel: Radio call 4619 Arusha. Telex: 42138 attention Lobo. A beautifully sited and boldly designed lodge built into the contours of a massive rock promontory overlooking the plains. The swimming pool is carved from the rock and fills from a waterfall. All rooms with bath and central heating. Restaurant, bar, lounge, shop. 345/- single, 460/- double, 645/- triple, suites 925/- to 1390/-, with breakfast.

**Seronera Wildlife Lodge,** address and telex as Lobo, but Tel: Radio call 4643 Arusha. Built on an outcrop of boulders at the centre of the park, ideally positioned for observing the great annual migration. All rooms with bath. Restaurant, also lounge and bar with panoramic view. Rock-hewn swimming pool. 530/- single, 690/- double, 820/- triple, suites 925/- to 1330/-, with breakfast.

There are **camping sites** within 4 kms of Seronera, but campers must be entirely self-sufficient and may not use the lodge facilities. No camping is permitted elsewhere because of danger from animals.

## TARANGIRE NATIONAL PARK

### Accommodation

**Tarangire Safari Camp,** c/o PO Box 1182, Arusha. Tel: Arusha 3625 or 3090. Tented accommodation. Restaurant, bar, lounge, gift shop. Game viewing vehicles available. 555/- single, 860/- double, full board.

**Camping** is permitted on application to the Park Warden. Campers must be self-sufficient except for water and firewood. For further information, contact Tanzania National Parks, PO Box 3134, Arusha.

# ACROSS CENTRAL AND WESTERN TANZANIA

## Morogoro

Lying at the foot of the blue Uluguru Mountains, Morogoro is 280 kms west of Dar es Salaam along the all tarmac road to Iringa and Mbeya. There is bird shooting on the mountain slopes and good trout fishing in the streams. An important agricultural centre, Morogoro can be reached by road, rail or air. The scenic drive from the capital can be broken at **Chalinze**, where fresh fruit can be bought from roadside stalls. The road after Morogoro towards Mikumi Park traverses impressive landscape with a mountain backdrop, and just before the eastern boundary of the park is a small village whose inhabitants display baskets and mats woven from reeds and frond of young hyphaenes.

## Mikumi National Park

Straddling the Tanzam highway just past Morogoro, Mikumi is the most accessible park from Tanzania's capital city. Although comparatively small in area (1300 sq kms), it is rich in wildlife with buffalo, wildebeest, zebra, impala, warthog and elephant to be seen in all seasons. The park's principal feature is the flood plain of the **Mkata River**, which averages 600 metres above sea level and is protected by a horseshoe of rugged mountains and forested hills.

Elephant, which are mainly of the grazing type, abound throughout the area, and buffalo totalling some 3000 are found on treeless grassland and in depressions near the swamps. A family of hippo lives at **Hippo Pool** 5 kms from the park gate. The Mikumi lion roams in pursuit of wildebeest and zebra, occasionally taking time off, like his Manyara cousin, to climb a tree for a siesta. Colobus monkeys can be spotted along the watershed of the Mkata River, and kudu are sometimes seen.

For visitors in a hurry, the area around the airstrip and Hippo Pool offers the best opportunities for game viewing. Those with more time should take a trip to Chamgore, a drive along the river, or the circuit of the hill drive to appreciate the variety of animals, terrain and vegetation.

It should be noted that at the park days are hot and nights cold. The Uhuru (Tanzania-Zambia) rail line marks the boundary of Mikumi with Selous to the south. The park has a landing strip for light aircraft. Accommodation is available at Mikumi Wildlife Lodge and at Mikumi Wildlife Tented Camp. Both have become popular stopovers for travellers between Dar es Salaam and Iringa. Camping is permitted only at a site 4 kms from the entrance gate.

**Selous Game Reserve**

**Largest unexploited wildlife area in the world**

The vast untamed paradise of Selous is the largest unexploited wildlife area in the world. Its general inaccessibility, combined with the fact that no human habitation is allowed within its boundaries, has ensured a magnificent refuge for animals, birds, insects and reptiles. Here some of Africa's finest virgin bush, unchanged throughout thousands of years, is inhabited by three quarters of a million wild animals. This is second in number only to Serengeti.

With virtually no man-made roads, the isolation of the area is accentuated by the Rufiji River system, East Africa's largest. Its massive tributaries, the Great Ruaha, Kilombero and Luwegu, flow through the centre of the reserve making effective communications almost impossible. Although opened in 1905, Selous has remained one of the least known reserves and is only just beginning to receive international recognition. The construction of safari camps has allowed penetration of certain areas, but much still awaits exploration.

The reserve was named in honour of Frederic Selous, naturalist, explorer and soldier who was killed in action against German forces in 1917. His grave lies close to the present Selous Safari Camp on the Beho Beho ridge.

Only the comparatively small portion of the reserve to the north of the Rufiji-Ruaha River systems has so far been explored, the vast area to the south remaining largely unfrequented.

The Great Ruaha flows into the Rufiji at spectacular **Stiegler's Gorge**, which is spanned by a cable car to provide the daring visitor with a breathtaking trip over the turbulent waters far below. Great herds of animals are attracted to these life-sustaining waters. The gorge was the site where German explorer Stiegler was killed by an elephant in 1907. Slightly further north the waters have formed a string of lakes where schools of hippo up to 50 in number are frequently encountered, together with a wealth of other big game animals and birds.

With its broad spectrum of game and bird life, Selous is perhaps one of the few remaining areas where the really big 'tusker' is still to be found. The reserve's estimated 60,000 elephant combined with some 30,000 in adjacent Mikumi and Kilomabero Valley form the largest known population of the species in Africa. Elephant may be seen bathing in the Rufiji River, browsing in the palm swamps, or crossing the track just ahead of you.

**And largest elephant herd in Africa**

Lion are frequent, as also are vast herds of buffalo, the most numerous animal in the reserve. A pack of wild dogs may be observed hunting wildebeest while a herd of zebra watch from a distance. Across the open savannah you are likely to see giraffe, wildebeest, waterbuck, baboon and eland, and in a quiet glade in the afternoon the shy bushbuck may appear. Woodland fauna are represented by over 70,000 Lichtenstein's hartebeest and some 14,000 sable antelope, and there are other rarities such as the great kudu, a possible 5000 rhino, and widespread southern reedbuck.

An extremely rich birdlife includes goliath heron, open-billed stork, hammerkop, fish eagle, secretary bird, a variety of sunbirds and kingfishers, and many others to excite the ornithologist and nature lover alike.

On the western boundary the Kilombero forms a large flood plain where, from March to May, the floods force elephant, buffalo, lion, leopard, crocodile, puku, buck, eland and sable to congregate. For the fisherman there are tiger fish and catfish. In the far south of the reserve, along the Luwegu River and its tributaries, alluvial flats and swamps provide food for great concentrations of elephant and buffalo. A river drive is almost invariably rewarded also with the sight of sable antelope, rhino and lion.

Although the altitude in Selous ranges only from 110 to 1250 metres, there is considerable variety of habitat. Much of the area is crisscrossed by small streams and valleys, and some 1700 botanical species have been identified.

Selous is best visited from July through to March as during the remaining months, which are rainy, a large part of the area becomes inaccessible due to flooding. The safari camps and lodges are closed from April to June.

**Getting to Selous**

The simplest method of reaching Selous is by air and all four camps within the reserve have well maintained air strips. Alternatively you can choose the Tanzam Railway which takes four hours from the capital and which runs along the northern boundary of the reserve affording excellent game viewing opportunities from the train window. It is possible to drive from Dar es Salaam, but a minimum of eight hours must be calculated and a four-wheel drive vehicle is mandatory. The journey can be undertaken only under optimum conditions in the dry season. One road leads to Selous from the east, one from Kibiti on the Kilwa road and follows the Rufiji upstream from Mkongo. The other road leads south from Morogoro along the striking Uluguru mountain chain to Kisagi village. Within the reserve safaris are conducted by Land Rover, or more adventurously by lorry. There are boat safaris along the river, and foot safaris for the intrepid, accompanied by an armed guard.

Bushtrekker Safaris operate the splendidly sited Mbuyu (baobab tree) Safari Camp on the banks of the Rufiji and offer exciting river and walking safaris. Selous Safari Camp, high on Beho Beho ridge, organises special three-day adventure safaris into unexplored bush. The oldest camp is the Rufiji River Camp just inside the reserve on the eastern approach.

## Iringa

Two hundred kms past Ikumi and 500 kms southwest of Dar es Salaam on the main Tanzam highway, Iringa is an important farming and tobacco centre at an altitude of 1635 metres. This is the district of the warrior Wahehe tribes whose chief Mkwawa won fame for his valiant and successful resistance against the Germans. At **Kalenga**, 15 kms from Iringa along the Mloa road, are the ruins of Mkwawa's capital with his mausoleum and a museum. Elephant abound in this area. In the southern highlands 23 kms southwest of Iringa, is the prehistoric site of **Isimila** where the old lake bed has been exposed, and with it thousands of Stone Age hand axes and cleavers of the Acheulian

*Wasukuma women bearing cotton, Lake Victoria*

period, still lying as they were found. **Lake Ngawazi** at Mufundi, 88 kms further on, will delight the ornithologist.

**Ruaha National Park**

Covering 13,000 sq kms this relatively new and undisturbed park is Tanzania's largest elephant sanctuary. One hundred and thirty kms from Iringa by good all weather road, its name derives from the Great Ruaha River which flows along its entire eastern border creating spectacular gorges and scenery. Its wooded banks of *acacia albida* (winter thorn) offer shade in the dry season for large herds of animals. Hippo, crocodile, turtle and fish inhabit the river itself. The park is also known for its concentration of kudu, its roan and sable antelope, and its rich bird life. Special photographic blinds have been built at strategic places where wildlife congregates.

Most of the park is undulating plateau country over 1000 metres in altitude with many rocky hills and outcrops. Tracks are passable only in the dry season from July to December, the best months for game viewing being July and November. Light aircraft operate to Ruaha from Iringa and Dar es Salaam. On the western bank of the river Msembe Camp offers accommodation, and camping is permitted at certain sites within the park. Hotels are available in Iringa.

### Mbeya

Lying between the two arms of the Great Rift Valley and only 114 kms from Tunduma, the small Tanzania-Zambia border town of Mbeya is an ideal centre for exploring the southern highlands. A scenic drive north takes you through **World's End**, a spectacular panorama over the Buhoro Flats to the ghost town of **Chunya** and the **Lupa Goldfields**, scene of the gold rush in the 1930s. There is good trout fishing in the streams of the **Mporoto Mountains** 72 kms east of Mbeya and in the ornithological and game viewing area of **Lake Rukwa** where crocodile and hippo abound 160 kms northwest of Mbeya. The road southeast from Mbeya leads through the tea country around Tukuyu to **Port Itungi** on the shores of Lake Malawi.

### Lake Tanganyika

Beautiful fjord-like Lake Tanganyika, second deepest in the world, offers excellent fishing for Nile perch, tilapia, tiger fish, yellow bellies and other species. The highland area of the Ufipa plateau at the southern end of the lake has an abundance of fauna and wild flora, the latter particularly in evidence in February and June. From the northern port of **Kigoma** round trips of the lake are sometimes operated, passing the country of the old mission stations and reaching Mpulungu in Zambia. At **Ujiji** 8 kms south of Kigoma, a plaque marks the site where Stanley found Dr Livingstone and from where they trudged 480 kms to Tabora. Large herds of elephant and buffalo can be seen in the nearby **Katavi Plain Reserve**, and the famous chimpanzees on the mountain slopes of **Gombe National Park**, 16 kms from Kigoma, where, due to scientific research, visitors are allowed only in small groups of five or six persons.

**Stanley and Livingstone**

Also located in the Kigoma region bordering Lake Tanganyika is **Mahale Mountains National Park**,

Tanzania's newest, which is scheduled for limnological (lake) research. Here chimpanzees are protected in their natural habitat. The Mahale area, which has been uninhabited by humans since the 1974 villagisation plan, is the home of tropical rain forest animals, savannah animals and other species endemic to miombo woodlands. The absence of dangerous animals allows visitors to explore the park on foot. At present there is no overland access to the Mahale region which can be reached only by a laborious 12-hour journey in a small vessel from Kigoma. It is proposed to operate a regular ferry boat to connect the park with the outside world.

**Tabora**, 320 kms inland from Kigoma but not connected by direct road, was founded in 1820 as a centre for Arab slave and ivory traders operating on the caravan route from the coast to Lake Tanganyika; the ruins of old Arab buildings can be seen here. Just outside the town is a reconstruction of the house in which Livingstone and Stanley lived and from where the former set out on his last journey. Travellers from Tabora to Mwanza may go via the famous Williamson Diamond Mines at Mwadui, now fast declining in production.

## Dodoma

**Proposed capital of Tanzania**

Five hundred and twelve kms west of Dar es Salaam, which it is scheduled to replace as capital, Dodoma lies 1133 metres above sea level in the arid centre of Tanzania, and on the Central Railway Line. The 84,000 Kongwa Ranch, a source of excellent beef and high quality breeding cattle, is located in this region, as also is the Dodoma Wine Industry started by the Fathers at Bihawana Mission. In the vicinity of Dodoma are many ujamaa villages of the Wagogo peasants who were weaned from their traditional life during the early 1970s by the government's radical agrarian policy. The Stone Age Kondoa Irangi rock paintings can be seen 185 kms north of Dodoma on the road to Arusha.

## Mwanza

The port at the southern end of Lake Victoria and lake terminus of the Central Railway Line from the capital, is not only the centre of a productive cotton area, but also handles much of the coffee grown in the western

**Speke's first sight of Lake Victoria**

part of the country. It was from Mwanza that Speke obtained his first sight of **Lake Victoria** and the nearby gulf has been named after him. Rock paintings have been found near both Mwanza and Bukoba.

**Rubondo** and **Saa Nane Game Reserves**, island zoo sanctuaries on Lake Victoria, can be reached by boat from Mwanza. More than 50 species of game animals and birds have been introduced on the islands.

**Bukoba**, founded by Emin Pasha, is situated on one of the country's most beautiful parks. On the western shores of Lake Victoria at the threshold to Uganda, it lies on one of the great migratory routes of the African birds. Vegetation is tropical with jungle, spacious green fields and banana plantations. Nearby **Biharamulo Game Reserve** is the northern limit of range of sable antelope, common reedbuck and steinbuck. **Rumanyika Orugundu Game Reserve** in the Kishanda Valley, has an exceptionally large concentration of rhino, besides numerous elephant, buffalo, lion, leopard, eland, roan antelope and other animals.

# PRACTICAL INFORMATION

See the *Accommodation* section in the *Tanzania Background* chapter for general information. The place listings that follow are arranged alphabetically.

## BUKOBA

### Accommodation

**Coffee Tree Inn,** PO Box 5. Tel: Bukoba 412.
**Lake Hotel**, PO Box 66. Tel: Bukoba 237.
There is also a **YMCA**.

## DODOMA

### Accommodation

Future capital of Tanzania this may be, but meanwhile it is not geared up for much.
**Dodoma Hotel**, PO Box 239.

## IRINGA

### Accommodation

**White Horse Inn,** PO Box 48. Tel: Iringa 30.
Also try the **Kilimanjaro Rest House**.

## KIGOMA

### Accommodation and Food

**Kigoma Hotel**. 110/- per bed. The restaurant is open to non-residents and is the best in town, at reasonable prices.
**Kigoma Community Centre**, 150 metres on the left as you leave the station. 30/- per night in a shared room. Fills up fast when the train or ferry arrives.

### Travel

Just south of Kigoma is **Ujiji** of 'Dr Livingstone, I presume' fame; a taxi there will cost you only a few shillings, and there is a water taxi service too.

## MBEYA

The new **Highlands Hotel** should be open by now, part of the Bushtrekker chain. For information: Bushtrekker Hotels, PO Box 88, Arusha. Tel: Arusha 3241. Telex: 42124. Or PO Box 5350, Dar es Salaam. Tel: Dar es Salaam 31957. Telex: 41178.

**Mbeya Hotel,** PO Box 80. Tel: Mbeya 223.
**Mbeya Guest House,** PO Box 153. Tel: Mbeya 202.
**Moravian Church Youth Hostel**, near the radio tower. 50/- per person including breakfast, and cheap evening meals available.

## MIKUMI NATIONAL PARK
### Accommodation
**Mikumi Wildlife Camp**, PO Box 605, Morogoro. For reservations: PO Box 1907, Dar es Salaam. Tel: Dar 68631. A comfortable, informal banda camp in the bush. The area is frequently visited by elephants. For most of the year you can use your own car for game-viewing as tracks in the park are good, but four-wheel drive vehicles can be hired: 375/- per hour for residents, 470/- per hour for non-residents, with each vehicle capable of carrying eight people. Vehicle and driver's park entrance permits are included in the rates. Accommodation rates are 350/- to 425/- per person in a banda with one or two beds, and 325/- to 310/- per person in a banda with three or more beds, full board included.
**Mikumi Wildlife Lodge**, PO Box 14, Mikumi. Tel: Mikumi 27. Telex: 41061. This is a modern safari lodge overlooking a waterhole in the park. All rooms with bath. Pool, shop, vehicles for game viewing available. 400/- single, 515/- double, 665/- triple, with breakfast.
There is a **camping site** 4 kms from the park entrance. Campers must be entirely self-sufficient except for water. No camping is permitted elsewhere in the park.

## MOROGORO
### Accommodation
**Acropole Hotel**, PO Box 78. Tel: Morogoro 41.
**Morogoro Hotel**, c/o Bushtrekker Hotels (see *Mbeya* listings). Located at the foot of the Uluguru Mountains just a few kms from the Zambia-Tanzania highway; Mikumi National Park is easily reached from here. Pool, tennis courts, shops at the hotel.
**Savoy Hotel**, PO Box 35. Tel: Morogoro 23. 185/- single, 315/- double, with breakfast.

## MWANZA
### Accommodation
**New Mwanza Hotel**, on Lake Victoria. Tel: Mwanza 3031. Telex: 41061 attention New Mwanza. All rooms with radio and air conditioning. The restaurant serves up fresh fish from the lake. There is also a bar and snack bar. 365/- single, 530/- double, suites from 660/- to 790/-, with breakfast.
The many **hotels** around the bus station charge 65/- single, 100/- double. There is a **Sikh temple** here that will put up travellers, and a **Catholic Mission** (but accepts Catholics only). Also try the **Victoria Hotel**, 230/- double with private bathroom, clean rooms, breakfast. And there is a **YMCA**.

## RUAHA NATIONAL PARK
### Accommodation
**Msembe Camp**, on the western bank of the Great Ruaha River. Limited accommodation in rondavels equipped with showers. Kitchen, beds, bedding and firewood provided. Advance booking: Park Warden, Ruaha National Park, PO Box 369, Iringa.

## SELOUS GAME RESERVE
### Accommodation and Travel
**Mbuyu Safari Camp**, beautifully sited on the banks of the Rufiji River. Bookings through Bushtrekker Hotels (see *Mbeya* listing). Luxury well-ventilated tents with makuti roofs, sisal mats, hotel-style beds, electricity, spacious verandah, en suite shower, flush toilet, mosquito nets and zipped in ground sheets. Bar and dining room with a magnificent baobab tree in the centre (*Mbuyu* is Swahili for baobab). Available: Land Rovers and jet boats for game viewing, also walking safaris, fishing safaris and air safaris. 360/- single, 600/- double.
**Selous Safari Camp**, at Beho-Beho. Bookings: PO Box 2261, Dar es Salaam. Tel: Dar 68631. Fully equipped safari

camp, the comfortable bandas with shower, flush toilet, electricity. Three-day adventure safaris into the bush can be arranged on the spot at attractive rates. Alternatively you can choose an all-inclusive three-day safari at 1725/- per person. You leave Dar at 11am Wednesday or Saturday by train to Fuga Halt, transfer by safari vehicle to Beho-Beho, with game viewing enroute, and get dinner and accommodation. The next day an early breakfast is followed by a three-hour safari, then lunch and an afternoon visit to the Maji Moto hot springs for swimming, and finally dinner and accommodation. On the third day you rise for a dawn visit to the Msine Gorge viewpoint and then go on a walking safari. After an early lunch you return to Dar, arriving at 5pm. Minimum four persons.

**Camping**: You can ask the Park Warden's permission to camp elsewhere in the reserve, but be sure to follow his instructions and advice.

## TABORA

### Accommodation

**Tabora Hotel**, PO Box 147. Tel: Tabora 47.

Also a **YMCA**.

# THE SEYCHELLES BACKGROUND

## Basic Facts

The Seychelles is a republic within the Commonwealth, an archipelago of 92 islands with a land area of 444 sq kms scattered over one million sq kms of the Indian Ocean, 1000 kms east of Kenya and Tanzania.

The population of the islands in 1977 was 62,000, of which 50,000 live on the island of Mahé, with 15,000 in Victoria, the capital, on Mahé. The principal islands are Mahé, 148 sq kms (about 24 kms long and 5 to 8 kms wide); Praslin, 41 sq kms; Silhouette, 16 sq kms; and La Digue, 10 sq kms.

English and French are the official languages, but Creole, derived from French, African and Arab sources, is the lingua franca of the majority of the inhabitants, who are mostly of French-African (Creole) mixture, with some Europeans, Indians and Chinese. Ninety percent are Roman Catholic, eight percent Anglican.

## Geography

**Islands of granite and coral**

The Seychelles consist of a group of 40 granitic islands (the Mahé group) and 52 outlying coral islands. The granitic have high hills and mountains, while the coralline for the most part ride just above sea level. All the islands of the granitic group lie within 56 kms of Mahé, which is the largest. They are rich in tropical vegetation and profuse with coconut palms, bananas, mangoes, yams, breadfruit and other fruits. Some vanilla and tea is cultivated, and cinnamon grows wild on the hills. Primitive rain forest lies on the upper levels.

The coralline islands have no permanent population, and some have no water. Contracted labour from Mahé produces copra, collects guano, birds' eggs, firewood, mangrove timber and salt fish, and grows small quantities of maize. The largest of the coralline islands is Aldabra, recommended for its flora and fauna, and where giant tortoises, indigenous to the Seychelles, can still be found wild. Aldabra ranges in width from 2 to 8 kms and encloses a lagoon of over 130 sq kms. Farquar, another coralline, is notorious for the number of ships that were wrecked there.

**Indigenous fauna and flora**

The islands were uninhabited at discovery and there was an absence of larger animals. A few harmless snakes can be found in the hills, and lizards are plentiful. There are flying foxes and nocturnal tenrec, a species of hedgehog. Of the larger animals only the sea turtle is not extinct. The Seychelles have 13 species of land bird that are not to be found elsewhere in the world, and the sea bird population is exceptional for its variety and density – terns, noddies, bridled tern and fairy tern, and shearwaters. There are 80 species of endemic trees and plants that range from the giant coco-de-mer to the small pitcher plant, an insectivor, and include the rare *bois Medusa*, a small tree so different from other trees that botanists have given it a family classification of its own.

### Climate and What to Wear

The climate is tropical and varies little throughout the year. March and April are the hottest months, but the shade temperature seldom exceeds 31° C. During the cool months of July and August the temperature can drop to 21° C. Southeast trade winds blow from May to November, the most pleasant part of the year. The period December to May, the hottest months and the rainiest, tend to be enervating because of high humidity and an even temperature day and night. Rainfall is high, with an average of over 35 cms per annum. The islands lie outside the cyclone belt, however, and thunderstorms are rare, and mild when they do occur. High winds seldom blow. Light cottonwear is advised for all hours, with a raincoat for sudden showers. Evening dress is usually casual, and the practical sarong can be bought locally. Visitors should refrain from appearing in swimwear in the town streets.

### History

Although probably visited in the Middle Ages by traders from Arabia sailing from East African ports with the monsoons, and later by both the British and

**The French**

the French, the Seychelles remained uninhabited until 1770, when at the urging of the French Administrators in Mauritius, the French sent Lieutenant Romainville with 15 soldiers and 12 slaves to establish an administrative headquarters on a site that was later to become Victoria, and shortly afterwards settlers began to arrive from Mauritius and La Reunion. Although they were meant to become farmers, they preferred to traffic in timber and giant tortoises, both lucrative trades.

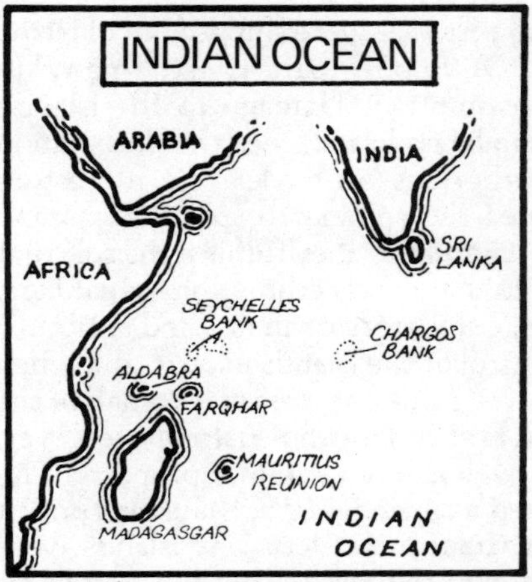
INDIAN OCEAN
ARABIA
INDIA
SRI LANKA
AFRICA
SEYCHELLES BANK
CHARGOS BANK
ALDABRA
FARQHAR
MAURITIUS
REUNION
MADAGASGAR
INDIAN OCEAN

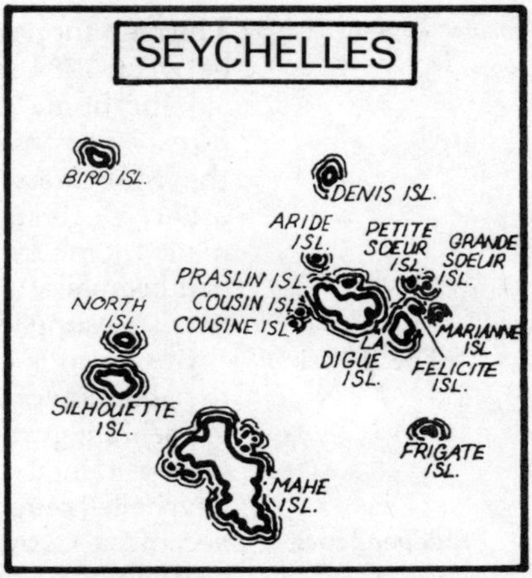
SEYCHELLES
BIRD ISL.
DENIS ISL.
ARIDE ISL.
PETITE SOEUR ISL.
GRANDE SOEUR ISL.
PRASLIN ISL.
COUSIN ISL.
COUSINE ISL.
NORTH ISL.
LA DIGUE ISL.
MARIANNE ISL.
FELICITE ISL.
SILHOUETTE ISL.
FRIGATE ISL.
MAHE ISL.

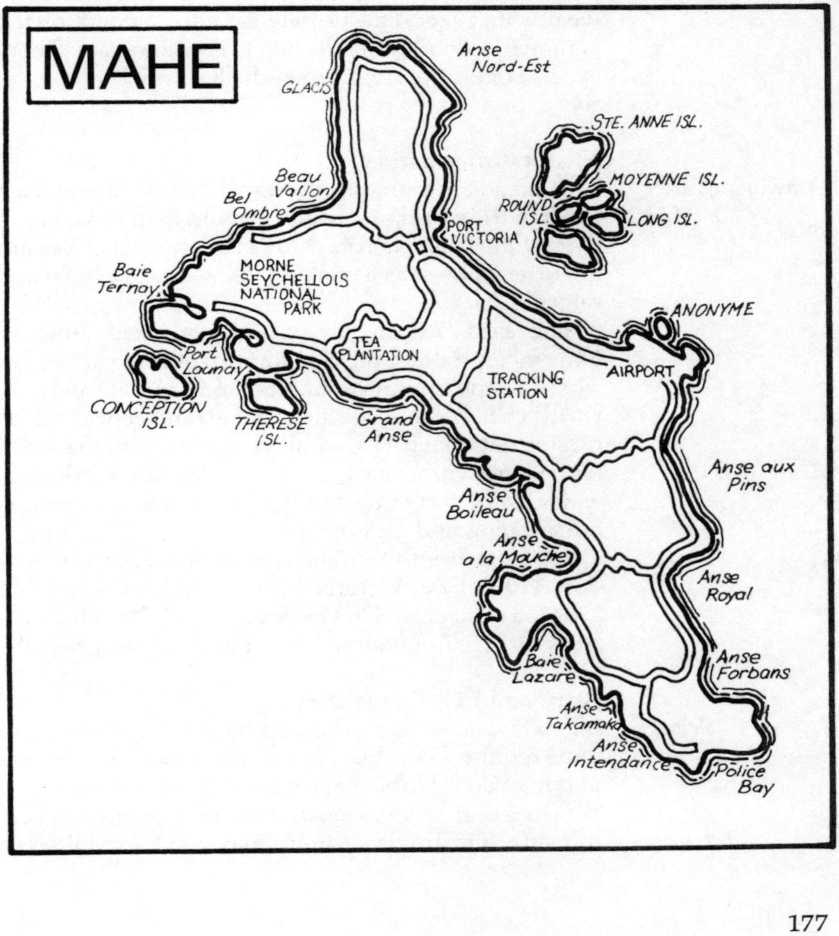
MAHE
Anse Nord-Est
GLACIS
STE. ANNE ISL.
MOYENNE ISL.
Beau Vallon
Bel Ombre
ROUND ISL.
LONG ISL.
PORT VICTORIA
Baie Ternay
MORNE SEYCHELLOIS NATIONAL PARK
ANONYME
TEA PLANTATION
Port Launay
AIRPORT
TRACKING STATION
CONCEPTION ISL.
THERESE ISL.
Grand Anse
Anse aux Pins
Anse Boileau
Anse a la Mouche
Anse Royal
Anse Forbans
Baie Lazare
Anse Takamaka
Anse Intendance
Police Bay

Thirteen thousand tortoises were shipped out of Mahé between 1784 and 1789 alone, apart from the many killed for home consumption. Damage to the island's forests was on a similar scale. In face of this devastation the Mauritian authorities sent Malavois to restore order. He restricted the settlers to special areas and made them farm. Thereafter they fulfilled the role that had been allotted to them and became ships chandlers, garrison suppliers, cultivators of maize and cotton.

**The British**

Britain took control of the islands in 1810 and when the abolition of slavery was enforced at least half of the French emigrated. French law and customs, however, were retained, as well as ownership of property. The Seychelles remained a dependency of Mauritius until it

**Independence**

became a Crown Colony in 1903. The islands were proclaimed a sovereign republic within the Commonwealth in 1976. The president and members of the National Assembly are elected every five years. There is one political party, the Seychelles People's Progressive Front.

## Visitors Information

**Unwinding after a safari**

The islands are among the most beautiful and least spoilt in the world, and being no more than three hours flying time from Nairobi, Mombasa and Dar es Salaam are often chosen as a relaxing follow-up to a mainland safari.

The best season for visiting is from June to November, though the climate is excellent year-round. There is the charm of traditional island life with its varied customs and cuisines, and magnificent beaches, marine national parks, coral reefs and exotic flora and fauna. Activities include scuba diving, snorkeling, water skiing, yachting and big game fishing, as well as horse riding and pleasant walks.

For further information, contact the Tourism Division, PO Box 56, Victoria, Mahé, The Seychelles. Tel: 22041. Telex: 2260. Or The Seychelles Tourist Information Offices in London, Paris, Frankfurt and Nairobi.

## Entry and Exit Formalities

**Visas**

All nationalities are admitted to the Seychelles and some require a visa, but visas will be issued on arrival to all bona fide visitors not seeking paid employment and in possession of a passport, onward or return tickets and sufficient funds. Visitors may also be required to prove they have suitable accommodation for their entire stay; camping is not allowed.

Immunisation for smallpox (officially eradicated worldwide), cholera and yellow fever is required only in the event of an epidemic. See the *Health* section, following.

**Customs regulations**

Visitors may bring in up to one litre of wine and one litre of spirits, 200 cigarettes, 50 cigars or 250 grams of tobacco. There are strict prohibitions on the import of arms and ammunition, spear-fishing equipment and drugs.

On departure a 50-rupee passenger fee is payable at the airport.

### Travel to and within the Seychelles

For all that they have managed to preserve their untouched character, the Seychelles have become easy to reach since the enlargement of Mahé's airport in 1972 to accommodate long-haul aircraft. Over 50 international flights arrive each week, yet the annual number of visitors to the islands is a modest 80,000 or so, capably handled by the developing infrastructure.

**Air**. There are direct flights from Abu Dhabi, Addis Ababa, Bahrain, Bombay, Colombo, Copenhagen, Dar es Salaam, Djibouti, Frankfurt, Hong Kong, Jeddah, Johannesburg, Khartoum, Kilimanjaro, London, Madagascar, Maputo, Mauritius, Marseilles, Mogadishu, Mombasa, Nairobi, Paris, Reunion, Rome, Tokyo and Zurich. Airlines include Air France, Air India, Air Madagascar, Air Tanzania, British Airways, Ethiopian Airlines, Kenya Airways, Lufthansa, Somali Airlines and South African Airways. Flying time from Kenya or Tanzania is no more than three hours, and little more than ten hours from any European city. Numerous package holidays include the Seychelles, often with East Africa and Egypt.

Air Seychelles operates regular services from Mahé to Praslin, Denis and Bird islands, as well as charters.

**Sea**. Cruise ships and cargo vessels call at Victoria, but not on regular schedules.

Ferries run three times a week between Mahé, Praslin and La Digue, and several hire craft maintain services between the islands.

**Land transport**: There is a bus service on Mahé and Praslin islands, and also about 140 taxis, their rates set by the government. Car hire is available on both islands, some with chauffeur, but advance reservations are advisable during the peak season. Drivers must be over 21.

Mahé's roads are almost entirely surfaced; some on Praslin are surfaced, though most are dirt roads; and some other islands have dirt roads.

### Accommodation

Accommodation ranges from large resort hotels to homely lodges and guest houses, and includes rented villas. The Seychelles Tourist Information Offices can provide two useful booklets, one a guide to hotels, the other a guide to guest houses. Reservations are particularly advisable at Christmas, Easter and during July and August. Note that camping is not permitted on the islands.

Accommodation rates in this Guide do not include service charges or tax.

### Food

The main restaurants offer European, Chinese or Indian dishes, but most visitors will probably wish to try Creole food in which fresh fish, lobster, crab, octopus, pork and chicken are served with rice. The food is well spiced and often curried, or simmered in coconut milk. There is tectec, a soup made from small shellfish, curried octopus, turtle steak, and flesh of coco-de-mer. Vegetables often on the menu are calabash, aubergine, choux choux, golden apple, palmiste (heart of palm) and green mango or patole. Fruits include bananas, pineapples, paw paws and mangoes.

**Creole cuisine**

Toddy is a local drink produced from fermented coconut sap and can become agreeably habit forming. Bacca, which comes from cane juice, is equally intoxicating. The local beer, of the lager type, comes bottled or on draught. Wines are imported from France and elsewhere, but are expensive. Likewise, most brands of imported liquor are available but at a price. The local fruit juices, coffee and tea are good.

### Health

Malaria and other tropical diseases are non-existent,

and the water is safe to drink at all hotels and in main towns and villages.

**Entertainment**

Nightlife is simple and unsophisticated. Hotels offer dinner dancing or beach barbecues, along with folk dancers and singers. The local Camtolet music is often accompanied by dancers demonstrating the old quadrilles of the Seychellois contredanse or the vibrant rhythm of the sega.

**Money Matters**

**Currency and rates** The unit of currency is the Seychelles rupee (Rs), divided into 100 cents.

The approximate rate of exchange is UK£1 equals Rs 9.7, and US$1 equals Rs 6.25. But rates are subject to fluctuation and should be checked.

There are no restrictions on the import or export of local or foreign currencies.

The principal banks are Barclays, Standard and Credit et Commerce.

**What to buy**

Local handicrafts include straw hats, sarongs and batiks. Jewellery and curios are made of tortoiseshell, oyster shell, mother of pearl, shark's tooth, green snail shell, coconuts and seeds. Raffia, bamboo, giant ray's tail and fish scales are worked into various items.

The rare and expensive tortoiseshell is frequently substituted by the polished plate of the hawksbill turtle, whose shell is graded by colour: the finest shell is orange without mottling, the next reddish mottle, then open mottle and finally dark shell.

**Coco-de-mer** The coco-de-mer palm is unique to Praslin island, though the strange double nuts, sometimes weighing over 25 kilos, were first found washed up on the shores of lands surrounding the Indian Ocean and were thought to have grown under the sea. They were attributed with magic powers and were highly prized by kings and chieftains. In some cases the penalty for lesser mortals possessing them was death. Today you can get them in the form of salad and fruit bowls.

**Hours of Business**

Shops are open from 9am to 12.30pm and from 1.30 to

5pm Monday to Friday, and are closed Saturday afternoon. Banks are open from 8am to 12.30pm Monday to Friday, and on Saturday from 8 to 11am. The main post office, in Victoria, is open from 8am to 5.30pm Monday to Friday, and from 8am to noon Saturday. Sunday is closing day. However, Telephone, Cable and Wireless Ltd operates a 24-hour link seven days a week with Nairobi, allowing worldwide communications.

### Time and Public Holidays

Seychelles time is Greenwich Mean Time plus four hours. Noon GMT is 4pm in the Seychelles.

Official holidays are 1 and 2 January, 4 and 5 April, 1 May, 5 and 29 June, 15 August, 1 November and 8 and 25 December.

### Weights, Measures and Electricity

Electrical voltage is 240 volts AC.

The Seychelles uses the metric system.

### The Economy

**Plantation agriculture**

For most of the history of the Seychelles the economy has been plantation-based, with cinnamon and copra the principal exports. Other crops such as vanilla, cloves, patchouli and tea are of less importance. Guano, mined on the outer islands, has had a fluctuating importance in relation to world prices, and the supply is becoming exhausted. Copra has been a lucrative export in years of higher prices, although plantation owners have never enjoyed long periods of prosperity that might have encouraged them to diversify their crops. Copra usually sells at a premium above world prices because the crop is gathered only after the ripe coconuts have fallen, a practice that renders the oil content higher than elsewhere.

When the Seychelles achieved independence in June 1976, after two centuries of colonial rule, the country faced a soaring trade deficit and seriously declining agricultural ouput. Production of food has always been inadequate for local consumption, and this shortage has been aggravated by the recent influx of tourists, with the result that the food import bill has increased more than fivefold since 1970. For some years yet, therefore, the Seychelles will continue to depend heavily on outside aid from Britain, the United

States and France, both to help offset the massive trade deficit and to provide job-creating investment, as unemployment also presents a major problem. A drain of skills brought about by numerous Seychellois travelling abroad for education and not returning has not helped the situation.

**Industry, commerce and tourism**

There is a move to develop local industries and agriculture, although there are few resources suitable for large-scale manufacture, except perhaps timber. Expansion is more likely to come about through the import of raw materials to be processed for export. Other economic possibilities include the further development of the tourist industry, the establishment of offshore banking, the creation of entrepôts for air and sea cargoes, and the building up of a fish processing industry.

**Fishing**

The sea is potentially the Seychelles' greatest source of wealth. The archipelago's surrounding waters are full of tuna, shark, sailfish, ray, bonito, marlin, red snapper and squid, which are regularly fished by fleets of Japanese, Taiwanese and Korean trawlers.

## Sports

**Underwater sports**

Goggling or snorkeling will reveal a kaleidoscopic underwater world in the Seychelles' marine national parks where natural life is protected and spear fishing is strictly forbidden. There are over 300 species of fish among the coral reefs, including the tiny irridescent blue demoiselle, the angel fish, parrot fish, slippery chick, wrasse, sergeant-major fish and the batfish, as well as more than 100 varieties of living coral, and shells of delicate, intricate markings.

**Game fishing**

Game fishing is a comparatively new sport in the Seychelles and there are records for the taking. The best time is from November to April, since the seas may be rough during the south-east monsoon and especially in July and August. Deep-sea fishing boats can be chartered by the day or week, but visitors are advised to bring their own tackle, which is usually in short supply. The Mahé group of islands lie on a shallow submarine plateau with a fall of 1000 fathoms over the edge, and these deep waters are exceptionally good hunting grounds for big game fish. Ocean giants such as black, blue and striped marlin abound, as well as sailfish, yellowfin and dogtooth tuna, speedy wahoo and barracuda, common and ocean bonito, dorado or dolphins and rainbow runners. In addition, on the offshore banks, colourful fish with Creole names can be landed, such as bourgeois, vara-vara, dame berry and captain rouge. Line fishing from the shore goes on all year with potential catches of bone-fish, milkfish, permit, caranx and job.

**Other sea and land sports**

Sea sports include scuba-diving, water skiing, yacht-ing and mini-sailing, and power boats or cabin cruisers can be chartered by the day, week or month. Land sports too are numerous and varied. There is a nine-hole golf course at Anse-aux-Pins and another at La Beoliere Country Club. Horse riding in the forests or along the beaches is popular, as also is walking along the mountain paths, through exotic groves or virgin paths. The larger hotels offer tennis, squash, badmin-ton, crazy golf and shuffleboard.

# THE ISLANDS

### Mahé Island

Home of 90 percent of the Seychellois and centre of tourism, Mahé is for the most part surrounded by a coral reef within which warm waters offer safe swimming and sea sports. Beaches abound, some isolated and wildly beautiful.

**The capital**

The charming town of **Victoria**, capital and only port, is on the northeast coast. At its centre stand a statue of Queen Victoria and a miniature Big Ben. Tin-roofed Chinese and Indian shops, their wide verandahs stocked with local handicrafts, line the main street, and the local market adds to the colourful atmosphere. Long Pier Road, running up from the foreshore to the heart of the town, houses most of the significant buildings and offices, including a hotel on whose open terrace social life centres. Just outside the town, to the backdrop of the splendid mountains of Morne Seychellois and the Trois Freres, stands State House, a classical-style white colonial mansion set amidst spacious green lawns. The Botanical Gardens are interesting for their display of unusual trees and shrubs, giant tortoises, and for a small aviary. There is also a museum.

**Touring Mahé**

For a tour of the island, climb up to the **Sans Souci Pass** to the rain forest and stop at the highest point where tea, cinnamon, cloves, nutmeg and black vanilla from the local plantation are on sale at a kiosk. As you descend there is a startlingly beautiful view of offshore islands before you reach **Mahé Beach**. The North East Point route affords views of Silhouette and North Islands. **South Mahé** offers a wild, unspoilt coastline with fine beaches that are often deserted. The island rises abruptly from the sea to a height of 905 metres, and several mountain roads traverse the landscape allowing magnificent views of bays, lagoons and inlying islands. Some roads cross through plantations, while others wind high into the forests of the **Morne Seychellois National Park**.

### Inlying Islands

**St Anne, Cerf, Round, Long** and **Moyenne Islands** in the **Marine National Park**, are just off Victoria. Creole lunches are served on day trips to St Anne and Cerf, and glass-bottomed boats can be hired.

**Therese Island** is a two and a half hour cruise from Victoria around the northern coast. The island has a long sandy beach, snorkeling is good, and there are enormous tortoises. Enroute the giant steps of Point Escalier on the west coast can be seen. Cut into the granite, they arouse speculation as to whether they were carved by nature or by the Polynesians from Madagascar in the cause of some ancient religious rite.

**Silhouette Island**, the third largest of the Seychelles and one of the most attractive of the granitic group, is two hours sailing from Victoria and one hour from Beau Vallon. It has 450 inhabitants. Life there remains much as it was a century ago; there are no vehicles, and the bacca press is worked by mule. The Plantation House, built early in the last century, is a fine example of wooden Seychellois architecture. The vegetation is luxuriant and the marine life abundant. The forest contains such trees as the rare bois noir, gayac and capucin. There are graves of Arab traders, and the family tomb of the Dauban family.

## Outlying Islands

**Bird nests and deep-sea fishing**

**Bird Island**, 96 kms north of Mahé, can be reached in half an hour by air. Here 1.5 million sooty terns nest, breed and hatch from May until November, not to mention the fairy and noddy terns, cardinals, ground doves, mynahs, crested terns and plovers. The island, which has a fine beach with numerous shells, is on the edge of the Seychelles bank with its 1000 fathom drop, marvellous for big game fishing. There is a lodge on the island for those who want to make more than a day trip.

**Home of the coco-de-mer palm**

The only place in the world where the coco-de-mer palm grows, **Praslin** is over three hours by boat from Mahé or 15 minutes by air. The Vallee de Mai is a botanical wonder with over 4000 coco-de-mer palms in the gardens, some over 50 metres high and 800 years old. At 25 kilos, the palm produces the world's heaviest seed. There are male and female trees, the male having catkins a metre long and bearing heavily scented yellow flowers. The seed-nut takes one year to germinate and seven to mature. The palm does not bear fruit until its twenty-fifth year, and it takes several hundred to reach full maturity. The coco-de-mer is protected by the state.

Also on Praslin can be seen various birds indigenous

*Seychelles sunset*

to the Seychelles: the Seychelles bulbul, the beautiful fruit pigeon and the elusive Praslin parrot. There are secluded beaches with safe swimming and excellent snorkeling. Accommodation is in short supply and should be booked in advance.

**Cousin Island**, one and a half hours from Mahé and also accessible from Praslin, is owned by the International Council for Bird Preservation and may only be visited on certain days. The Seychelles fody, the Seychelles turtle dove, the long-tailed tropic bird, the wedge-shaped shearwater, the fairy tern and the Seychelles brush warbler can be seen here.

**La Digue** is about two and a half hours sailing time from Mahé or 30 minutes from Praslin. Oxcarts are used to transport visitors to the beachfront hotels and for excursions over the more picturesque parts of the island where fine examples of traditional planters' houses can be seen. Footpaths give access to all parts of the island, and there are bicycles for hire. Wide, deserted beaches offer safe swimming, and snorkeling and fishing can be enjoyed from a *pirogue*, the local sailed craft. The woods of La Digue are the sole remaining sanctuary of the rare black paradise flycatcher, which was once thought to be extinct. The island is also rich in cycad plants, which include sago and tapioca. Creole cooking is a La Digue specialty.

**Fregate Island** gets its name from the frigate bird, its shape resembling the bird in flight. It lies 51 kms east of Mahé and can be reached by fast boat in two hours, longer by traditional schooner. An airstrip is planned.

**Pirate base**

Fregate was once a base for pirates and there are tales of hidden treasure. Some of the rocks bear cabalistic signs and Arabic inscriptions. The magpie robin, a rare tame bird, is found only on Fregate. An overnight stay is recommended on the island.

# PRACTICAL INFORMATION

Accommodation is generally very expensive on the islands, though this Guide does list several of the cheaper places. Also, because meats and dairy products have to be imported, meal prices are high too (Rs 100-200 for lunch or dinner at the better restaurants), though the quality is excellent.

## MAHÉ

### Accommodation

A **Sheraton** is abuilding on the island and should be open by now, but rates are not yet available.

**Barabarons Beach Hotel**, PO Box 626, Barbarons. Tel: 78310. Telex: 2258 BBCH SZ. Beach hotel on the west side of the island. Accommodation is bungalow-style, the dining room opens onto the sea, and there is a pool, plus golf, tennis, and a disco. Rs 530 single, Rs 725 double, with breakfast.

**Mahé Beach Hotel**, PO Box 540, Port Glaud. Tel: 78451. Telex: SZ 2455 Porglo. Built into a granite cliff, 19 kms southwest of Victoria, all rooms with bath, air conditioning and ocean view. Several restaurants, bars and disco. Pool, putting green, tennis squash, boat hire. Rs 440 single, Rs 550 double, with breakfast.

**Residence Danzilles**, PO Box 267, Bel Ombre. Tel: 23901. A charming, informal hotel set in a tropical garden by the sea. Bungalow accommodation, all rooms with bath, some with air conditioning. Restaurant, pizzeria, bar and pool. Rs 440 single, Rs 595 double, with breakfast.

**Casuarina Beach Guest House**, PO Box 338, Anse-aux-Pins, Victoria. Tel: 76211. Telex: 2321 Carina SZ. Excellent facilities, but cheaper (and more intimate) for being a guest house rather than hotel. All rooms with bath and air conditioning. Creole cuisine. Rs 275 single, Rs 360 double, with breakfast.

**Pension Bel Air**, PO Box 116, Victoria. Tel: 22616. Just outside of town, with a fine view over the harbour and inlying islands. Rs 175 single, Rs 240 double, with breakfast. Add Rs 45 per person, half board; Rs 75 per person, full board. Children half price.

### Information

The **Information Office** is just after the museum on Long Pier, the road running out to the inter-island ferry terminals.

### Travel

See *Seychelles Background* chapter for general information.

All arrangements for island-hopping can be made in Victoria through agents, eg **Coralline United Touring**, PO Box 115, Premier Building, Victoria. Tel: 22821. Telex: SZ 2223. This company can book hotels, arrange coach, boat or air excursions, also glass-bottomed boat trips to the Marine National Park, and it charters yachts, organises fishing and diving expeditions, and is the Hertz car hire agent.

There is a **taxi stand** in Gordon's Square, at the centre of Victoria.

The **airport** is 11 kms to the southeast of Victoria.

## BIRD ISLAND

### Accommodation

**Bird Island Lodge**, PO Box 404. Tel: 76733. Telex: SZ 2334 Bird. Palm-thatched chalets of island timber, facing the sea, with shower and terrace. Creole cuisine. Rs 695 single, Rs 990 double, full board.

## PRASLIN

### Accommodation

**Chateau de Feuilles**, Pointe Cabris Estates, Baie Ste Anne. Tel: 33316. Telex: 2255 Cabris SZ. A chateau built of white granite with palm-thatched roof, hardwood floors and beamed ceilings, beautifully situated in a hilltop palm grove with panoramic views over the long white sand beach on the east side of the island. International and creole cuisine, bars, library, pool. Rs 525 single, Rs 725 double, with breakfast.

**Cote d'Or Lodge**, set in tropical gardens one km from the village. Tel: 33551. Telex: SZ 2246. An informal place with accommodation in rondavels, each with bath and patio. Rs 350 single, Rs 510 double, half board.

**Indian Ocean Fishing Lodge**, Grand Anse. Rs 200 single, Rs 280 double, with breakfast.

## LA DIGUE

### Accommodation

**Gregoire's Island Lodge**, Anse Reunion. Tel: 34233. Telex: 2292 SZ. Chalets with thatched roofs amidst coconut and takamaka trees on the beach, all with air conditioning and bath or shower. Creole cuisine the specialty. Rs 495 single, Rs 700 double, half board.

**Choppy's Bungalows**, Anse Reunion. Tel: 4224. The cheapest on the island, Rs 110 single, Rs 280 double, with breakfast. Full board available.

# INDEX

After each place listing is a letter: K for Kenya, T for Tanzania, S for the Seychelles.